Beyond the Mountains of the Damned

Beyond
the Mountains
of the Damned

The War inside Kosovo

MATTHEW McALLESTER

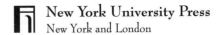

New York University Press
New York and London

NEW YORK UNIVERSITY PRESS
New York and London

Library of Congress Cataloging-in-Publication Data
McAllester, Matthew, 1969–
Beyond the mountains of the damned : the war inside Kosovo /
Matthew McAllester.
p.   cm.
Includes bibliographical references.
ISBN 0-8147-5660-3 (cloth)
1. Kosovo (Serbia)—History—Civil War, 1998– 2. Pec (Serbia)—
History, Military—20th century. 3. Kosovo (Serbia)—History—
Civil War, 1998– —Personal narratives, Albanian.
I. Title: War inside Kosovo. II. Title.
DR2087.2.P43 M33 2001
949.7103—dc21   2001004370

New York University Press books are printed on acid-free paper,
and their binding materials are chosen for strength and durability.

Manufactured in the United States of America
10 9 8 7 6 5 4 3 2

For my mother and father

Contents

Acknowledgments   ix

Introduction   1

1. One Town, Two Lives   4

2. The Ghosts of Kula Pass   20

3. Staying Behind   39

4. The Serbian Canterbury   51

5. The Friendly Lion and the KLA   66

6. In the Trunk of a Gray BMW   88

7. Coffee with Zejnepe   103

8. Burning   118

9. Agreements   132

10. The Illyrian Wolves   141

11. A Silent Town   150

12. The Killing   159

13. A White Plastic Bag in the Long Grass   179

14. New Roofs, New Coffins   196

15. The Butcher's Business   212

Bibliography   225

About the Author   227

All illustrations appear as a group following p. 100

Acknowledgments

For their support, friendship, and help, many people deserve thanks: Isaac and Barbara Guzman, Alex Bellos, Jane McAllester, Richard Poureshagh, Mick Smith, Michael Muskal, Heathcliff O'Malley, Viorel Florescu, Conal Urquhart, Andrew Smith, Michael Montgomery, Michael Slackman, Les Payne, Janine di Giovanni, Fred Abrahams, Haleh Anvari, Dominic Cooper, Tony Marro, Charlie Sennott, Jessica Kowal, Blaine Harden, Charlotte Hall, Richard Skinner, Jo Bloom, Alex Cooke, Jamie Talan, Peter Davies, Mark and Isabel Woldin, Alex Martin, Ron Haviv, Jim and Carol McAllester, Harvey Aronson, Robin Topping, Sandro Contenta, Richard Miron, Crispian Balmer, Nick Goldberg, Steve Crawshaw, Ed Gargan, Michael and Megan Schurter, Ira Silverberg, Andrew Metz, Mohamad Bazzi, Miriam Pawel, Jennifer Pirtle, Patricia Falvo, Kristin Kelley, Jessica Steinberg, Skiddy and Elizabeth Von Stade, Ron Goldfarb, Matt Rees, Michal Schonbrun, Mary Burke, Bob Souter, Daniel Klaidman, Monica Selter, Sophie Garnham, Larry Kaplow, Somini Sengupta, Leonard Newmark, Laurie Garrett, Kate Goldberg.

Thanks also to all those in Kosovo and Montenegro who were so generous with their time, especially the Bala family.

There are some people without whom this would not have come together: Tim Phelps, John Maingay, Roy Gutman, Phil Sherwell, Julian Simmonds, Liam Pleven, Rebecca Sutherland, Stephen Magro, Kristen Auclair, Laurie Muchnick, Enver Doda.

One person in Yugoslavia was invaluable. He helped me endlessly but cannot be named for his own safety. There are others there who performed similar roles and they know who they are.

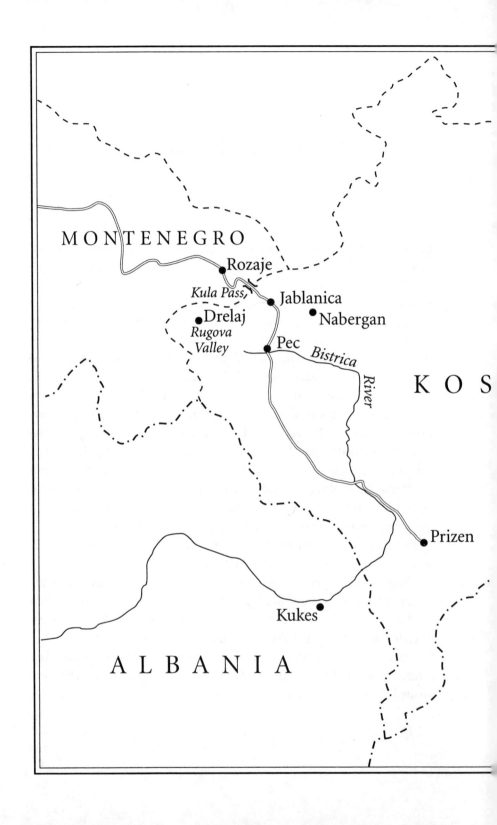

MONTENEGRO

Rozaje

Kula Pass

Jablanica

Drelaj

Nabergan

*Rugova
Valley*

Pec

Bistrica

River

K O S

Prizen

Kukes

A L B A N I A

S E R B I A

● Pristina

O V O

● Skopje

M A C E D O N I A

Introduction

In March 1999 the world watched thousands of Albanian refugees pour out of Kosovo, telling stories of the terror that drove them from their homes. This is the story of one family who stayed behind in the darkest part of Kosovo and lived the war that was unseen by the world.

To the Bala family and other Albanians who stayed in and around the Western Kosovo town of Pec during the seventy-eight days of the NATO bombardment, the war in Kosovo was not about cruise missiles and geopolitics and fields full of refugees. It was about tiptoeing between survival and death in the town that saw the fiercest destruction, the most thorough eviction of the Albanian population, and killings whose brutality begs explanation.

This is also the story of the Serb paramilitaries who terrorized Pec. They ruled with murder. Today, most of them are alive and well in the new Yugoslavia. So unconcerned are some of Yugoslavia's paramilitaries about the prospect of ever being held accountable for their crimes that they could sit down over coffee and beer after the war to discuss in detail their brief, brutal reign in the hell that was Kosovo.

The unseen war, the war inside Kosovo, has remained largely untold.

A handful of journalists, including myself, crossed over the borders into Kosovo during the conflict to provide brief glimpses into the war zone. Others saw more central parts of Kosovo, often under the watch of the Serb authorities. All our accounts were hampered by concerns over safety and the lack of free movement. Mainly because of Yugoslav President Slobodan Milosevic's determination to keep most foreign journalists out of Kosovo during the war, the great majority of reporting during those seventy-eight days relied on the testimony of the Albanian refugees who were expelled to Albania, Macedonia, and Montenegro. The witnesses provided extraordinary tales, but after a period the world found these stories from the margins of the war zone repetitious and lacking in immediacy.

What was left by the end of the eleven weeks of NATO's bombing campaign was an incomplete, detached, and unsatisfactory chronicle of the largest European war since 1945. Most people viewed that story at a distance that is becoming ever more common in large modern wars: Through the video cameras attached to NATO missiles and the mosaic of accounts by refugees.

Small wonder, then, that one of the first books to be published after the war was Michael Ignatieff's insightful *Virtual War,* in which he suggests that Kosovo will set a pattern for the wars of the future: Television, public opinion, domestic political concerns, an absence of self-sacrifice, computer hacking, and the approval of military lawyers vetting all targets will characterize future wars. Ignatieff correctly writes that there was no traditional war in Kosovo. There were no battalions of infantry sniping at each other, no tank divisions picking each other off from hilltops, and not a single NATO casualty. To the frustration of NATO's generals, the President of the United States, Bill Clinton, repeatedly said that there would be no ground war in Kosovo.

But there *was* a ground war in Kosovo. In fact, it was the struggle on the ground that caused the air war. There was a relatively clear chain of events: The Yugoslav authorities brutalized Kosovo's Albanians for a decade. Some Albanians formed a guerrilla army, the Kosovo Liberation Army, to fight back. In 1998, during a brutal campaign to stamp out the KLA, the Serb police began to massacre Albanian civilians. Fearing interference from Albania, the Western powers tried to negotiate a peace settlement between Milosevic and the KLA. After Milosevic refused to accept a peace deal in early 1999 that Albanian leaders had signed on to, NATO bombed Yugoslavia to stop the Serbian violence that was threatening to cause a wider war in the Balkans. Strategic concerns became moral when the Serb forces began to massacre and expel the Albanian population.

The war was very real, not at all virtual, to the Bala family. It was real to the Albanian guerrillas who fought around Pec and to their enemies in paramilitary units. It was real to the dead and it was real to their survivors. While it was unfolding, the world did not see this war. And so it is a view of the war inside that I offer in this book.

The story of Pec, in many respects, is the story of Kosovo during the war. No one can tell it better than the people who were inside and around Pec during those seventy-eight days.

Some notes on the sourcing of the book: Unless otherwise noted in the text, the chapters that evolve around the Bala family are based entirely on the recollections and words of the family and their neighbors offered during many interviews. Sometimes, in different interviews, the Balas gave slightly varying versions of the same events. In those cases, I sought a final version. When doubts and failed memories persisted, I have chosen the detail that makes the most sense in the context. Where people's thoughts are depicted, they are the recollected thoughts of people who are still living or the memories of what was being discussed at the time. Information on Nebojsa Minic and those paramilitaries who were not interviewed for this book but who feature in it comes from a variety of sources, including photographs and interviews with other paramilitaries, Yugoslav officials, family members, and neighbors. I am grateful to Riza Loci for allowing me to quote from his diary.

Many places in Kosovo have Albanian and Serbian names. To use one or the other can be seen as conferring a kind of ethnic primacy to one group or the other over a place. It is an impossible job to be absolutely fair. So I have followed the style of the many international visitors to the region, which is to say that I have been guided by common and random usage of Albanian and Serbian names. For example, I have used Pec rather than Peja because I first heard the town referred to as Pec.

For the sake of simplicity, I have not used accents for either language.

Chapter 1

One Town, Two Lives

It is just past seven in the morning when Isa Bala arrives at the cattle market outside Pristina. The fog that lay a few feet above the plains of central Kosovo has gone, burned off by a marigold sun. Isa gets out of the car, takes a pee by the side of the road, and goes to work, the right-hand pocket of his jeans stuffed full of twelve thousand deutsche marks.

Isa is a butcher. He's here to buy cows that he will sell later in his shop in Pec, sliced into steaks, ground and rolled into chippolata-sized morsels called *cebob*, or mixed up and stuffed into sausage skins in a spicy recipe he swears he'll never reveal to anyone but his son.

Kosovo's cow population, like its human population, has decreased dramatically in recent months. Isa estimates that there are now 20 percent fewer cows than there were before the eleven-week war in Kosovo. Some were shot by Serbs, some were stolen and taken to Serbia, some just died from neglect. But at this time, eight weeks after the war has ended, everyone needs money. So there are plenty of cows for sale at the market and plenty of eager sellers.

"Isa, Isa, look at my cows," calls out a dealer as soon as the heavy-boned butcher ploughs between the first row of horned brown and white cows. The animals are tethered by ropes and chains to the rusty metal barriers that form parallel lines down the center of the field where the market takes place early every Tuesday morning.

"Ees, Ees," shouts another seller like a whining child desperate to attract his father's attention. The man tilts his head to one side, his eyebrows so pleading that they're almost touching above his nose. No one allows himself to be robbed in the Pristina cow market. Everyone's looking for a deal. Everyone's an actor and no one's a fool.

"Isa, Isa, stop, stop. How much will you give me for this one?"

Isa's in no hurry. In the car on the way to Pristina he was unexcited about the prospects at the market. "I'll buy four, five, maybe six cows," he mumbled from under his thick, teak-colored mustache with its few strands of gray. "We'll see. It depends on the price."

Hands of old friends grab Isa's as he walks over the pebbles, dirt, and cow dung of the field. "How are you, Isa?" sellers ask. "How's business?" They avoid the customary Albanian politeness of asking how his family is.

The hands that grab Isa's are more than hands of friendship. More than ever, the market is about making money in lean times. Once the first seller succeeds in keeping Isa's T-bone-sized hand in his own the seller pulls the butcher, quite roughly, toward his cows. Isa leans his body back as if in a gentle tug of war and his poker face takes on a look of reluctance. "Jo, jo, jo," he says, pronouncing the j as a y. "No, no, no." But he lets himself be led between the dung-smeared rears of dozens of cows to a medium-sized brown and white. Isa's first rule of buying: Never look in the mildest bit enthusiastic about a cow, even a bargain on four legs. It's like knowing how to react when you're dealt a royal flush.

Between his thumb and fingers, Isa squeezes a flap of flesh next to the cow's anus. He steps round and pinches the side of the cow, testing for fat content, something he's been doing since he bought and slaughtered his first cow at the age of eleven. There's a step-on weighing scale in the market that has a long line of cows and bulls waiting beside it but Isa never uses the scale. He knows how much a cow weighs and how old it is just by looking at it. And he knows how much fat it's carrying by giving it a good feel.

5

"Nine," says the man, referring to the asking price, nine hundred marks.

"Seven."

"Come on, eight point five," barks the man, still holding Isa's hand, refusing to let go.

"Seven."

Isa walks away. The man won't let go of Isa's limp hand and Isa has to yank it away and still the man comes after him and grabs his hand again, calling out his name, "Isa, Isa." But the butcher breaks away and the seller gives up. Isa had no intention of buying the cow. He's just showing his mettle to the crowd that swarms around him at all times.

Two bigger cows idle next to each other in the next row. One of the half dozen small boys selling cigarettes—counterfeit Marlboros and Winstons from neighboring Montenegro and Macedonia, cigarette-smuggling centers of the Balkans—pops up beside the cows. Isa doesn't smoke and wags his index finger at the boy, the silent Albanian way of saying no.

"Both of these, twenty-two," the seller, a wiry, middle-aged man in a black beret tells Isa. Twenty-two hundred marks. One of the cows starts to low forlornly as the men haggle over its fate. Slobber drips from its mouth onto the earth, rolling into dust-covered balls. Someone kicks it hard in the side to get it to shut up. Again, Isa walks when he doesn't get his price and has to wrench his hand away from the owner of the two cows. Perhaps his pessimism in the car was justified and the prices today are too high.

"You're shaving us, Isa," another seller calls out to Isa, using an Albanian expression to complain of Isa's firm grip on those twelve thousand marks in his pocket. "You're putting your razor right up against our skin."

A single black and white is the next to have its rear end squeezed. Its owner slaps Isa's hand with a smack.

"Nine."

"Seven."

The seller yanks Isa's arm up and down in a wild handshake and the two men raise their voices, facing off against each other, bellowing out numbers, persuasions, and refusals, and other men surround them, encouraging the deal, suggesting compromises, and still the exaggerated and aggressive handshake continues until suddenly Isa's arm tenses and after a final downward movement of the now gripped hands the men cast their arms wildly apart and it's a deal. Eight. For the first time since he entered the market, Isa pulls out his wad of marks and flips over eight blue one hundred mark bills to the now impassive seller. The butcher unwinds the dirty rope and leads the cow away.

It turns out he's just getting started. As a flock of pigeons arcs around the nearby field of golden sunflowers and the smell of dung floats on a slow wind, Isa stomps around the market and an hour and a half after arriving he's bought nineteen cows and four calves. He's arranged for a friend to take them back to Pec in a truck.

On the way home, Isa's voice fills the car. He nearly always talks fast and loudly and slightly slurs his S's as if his tongue is slightly too big for his mouth. He's delighted. He hadn't expected the cattle to be so cheap and that's why he spent every mark he had and took some cows on credit. Isa's the type who won't allow any hard-up soul he knows to go hungry when he has meat left in his shop at the end of the day. But first and foremost, he's a businessman. "When you do business, do it for profit or don't do it at all," Isa says. "We have a proverb: It's bad to be a cat for a thousand years and not catch a mouse."

He explains that he makes more money than other, less experienced butchers do, because he thinks about the seasons, the weather, and how people eat. He explains that he picked out the leaner, skinnier cows, leaving the heavier ones for another day. "In the summer people don't like eating fatty meat. In winter people want a bit more fat," he says.

Part of being an old hand at butchering is not caring in the slightest that you've just bought nearly two dozen animals for the purpose of slitting their throats and cutting them up for people to buy, cook, and eat. Some people work with pipes, drains, and taps, others with computers, Palm IIIs, and fax machines. Isa happens to work with knives, blood, and flesh. At the end of a day in the shop his short-sleeved cotton-nylon mix shirt and jeans are nearly always splashed and smeared with blood. Sometimes, little flecks of fat or muscle get caught in his short, spiky dark hair. Often, he wears the same shirt and pants for two or three days, the scarlet stains turning russet over time. It doesn't enter his mind that chopping up dead animals might be somehow unsavory. For him, it's not about death. It's about life, feeding people—especially his family.

Isa has recently gone into partnership with another butcher's shop in Pec and they look after the animals until they're needed in the shops. The other butchers do the slaughtering. Isa's forte is chatting up the customers, passing on the news, and being the trusty face on the business. He's also the master of the sausage and can find more meat in a brown and white than most. Isa makes one cow go a long way.

It's close to noon when he returns to Pec. He says he doesn't have time to stop at his house on Dushan Mugosha Street to say hello to his wife Halise or to grab a bite to eat and he accepts a ride right to the front door of his shop where he chops and sells until nine at night. The lettering on the glass door says the shop closes at eight. After he's wiped down the surfaces, mopped the floor, put the remaining meat away in the refrigerator, and locked the door, he sits outside with friends, playing cards on the steps of the apartments above his shop, chatting well into the night. Only when his friends clear off and go home to their families, when he's run out of excuses to stay at the shop, does he go home.

As he walks toward the house he glances up at the second-floor windows of his living room. It's dark but there they are, the bullet holes in the double glazing. His heavy shoulders sloping forward, Isa opens the metal gate in front of his house and walks up the concrete path to his front door in reluctant silence.

Like all Albanian business owners operating in the Serb-controlled Pec of the 1990s, Isa learned to be wary of Serbs who came into his shop, especially young men. Against these young men there was no recourse in the law. They were the law. So Isa made it a point to remember their faces.

Nebojsa Minic's face was long and wide, just like his body. He had dense black hair, naturally wavy but usually cut short, and furry black caterpillars for eyebrows. Narrow eyes sat on either side of a large, straight nose that made Minic look like he was leaning toward you even when he wasn't. Years of working out in prison had made his forearms and shoulders solid and powerful. While most Serbs tend to have pale, classically Slavic skin, Minic's face was light brown and leathery, his black stubble often noticeable.

Seven or eight years ago Minic came into Isa's shop a couple of times to buy Isa's famous sausages. He was polite, didn't say much, just asked for his sausages, paid, and left. Isa was flawlessly polite in return because Minic's large build had caught his eye. He took a mental snapshot and filed it away.

"I thought he looked like a criminal, a thief," Isa said.

On his identity card, Minic listed his profession as "laborer." But Isa was right. Minic was a criminal and a thief.

Born on March 1, 1964 in the village of Rosulje just to the east of Pec, Nebojsa Minic was a pretty normal kid for his first decade. His parents, Vojin and Gordana, moved the family to a small, single-story house at 22 Urosa Djurovica Street in the Brzenik neighborhood of Pec when he was an infant. The young Minic became good friends with the Albanian boys next door, Nuredin and Isuf Ramaj. Nuredin was three years older than Minic, Isuf three years younger than their Serb buddy.

"We never had problems with each other because we were Albanian and he was Serbian," Isuf remembers. "We didn't hate each other at all."

Minic was a tough kid, though. An old black-and-white photograph shows him at the age of about thirteen with his left arm slung over the shoulders of a friend as he stares sullenly into the camera. The Ramajs remember that as they grew older Minic used to rough up his big brother, Ljubisce. He would argue a lot with his older sister, Ljiljana. He got lousy grades in class.

He was eleven when he first got into trouble with the police. He had started to steal. It wasn't just Albanians who began to keep an eye out for young Minic. Serbs suffered his muggings, his theft, too.

The Ramaj family became wary of him but not wary enough. In 1985, they agreed to buy the Minic house. They paid Minic and his family the asking price but Minic, now twenty-one and the dominant force in the household, declined to move out. To this day they have the receipts. There was little the Ramajs could do except look forward to the many times that the police caught Minic and took him off to prison.

It was behind bars that Nebojsa Minic learned his flawless Albanian. With his dark complexion, you could easily mistake him for an Albanian when he spoke the language. What's more, his fellow inmates taught him how to play the two-stringed Albanian plucking instrument called the *ciftelia*. And he would impress his Albanian neighbors with his knowledge of their folk songs, including one that goes on for thirty minutes. Even most Albanians cannot sing the full song. He also came out of prison with a drinking problem.

"He is the kind, the type who cannot live without Albanians," Nuredin Ramaj remembers. "When he has no drink, no clothes, no cigarettes, he can even get down on his knees and cry. In a way he loved Albanians because only the Albanians would be with him. The Serbs rejected him."

In the late 1980s and early 1990s, Minic began smuggling cigarettes and oil—such standard enterprises in Yugoslavia for many years that the current President of Montenegro, Milo Djukanovic, was one of his republic's best known cigarette smugglers. Minic's line of work took him to other European countries, including Germany and Austria, but he was never more than a bit player in the Yugoslav criminal world. But in the early 1990s, Minic took a step up the smuggler's hierarchy, according to a relative of his.

Minic graduated from oil and cigarettes; he started handling drug shipments. At that time, the drug trade in Kosovo was firmly in the control of Albanians, who only collaborated with Serbs because the Serbs could provide access to the large markets in Serbia, Montenegro, and beyond to other parts of central and Eastern Europe. The main contact among the Serbian underworld was a man called Darko Asanin, who is now dead. Asanin was a lieutenant of Zeljko Raznatovic, more commonly known as Arkan, the most famous—and most famously assassinated—paramilitary leader in Yugoslavia. It was not the last time that Minic would find himself under Arkan's ultimate control. But at that point, Minic was just another circuit in the complex machinery of the Albanians' and Asanin's drug business. Arkan himself had at this time almost certainly never heard of Minic.

Like many criminals in Serbia and Montenegro, especially those with links to Arkan's well-oiled organized crime concerns, Minic took a sabbatical in Bosnia, say his family, neighbors, and former paramilitary comrades. It was just his kind of war—profitable and easy. Bosnia was most rewarding to those who laughed at the laws of warfare. And no one worked as efficiently there as those who had always laughed at the laws of peacetime.

"He was fierce and out of his mind," recalled his relative, who heralds from the Minic family seat Podbisce, a village in the rocky north of Montenegro, where Serbian nationalism has become as instinctive as drinking a shot glass of throat-burning *raki* with breakfast. "He came a few times to Podbisce to see his cousins. He was showing us these photos of slaughtered Muslims and he was doing it with glee. He didn't spare anyone. My father started to hate him, as did many other relatives. After that he started making trouble everywhere in Montenegro—in Budva, Podgorica, Herceg Novi. He started so many fights in the cafés."

It was in Bosnia that Minic's violent side blossomed. He operated in a unit under the Bosnian Serb army, according to his comrades, who spoke after the war in Kosovo. One Kosovo paramilitary, "Tony," said that Minic was in the Drina Wolves unit and that there he met five or six guys who would later become key friends in Kosovo. The friends used to use the code word of *Munje,* Lightning, over their Motorola radios in the field. It was a name they liked and would resuscitate in Kosovo.

Led by Radislav Krstic, a Bosnian Serb military leader who has been indicted by the International Criminal Tribunal for the former Yugoslavia, Minic was one of the killers at the July 1995 Srebrenica massacre, the worst single atrocity committed in Europe since World War II. After seizing the town, designated a UN safe haven, Serb soldiers killed thousands of Muslim men.

"There were killing trucks" in Srebrenica, said the paramilitary Tony, who served under Arkan in the Pec region during the Kosovo war. Tony is a calm man with utter contempt for Minic, whom he still regularly encounters. "Minic was one of the men escorting the trucks to a site and executing the men. They would massacre them in the truck or as they were getting off the truck, one by one. They did seven to eight thousand in five days. Imagine—everyone must have individually done a lot of killing. Later he was boasting about how he was fucking girls there, too, exulting in how the girls scream as he was raping them. Killing was a kind of routine for him. The day after he forgets all he's done. He was quite well known, famous, for raping in Bosnia. Not only rape. He liked to physically abuse them, too, and he liked to boast about it. He isn't a normal guy."

When the war in Bosnia was over, Minic, with his pocket full of loot and horrific vacation photos, came to Montenegro arrogant and aggressive. It was hard to give up the power that came with being a paramilitary. But in Montenegro, he encountered an established criminal culture that had no patience with cocksure newcomers. One day, in the mid-1990s, under one of the awnings of the seafront cafés of Budva and Herceg Novi, Minic started one fight too many, this time crossing someone in the Montenegrin organized crime world. It was explained to him that he was no longer welcome in Montenegro. Driving quickly through the tunnels and gorges on the road north to Pec, he fled to his Albanian drug connections in Kosovo.

Back home, he suffered from the same problem. Neither he nor his fellow Kosovo Serbs were in charge of the criminal world, his world. The Albanian criminals weren't impressed by his new Bosnian résumé. For sure, Belgrade ruled the town halls, industry, and the police stations of Kosovo by this time, but the Albanians were still the bosses of the drug trade. For a while, the Ramajs recall, their old playmate opened a small kiosk near the house and tried to go straight, selling newspapers and cigarettes. He was calm, polite. He had a new girlfriend and perhaps she and Minic were trying to settle down. It did not last long. Minic gained the confidence of the local Albanian drug kingpins. He set out to become a crucial distributor for them, opening up new routes in Europe and becoming the player he had sought to be for years. He had finally gained some respect.

Exactly what happened to split Minic from his Albanian partners is unclear. But several people, including his relative, say the bust-up came over a substantial heroin shipment to another country, probably Italy. Possibly the Albanians tried to cut their Serb friend out of the routes he had opened up and controlled. One large deal went wrong somehow and the man who came out feeling cheated was Minic. Already shunned by many local Serbs as a criminal, a lout, and a blockhead, Minic felt alienated by losing his Albanian friends.

"From then on, he hated, absolutely hated Albanians," said a Montenegrin man who worked as a paramilitary under Minic during the war in Kosovo.

Soon after Minic's split with the Albanian drug lords of Kosovo, he joined the Pec police force. That was in 1997 or 1998. He had had enough of working with anyone other than his own kind and at last he was happy in a job whose responsibilities perfectly matched his talents and experience.

Minic's career unfolded without the Albanians of Pec really noticing the changing stature of a man who was, to most of them, just another bigoted Serb to avoid on the street.

Minic lived just a short walk away from the Bala family, down Dushan Mugosha Street and right through some narrow dirt tracks of streets to what was renamed Dardania II Street after the war. The street is in a less well known part of Pec. Minic family's house was a cinderblock bungalow surrounded by an overgrown yard and a low brick wall. His girlfriend, a Bosnian Serb refugee named Rada, lived a few hundred yards from Isa's shop. A couple of Minic's friends who had similar views to him lived about a hundred yards away, back toward Dushan Mugosha Street. On the other side of town were another two of his good friends, Vitomir Shalipuri and Miljan Kaljevic. They were all becoming very close and were soon to be partners in the war.

Isa heard things about Nebojsa Minic. Isa's shop is one of Pec's gossip salons. When people come into Isa's shop, they tell him the latest and he passes it on to others. The meat costs but the gossip is free. There were quite a few rumors about Minic and none suggested that he was the kind of guy who would be a good neighbor to an Albanian. So, like most Albanians who knew about Minic, Isa tried to keep his distance from the big Serb.

Around 1997 or 1998, he noticed Minic walking and driving around the streets of Brzenik in a blue camouflage police uniform. The drug smuggler and veteran killer from Bosnia had joined the police. He was now doing his duty for Belgrade. And it wasn't to serve and protect.

Fifty-two-year-old Myrteza Vokshi owned a kiosk on Dushan Mugosha Street, about half-way between the Bala and Minic households. One day he sat inside on a rickety chair, the back door of his shop open for ventilation during the summer. A quiet man with a young family, he sold newspapers, candy, stickers of Yugoslav soccer stars, and cigarettes. It was early afternoon. Minic walked past and stuck his big nose and narrow eyes in through the low rectangle from which Vokshi handed out his change and goods. Minic bought something, Vokshi can't remember what. But he remembers what Minic said, apropos of nothing. "I'd kill you for ten marks," he told the Albanian kiosk owner.

This time, Minic walked away.

"My father was a butcher, my grandfather was a butcher, my great-grandfather was a butcher, my great-great-grandfather was a butcher. The Balas have been butchers for a thousand years."

Isa's paternal grandfather Musa Bala was indeed a butcher but he was not a great businessman. He drank too much and partly as a result of that he lived in Pec but had a shop in the nearby village of Vitomirica, where the rent was cheaper.

His son, Isa's father, Shaip Bala, didn't fare much better. He too lived in Pec but ran a shop in Klina. He took the train to work.

"My father became mentally ill. I was only fourteen when my father died. We were living in Pec but when my father got ill when I was six we had to close the shop in Klina."

The Bala family had very little money. Like his father before him, Shaip Bala had a weakness: He played and lost at poker. When he was at home with his madness, he would sometimes curse at his family, then fall into dark, silent depressions. His big butcher's hands never went to work with a cleaver and a carcass again after the shop closed. He knew only one trade and so the Balas' income dried up almost completely.

In Albanian families, particularly in those days, the woman's duty was to look after the family and it was the man's role to work. Mahie, Isa's mother, began to buy and sell things to help the family survive but Isa, at the age of six, became the man of the house. He had three sisters and a baby brother.

As long as he can remember Isa had worked in his father's shop. His father would give him small jobs, like skinning a part of a cow or a sheep. Slicing up the actual meat was too important a job for a small boy. No one buys a steak that looks like it has been hacked into shape with a blunt ax.

Isa soon learned to respect the knives and implements of the trade. He'll never forget one early lesson.

You can feel that lesson when you shake his hand. His is a disconcerting handshake. That's partly because he takes your hand very loosely in his own powerful palm. But it's also because part of his hand is missing. The index finger on his right hand is about half an inch shorter than it should be and his fingernail is curved over the tip like an ice cream scoop.

One day, when he was four years old, Isa was watching his father make sausages with the hand-driven meat grinder in the shop. His father said that he could have a go and the little boy promptly pushed his fingers too far into the grinder. In a second the top of his finger was off.

Later the fingernail grew back, curling over the tip of the shortened finger. When Isa's little brother Musa was almost exactly the same age, he too stuck his right index finger into the grinder and lopped the top off. Isa told his kid brother later that their fates would always be linked.

Isa couldn't afford to be put off the family trade by his accident. When he was seven, a year after the shop closed, he cobbled together enough dinars to buy a sheep from a friend of his father's. He slit its throat, used his father's knives to cut it up and went from house to house selling the mutton. He doubled his money and headed to the sheep market to buy more. But the villagers there wouldn't take the little boy seriously.

"Bugger off," they told him. "What are you doing here? You don't know anything."

Someone eventually sold him another sheep. Later the men realized that the kid who showed up to buy a sheep ever more frequently wasn't messing around and they started dealing with him as an equal.

While his father went out gambling or stayed at home sitting in a silence perforated by shouting, Isa graduated to buying his first cow. By the time he was eleven, he was unusually big and strong for his age and so the large beasts did not intimidate him. As fast as he could kill them and cut them up he would sell them door to door to his now regular customers.

It's not easy to balance being a pubescent butcher and door-stepping meat salesman with the usual load of classes and homework and so, not surprisingly, Isa fell behind at school. He did well when he applied himself but he knew that geometry and history were not going to help him in his life. He could read, write, and knew numbers well enough to work out in a heartbeat when a sly cattle dealer was trying to put one past him. He had a family to feed and beyond that, a business to run for the rest of his life. He had a private chat with the head teacher to explain how things stood with the Bala family, and at thirteen he left school.

Even with lessons a thing of the past, Isa's intensive work life didn't leave much time for making friends. He never had time to play. Or perhaps, having seen how his father and grandfather had used their spare time, he never gave himself time to play. The other kids in his neighborhood seemed to resent his adult role.

Isa's father was clearly sick. His behavior was erratic, crazy. But for Albanians, your father is your father and he deserves respect. According to tradition, Isa gave him some of his earnings and never dreamed of questioning the wisdom of what his father spent the money on. It went on poker games and cigarettes, five packs a day. At the age of forty-eight, his father died of lung cancer.

"I never drink or gamble or smoke," Isa says. "I have three coffees a day."

In the few years since Isa had taken on the responsibility of providing for the family, he had saved quite a sum of money. At the age of sixteen or seventeen, he had enough to buy his first house in the Pec neighborhood of Kapesnica. Two or three years later, he took over the shop on the Yugoslav People's Army Street where he still works. Like most business owners in Pec, he paid his rent to the state.

While Isa was doing his obligatory national service in the army, the teenage Musa ran the shop. The older Bala brother would rather have stayed in Pec working in his shop but he did not object to serving in Tito's multiethnic army.

"In Yugoslavia before Tito died it was just like the United States," he says. "Everything was fine. You could sleep well. You had a passport and could go anywhere in the world. You had freedom. At that time no one asked you if you were Albanian or Serbian. I used to go into Serbia to buy cows, to Novi Pazar, Vojvodina, Novi Sad. We even slept in Serbs' houses. No one asked you anything. They weren't friends but they were fine. It was business. We would go up there to buy cheaper cows. When Tito died everything changed."

When Isa decided it was time to get married—and at twenty-four, he was beginning to look like a suspiciously old catch—his mother went to work. She came up with Halise, three years Isa's junior and the relative of an in-law. "If I'd just taken a girl from any old place it would have been disrespectful."

Unlike the dark-haired, pale-skinned Isa, Halise was blond and had the kind of tan, rosy skin that makes so many Albanians seem ruggedly healthy and outdoorsy and attractive. Isa explains the look: "Albanians have always lived in the mountains. It's the mountain air, the exercise."

Isa was building the simple pillars he would rest his life on: work, family, and God.

To Disraeli, "man is a being born to believe." Isa is such a man. Disinclined to proselytize, he nevertheless believes so strongly in so many things that it is pointless to argue with him. He has unwavering views on everything from the Albanian complexion to the existence of God and the rules of marriage.

"Women should stay at home," he says, without a second's hesitation. "We Albanians don't get divorced. Only for cheating and if your husband is a thief. We don't argue a lot with women. Women in the United States don't want kids. If you don't have children what's the point in living? You need children to take care of you later in life. When you have good kids and a nice wife you love to go home. You get your dinner set and your bed made. When you're alone it's like being in the woods. A man who dies without kids would be better not to have lived at all. When you want to get married it's not important to find a beautiful woman. Beauty lasts about two days. You have to find the kind of woman who knows how to love you. She has to know how to be with your guests, how to manage the house. She's not just for sex."

He is amazed that some Western countries like Italy actually have declining birth rates. "Kids and money—you can never have enough," he says.

"It's just wonderful when you're all together at dinner and you bless the food. When you're all alone and you sit at the table to eat there's no use blessing the food. That's just like living in the jungle."

Halise, brought up to produce children and be provided for by her husband, set about her marital task. First came Hajri Isa Bala, in 1986. He was the first son, a great joy to Isa. Then Halise gave birth to a little girl,

Dardane Isa Bala, in 1988. She would soon learn from her mother how to help about the house. The second boy, Veton Isa Bala, was born in 1991. A little imp with thin legs and a wide smile, Veton was always out on his bike, playing in the streets.

And in 1993, Halise gave birth to a third son, Agon Isa Bala. Isa couldn't help it. He was even-handed with all his kids but Agon was his favorite. They had one of those irresistible father and son bonds. They even looked the same. From the moment he was born, Agon had Isa's thick neck. People called Agon "Little Isa." It was Agon who waited every day at the front door for his lumbering, blood-spattered father to come home, running to hug Isa's legs when he finally arrived.

The family was of average size for Albanians and the young couple and their babies had more than enough room in the house that Isa had bought half-finished on Dushan Mugosha Street in 1990. Isa bought it with family and business in mind. On the ground floor facing the street was space for two stores. One he would use for himself as a *cebob* shop. The larger one he rented out to an Albanian travel agent.

The shops had a separate entrance from the house, whose front door was at the end of a concrete pathway to the right of the three-story building. A footpath led to the backyard. Four and a half tiled steps brought you up to the pine front door. Visitors waiting to be let in could rest against the whitewashed neoclassical banister that ran alongside the steps and supported two concrete urns.

It was a modern house, simple and well built. Neither the previous owner nor Isa stinted on the interior, lining the solid pine stairway with more pine paneling on the walls. The doors were solid and stained russet. The floors were pine, too. Isa splashed out on double-glazing to protect his kids against the harsh Pec winter. For the summer there were three balconies to sit out on. He had the walls painted a simple white. With the whole of the top floor left open plan and flooded with light and a dark basement below the three main floors of the house, it was a home for kids to run about in and play hide and seek. It was the home with the "good kids and a nice wife" that Isa liked to go back to in the evening before the war. And it was the home that Isa wanted to get rid of or tear down after the war.

～

Hanging on the white-tiled wall above the heads of customers who walk in through Isa's shop door is a large faded photograph of Pec in 1936. The framed sepia image shows a town of stone houses with tiled roofs. In the foreground, people go about their business on one of the town's main streets. Beyond the city, lurking motionlessly like a cat above an oblivious mouse, a range of snowy mountains rises from the Dukagjin plain.

In Albanian, they are the Bjeshket e Namuna. In Serbian, Prokletje. Their name can be variously translated as the Accursed Mountains, the Damned Mountains, or, a little more liberally, as the Mountains of Ghosts or the Mountains of the Damned. The first time I heard about them someone referred to them as the Mountains of the Damned. It seemed appropriate.

Accounts vary as to how the mountains got their name. People around Pec tend to shrug and tell you to take a quick look at the peaks to the west of the town for an answer. You can see them from nearly everywhere. From the main square, known as the Korzo. From the Hotel Metohija in the Korzo, where many Yugoslav Army soldiers lived during the war. From the windows of Isa Bala's house. From Nebojsa Minic's front yard. From the Yugoslav People's Army bridge that joins the northern and southern parts of the town across the Bistrica River. From nearly every garden and every street. What you see are mountains as graceful as the Alps and as forbidding as the desert Rockies of New Mexico.

The mountains have seen much suffering and death over the centuries. During the 1930s, when the photograph in Isa's shop was taken, they towered over Pec as Albanians and Serbs continued their age-old struggle for political dominance. During World War II, Tito's communist Partisans tormented their Italian occupiers from cave and cliff top.

After World War II, the mountains saw a strange kind of peace. The farmers who carved out a life on the slopes of the foothills and the villagers and townsfolk who lived down below on the plain worked on together under the enforced ethnic harmony of communism. It was a largely artificial ethnic harmony, and in the first half of 1999 violence returned to the mountains like never before.

Chapter 2

The Ghosts of Kula Pass

Aeneas: We know each other well.
Diomedes: We do; and long to know each other worse.
                                    —William Shakespeare, *Troilus and Cressida,* IV.i

When I walked off the front loading bay of the rusty freight ship *Alba* onto the harborside of the Montenegrin port of Bar, the concrete quay was beginning to warm under the first hours of sunlight. The air was salty and clean and had the early smell of a hot spring day. Curving around the port, now the most important in the much-reduced territory of Yugoslavia, were hills of ragged stone. Dabs of a breeze came off the Adriatic into the sheltered bay and tiny waves slapped against the hull of a small Yugoslav navy gunship moored to the dockside. The Adriatic is the clearest sea I have ever seen and you could see the hull of the boat below the surface. The whole craft was old and unthreatening, its paint peeling, rust showing. With modern allied battleships prowling the Adriatic, it was no wonder the Yugoslav navy was keeping a low profile. Three or four soldiers guarded the boat. This day would make them sweat in their khakis unless they found a spot in the shadow of a nearby winch. A few hours earlier, NATO had bombed some military installations around Bar. I wondered how welcoming these soldiers would be if they knew that among the passengers were two journalists from NATO countries.

Yugoslavia was not on my beat. In fact, two days before I landed at Bar I didn't really know where Montenegro was. Unfortunately but unavoidably, the world's war zones are often visited by drop-in journalists who know precious little about the places they are going to. I had just been sent to the Middle East by my newspaper, *Newsday*, and had spent my first five weeks there living in a hotel in Jerusalem and trying to learn Arabic. Balkan wars were not meant to be on my agenda for the next three years. On Tuesday, March 23, 1999, my editor, Tim Phelps, called me as I was having dinner in Jerusalem with a friend and said that he would like me to fly to Rome the next day. The war was clearly about to begin. From Rome, I was to head south to the Italian port of Bari, where I should pay a visit to the Yugoslav consulate to try to obtain a visa. My *Newsday* colleague and Balkans expert Roy Gutman knew that this Yugoslav consulate happened to be manned by Montenegrins, not Serbs. For the Montenegrin government, at odds with the dominant federal and Serbian governments in Belgrade, the more foreign journalists who showed up to chronicle any threatening action from Belgrade, the better.

I packed a small backpack, picked up five thousand dollars in cash from my money changer and slept one last night at the hotel in Jerusalem. Early the next morning, March 24, I took the flight to Rome. Along the way to Bari, I bumped into my friend Charlie Sennott, the *Boston Globe*'s correspondent in the Middle East and he came with me to the consulate.

"There is one more ship out tonight," said the consul-general, who could not give us a visas because the Montenegrins had been stripped by Belgrade of the power to issue them. "Two of our government ministers are going to be on it."

The *Alba* was an old boat with throbbing engines that carried us through the night toward the bombing. As we ate dinner with the Montenegrin ministers of industry and culture and their wives, friends, and aides, they listened to their radios and heard the news that NATO had started to bomb the airport near their hometown of Podgorica, a base for the Yugoslav Army.

"Why are they bombing us?" Milosevic's Montenegrin enemies asked us as we all ate schnitzel and potatoes in the freighter's bare dining compartment.

And now we were in Montenegro, hiring a taxi, passing through immigration without visas, visiting a man whose home had been damaged by the previous night's bombing, and driving north to Podgorica past men in fatigues with AK-47s. We assumed they were Yugoslav soldiers but it turned out that these tall commandos with close-cropped hair were Montenegrin police and that's why they all cheerily waved us on to the capital.

In Montenegro's capital, Podgorica, once Titograd, winter was still hanging on. Slushy snow filled the streets. The shops, struggling with the embargo on Yugoslavia, stocked Yugoslav and smuggled products and food. Most people lived in apartments in the concrete blocks that Tito had left all over the country, buildings that sucked the light out of the sky.

Over the next few days, the dark brown rooms in the Hotel Crna Gora in Podgorica began to fill up with foreign journalists. Charlie and I had found a good translator, Katarina, and a dynamite driver, Nermin. (I have changed their names.) A lot was happening. Bombs fell at night on the outskirts of the city, mainly south toward the airport. During the day, with expectations of a Belgrade-led military coup growing every hour, we stood and watched an anti-American demonstration in downtown Podgorica and Katarina wiped away tears of fear from her eyes as the pro-Serbia crowd threw rocks at the window of the now-deserted American cultural center. We visited the pro-Milosevic newspaper, *Dan,* and were shouted out of the newsroom by some of the busy staff. And in his high-ceilinged office, Slobodan Tomovic, the Montenegrin minister of religion, began to explain to us the religious significance of Kosovo to the Serbs. It's the heart of the church, of the Serb people, he said. Its history is perverted with myth and exploited by killers, he said, but the history is part of every Serb's worldview. "I learned about it before I learned to read," said Tomovic, a Montenegrin. In Kosovo, this special region, he said, there is a very special town called Pec, just over the mountains. That's where the Patriarchate of the Serbian Orthodox Church is situated. Just outside the mainly Albanian town of Pec, this beautiful walled compound of churches and dormitories is the spiritual center of the church. He pointed to it on our tourist map and it looked only a few miles away from Montenegro and I asked if we could visit there before it became too dangerous and the minister said it was already too late for that. He was polite and sad.

Katarina's brother had a friend named Ibrahim who lived in the dour logging town of Rozaje on the western edge of Montenegro, the part that borders Kosovo. The road to Pec leads from Rozaje. It was the last stop before Kosovo and Ibrahim knew the place and its people better than anyone. He also knew Pec, having performed in a band there many times. Ibrahim's father, now dead, had been Muslim and his mother is Albanian. He speaks Serbian and Albanian.

On Friday night, two days into the first war that NATO had ever waged, Ibrahim sent word that a few Albanians had come over from Pec and we decided to drive up there early next morning. So far, the war had been about bombing, but on that Saturday there was the feeling of a beginning.

Before an Albanian enters someone else's house he or she will slip out of his shoes or boots and line them up just inside or outside the front door, then stepping cleanly and quietly on sock-covered feet into the living room. Fatime Djanbaja did not have to observe the polite custom this time because she was already shoeless on the afternoon of Saturday, March 27, 1999, when she arrived at the front door of a relative's home just inside the territory of Montenegro. The five Serb men in fatigues who, in a matter of a few minutes, had fired machine gun bullets through her front windows, smashed up her home, beaten her husband, robbed her, and forced her to leave her house had not given her enough time even to find herself a pair of sneakers to keep her feet dry in the snow. Her toes curled inside her damp white socks. A gas fire purred in front of her. Her face was empty as she stared at the flickering heat.

Fatime sat on a couch in the half-finished house of her relative in Rozaje, which lies a few miles inside Montenegro along the road that leads over the Mountains of the Damned from Pec, through a high, ex-posed pass called Kula. Her neatly cut blond hair pointed to her origins among middle-class Albanian society in Pec, one of the wealthiest cities in Kosovo. On the skin of the lower part of some of her fingers were the round marks where gold rings had comfortably squeezed her flesh for decades. The holes in her earlobes were empty of earrings. Her neck and wrists were without gold chains. For Kosovar Albanian women, and in particular the Albanian women of Pec, it is traditional to be given large amounts of gold as wedding presents and to wear much of that jewelry on a daily basis. Gold is one of the things Pec does well. People drive there from all over Kosovo to shop for gold jewelry. There is a section of the old town, or Haxhi Zeka, full of jewelers' shops called the Long Quarter. There, narrow stores with wide profit margins bunch together along the streets like the jewelry stores on the Ponte Vecchio in Florence. It's so crucial to the prosperity of the town that locals call the area the Suez Canal. Its gold was also part of many Albanians' financial planning. To many of Pec's Albanians, long used to sudden devaluations of the Yugoslav dinar and suspicious of the Serb-controlled banks, gold was their favored investment. It was portable, easy to hide, and rarely lost its value. Unless it was stolen, of course. The Serb men who dressed like soldiers but were not soldiers had made Fatime take off all her jewelry, her investments. Even her wedding ring. They wanted still more, so she showed them where she kept her other jewelry and the family's cash savings, a few rolls of deutsche marks. And they took her husband Rexhep's Rolex off his wrist.

"We came to kill you," one of the men said. "We have an order to kill you."

"Kosovo is Serbia's territory and Serbia's land," another one told them, as he held a gun to Rexhep's head. "All of you Albanians must leave."

The Serb men chose to evict the couple rather than murder them. But before the Djanbajas left their home, the men decided to make their message very clear. With the butts of their Kalashnikovs, the Serbs started to beat Rexhep. The blows came to his face and head. He closed his eyes and his wife watched and the men beat him as he lay on the ground. Silent and wondering if she was watching her husband's death, Fatime tried hard not to look in the eyes of one of the men beating her husband. He was a neighbor, a Serb they had known for years. She didn't want to anger the man with a look of recognition. What is it they say about how you should behave if you meet a bear in the woods? Stare at the ground in front of you. Don't look the bear in the eye. Fatime stared at the kitchen floor. She was sure he and the other four were drunk or on drugs but maybe it was a more natural fury, born of resentment, myth, language, revenge, religion, their own exploitation by their own leaders. Whatever fueled them, they worked like people from a rival tribe, not like soldiers or townsfolk. Knowing from the neighbor that Rexhep was an observant Muslim, they unscrewed the top off a bottle of alcohol and told him to open his mouth. And they poured, the clear liquid racing down his throat and overflowing from his mouth and down his chin.

"Get out," the men told the middle-aged couple.

Fatime and Rexhep, she shoeless, he quivering in pain, ran through the muddy street to their red Yugo car. Behind them the Serbs were shaking cans of spray paint and began emblazoning a sign on the front wall of the Djanbajas' house. Four Cyrillic S's divided by a cross appeared on the brickwork. Every Serb knows what that sign means. Kosovo's Albanians know too. "Only Unity Saves the Serbs." The cross is borrowed from the Serbian Orthodox Church, the institution that has done most to bind the Serb people together over their troubled centuries. The Djanbajas turned the ignition and made for the road to Rozaje, over the Mountains of the Damned. The Serb men had arrived at the Djanbajas' home in Pec at noon. Three hours later the couple were homeless in Montenegro.

Helping them along the road inside Kosovo were soldiers and paramilitaries like Dragan, a less than thoughtful, heavily tattooed career criminal and sometime foot soldier for Serbian nationalism. Operating in the Pec region, he was a member of a paramilitary group called the Pit Bull Terriers.

"When the bombing started all the Albanians started to flee. Most were women and children and older people leaving on tractors. Some we helped. The men were hiding in the forests and others were pretending to be injured or handicapped. We were on the outskirts of Pec, controlling the stream of traffic, trying to make it go smoothly."

That Saturday afternoon, the NATO bombardment was three days old. In the United States, President Bill Clinton was vowing to protect the Albanians, whose leaders had agreed to an American-brokered peace deal a few weeks earlier. "We promised we would stick by them if they did the right thing," Clinton said in a radio address. "And they did. We can't let them down now." In Belgrade, President Slobodan Milosevic, who had rejected the deal, went on television to promise his people that NATO troops would never occupy Kosovo, one of the key parts of the proposed deal.

In the quiet of Rozaje that day, as icy rain fell on snow and mud, the wealthier Slavic Muslim residents of the town were butchering the sheep they would eat and give to their poorer neighbors in celebration of one of the two annual Muslim feasts. Men stood outside their homes in the downpour slicing through the bone, muscle, and ligament of sheep. A stripped carcass rushed along the surface of the bloated and frothing Ibar River. It was time to celebrate the feast, a time of family, peace, plenty of good food, and respect for God. As the preparations continued, a handful of people like Fatime Djanbaja were filtering through Kula Pass from the mountain road in Kosovo called Savine Vode and into the homes of friends and relatives in Rozaje. That afternoon, hardly anyone in town noticed the newcomers. Fatime and Rexhep and a few other families were the first sign of the exodus that was to come the next day and would continue for days and weeks after that.

Unlike the hundreds of thousands of Kosovar Albanian refugees who fled to Macedonia and Albania, Fatime Djanbaja and the nearly seventy thousand who followed in the following days sought refuge in another part of Yugoslavia. An extremely volatile part. The Yugoslav republic of Montenegro was in a bind during the war of 1999. The only remaining partner of Serbia in what was left of Yugoslavia found itself being bombed by NATO, threatened with a military coup by Belgrade, and flooded with Albanian refugees over the course of eleven weeks. The bombing and refugee crisis were disasters for Montenegro's young president, Milo Djukanovic, who had turned away from socialism and had recently begun to seek and obtain invitations for tea with Western leaders. Democracy and independence from Yugoslavia, Milosevic, and Serbian control was the future for his 650,000 people, he had decided.

An independent Montenegro was anathema to Belgrade and any Serb who, after a decade of Serbian wars, still believed in the dream of a Greater Serbia. Djukanovic's challenge was to start the process of securing independence without starting another war. The last thing Djukanovic wanted was a fight with Milosevic, but he had amassed his own heavily armed and very loyal police force to defend him if it came to war.

The unique problem for Djukanovic the separatist was this: Unlike all the other independence-minded non-Serbian peoples of the former Yugoslavia—Slovenes, Croats, Bosnian Muslims, Macedonians, Albanians—about half of all Montenegrins consider themselves Serbs and would likely fight against the other half to remain within Yugoslavia.

That other half, the supporters of separation from Serbia, look back to 1918, when Montenegro lost its independence and became part of the brand new Kingdom of Yugoslavia, thanks to the whims of the Great Powers who reshaped much of the world after World War I. Serbia, as the largest nation in the new country, dominated Yugoslavia. Many Montenegrins found justice missing from this arrangement. For centuries, Serbia had been under Ottoman rule, only regaining its independence in 1878. Montenegro, as nationalist Montenegrins tend to remind you every few minutes in political coffee-talk, never fully succumbed to Ottoman domination. What kind of just desserts was this, to be in a new country dominated by Serbia, a country that could not look after itself for centuries? And then, in 1918, in an immediate sign that Serbia wanted to absorb Montenegro into its own world, the Serbian Orthodox Church unilaterally declared that the Montenegrin Orthodox Church was no longer.

Such events have not been forgotten. Generations after losing their independence, many Montenegrins are quite willing to fight Yugoslav forces to regain it. During the war in Kosovo, bunches of young men in the southern town of Cetinje, where old portraits of Montenegrin kings and church leaders appear on the walls of cafés and bars, formed armed groups whose purpose was to scare off the Yugoslav soldiers who came knocking on doors and visiting those same cafés trying to draft unwilling young men into the Yugoslav Army. To these Montenegrins, Serbs are uncultured, uncouth, and unwelcome.

A civil war in Montenegro, Djukanovic knew, would not be a fistfight. Of all the well-armed peoples in the Balkans, the Montenegrins are perhaps the most obsessed by guns. Firearms are everywhere. Among many families, the old Montenegrin tradition still holds that a baby boy must sleep with a gun under his pillow on his first night in the world. That gun remains his for life. Many Montenegrin men do not stop with that first acquisition.

Not that you would think most Montenegrin men would need a gun in a fight. Montenegrins like to say that after the Dinkas of Sudan they are the tallest people in the world. And for sure, a six-foot man in Podgorica is like a pine in a forest of redwoods. Anyone of any importance— Djukanovic is the best example—seems to be a giant. Hence the national interest in basketball. But hence also, perhaps, a certain fearlessness in battle.

Making matters even more volatile for Djukanovic in the spring of 1999, many Montenegrin men were battle-tested. The little republic was full of men who had had recent experience fighting for the Yugoslav Army in Milosevic's earlier wars. They had killed Croats and Muslims and they knew how to kill each other.

Montenegro's towns and villages were also the breeding ground of numerous celebrated paramilitaries and Serb-nationalist politicians. The Bosnian Serb leader in the Bosnian war, Radovan Karadzic, was born in Montenegro. Milosevic's parents were Montenegrin and he used to spend boyhood summers in a mountain village called Lijeva Rijeka where the last name of every second person seems to be Milosevic. One Milosevic cousin chased four visitors off with a knife—myself included —one afternoon during the war. These people's political allegiances are to Belgrade. Their souls are Serbian. They too were ready to fight.

For Djukanovic, a war with Serbia, then, would also have meant a war between the towering separatists of Cetinje and the short-tempered Serbs of Lijeva Rijeka. Both groups had about the same numbers. Both were heavily armed. Djukanovic would do almost anything to avoid a civil war. Even if his side won, he would not have much of a country left to rule.

And now, all of a sudden, just as he was trying to persuade his people that their future lay in good relations with the West and not in a cozy isolationist alliance with Belgrade, his new friends at NATO had started to bomb his country. It was a disaster. Every day in Podgorica brought new rumors of a coup. Milosevic and his political allies in Montenegro smelled an opportunity to topple Djukanovic, who had won election over the pro-Milosevic president, Momir Bulatovic (the Prime Minister of Yugoslavia during the last Milosevic years), by a few villages' worth of votes. From day one of the war, Montenegro was quivering with the fear that what was going on in Kosovo was modest compared to what could happen there.

I had always considered the word "paramilitary" to mean an accessory military force that works alongside a true military. The dictionary suggests that it can also mean a diversionary or auxiliary force, sometimes existing when there is no regular military. From the first days of the war, the Serb paramilitaries in Kosovo stretched the definitions. Becoming the vanguard rather than the backup in the ethnic cleansing campaign, they did the dirty work and the profitable work.

The paramilitary groups came under the ultimate orders of Milosevic and through the command control of the Ministry of the Interior, or MUP (Ministarstvo Unutrasnjih Poslova), according to many Yugoslav military and paramilitary sources. The MUP was the nerve center for Serbia's war in Kosovo. There were absolutely no freelance paramilitary groups in Kosovo. There was too much at stake politically and too much money to be made to allow uncontrolled opportunists to run wild inside Kosovo. It was all run from Belgrade, where the criminal world of Arkan was barely distinguishable from the official world of the state security services. Milosevic had the final word on the running of the ground war.

Testimony from the paramilitaries makes it absolutely clear that months before the NATO bombardment began, Milosevic had planned to conduct a campaign of terror against the Albanians. It was no opportunistic tactic prompted by the NATO bombardment. Even low-level paramilitaries were told weeks in advance by their commanders and recruiters about the looting and killing that would soon happen.

All this was orchestrated by the complex command structure of the MUP, Milosevic's main tool in Kosovo.

There were and are two sometimes competing strands of the MUP, which oversees all policing in Yugoslavia. One pillar of the Interior Ministry is the Sector of Public Security, or RJB (Resor Javne Bezbednosti). This sector includes all policemen in blue and green camouflage uniforms. A part of this sector is the much feared PJP (Posebne Jedinice Policije)—the Police Special Units. By this stage down the ladder of police organizations, lawlessness has entered the ranks of discipline: *Munje*, or Lightning, a PJP group made up partly of some of Yugoslavia's most dangerous criminals, was the elite unit within the PJP before and during the war in Kosovo.

Given the power that each arm of the security services possesses in Yugoslavia, a careful balancing act has to take place so that no one group or individual becomes too powerful. Incidentally, the same was as true now in 2001 as it was in the Milosevic decade.

Offsetting the awesome power of the Sector of Public Security within the Ministry of the Interior is the State Security Service, or RDB (Resor Drzavne Bezbednosti). Within the State Security Service are the official Red Berets, an elite group of policemen, and the Frenkis, a thuggish unofficial paramilitary group named after their leader, Franko Simatovic. Like *Munje*, the Frenkis are a mixture of criminals and hardened police officers.

In the special circumstances of the war in Kosovo, the balance was even trickier to strike. Into the mix came Arkan and his highly organized Tigers, working at the same time for Arkan and the MUP. Smaller paramilitary groups worked under the auspices of one or other of the two strands of the MUP.

And of course, given that Kosovo was a war zone, there were forty thousand troops from the Yugoslav Army, or VJ (Vojska Jugoslavije) in the field. Two vitally important units in the VJ were the Military Police and their sister unit, the Counter Intelligence Service, or KOS (Kontra-Obavjestajna Sluzba). These groups controlled the borders.

If all this sounds like a typically confusing Balkan, postcommunist mess, that's because it was. Deliberately so. It was a classic leadership gambit of Milosevic's: Have all the loot and burning and killing ultimately and efficiently channeled through the MUP, and to a lesser extent through the army, while keeping the lieutenants and foot soldiers in his enormous crime family competing with each other over the spoils and power.

It was highly effective at the time but its long-term consequences were less helpful to Milosevic. The feuding paramilitary groups killed many of each others' members at the end and after the war (Arkan was the most famous victim); the army felt cheated; and some of the Milosevic thugs started to talk about their experiences in Kosovo in order to expose the system that they felt had exploited them.

One was a recently retired senior Yugoslav Army officer who spoke after the war on condition of anonymity. A veteran of the fighting in Kosovo, the officer was disillusioned and disgusted with Milosevic and the army by August 1999. The regular soldiers, many of them conscripts, were paid a pittance of state wages to hang back and protect the marauding paramilitaries from KLA ambushes, he said. And for their efforts, the regulars were bombed by NATO in the field while the mobile paramilitaries in their small groups moved with almost complete freedom and impunity.

"The Yugoslav Army consciously and deliberately protected [the paramilitaries]," the officer told me over coffee one day in Montenegro. "Basically, the role of the army was to pick up corpses and organize mass graves and burials. For example, the Frenkis would rush into one town, massacre people and do whatever they wanted. The army was not allowed to enter. When they had finished the army would go in and bury the corpses and burn them as it was in Germany a long time ago."

In Pec, the delicate balance of power had several paramilitary groups and the police ruling the town.

"My first cousin was with [Arkan's] Tigers in Croatia and Bosnia," twenty-six-year-old Tony, the Arkan associate, explained after the war as he sat in a café in Montenegro, sifting through his memories and the guilt that tormented him. "Through him I went to Kosovo. We are very close. He said to me, 'Do you want to make money? A lot of money?' It's not a nice way to make money but such were the circumstances. When this action on Kosovo started he was there on the first day. I went a bit later. Our job was to gather and send all the spoils and to transfer them to Belgrade. The majority of the spoils went to Arkan. The spoils were divided up in Belgrade. The state took part. We were backed up by the units who did the cleansing.

"We operated in small groups in different regions of Kosovo. We had good equipment, good jeeps. There was very fast movement from place to place. After we finished taking the loot from one place we would go to another place."

Tony described how individuals were not allowed to keep more than approximately 10 percent of the loot they had gathered. The rest had to go to Belgrade. "The heavy things went immediately to Belgrade. TVs, fancy furniture, refrigerators, all white goods. There was no need for them to stay in Kosovo. We knew Kosovo would be lost. At least we knew that while those other fools were fighting. It was very sad to see the regular troops sitting in tanks and antiaircraft positions exposed to high risks of getting killed every day when they didn't earn a dinar or a penny. They were supposed to take orders and they did because of their political persuasions.

"The paramilitary units I met were composed of all kinds. There were junkies, prisoners, people picked up off the streets of Belgrade, people possessed with patriotic, nationalistic ideas who thought they could beat NATO with guns. They believed in that. . . . There were drugs, as many as you wanted. Coke, heroin, LSD—everything you want. The whole range. Some of them asked to be paid in drugs.

"We had gypsies assigned to us to take the goods out of the houses. My team was composed of businesspeople. Those who were directly involved in the cleansing were considered pawns by us, frustrated people who could pour out their fury and rage at someone."

Under Arkan's direction and with the cooperation of the Interior Ministry, Tony's group had primary dominion over the Pec region's wealth. To begin with, the process of emptying out Pec and its villages of their goods went smoothly, Tony said. But as NATO struck at main roads and army communications centers, his small group had to rely on the army to build temporary bridges and on back roads that had not been bombed. In the early days, they communicated by satellite telephone with Belgrade but later the Yugoslav authorities became convinced that NATO could listen in on the phones and so locate their military positions. Tony's group and others switched to using Motorola radios.

It was also easier in the beginning because his group had lists of the richest Albanians in Pec. The lists had been compiled over the years by the local Serb authorities in Pec, Tony said.

"The information was concise. First name, last name, address, who the head of the family is; how many family members there are; whether there was someone working abroad; whether they owned a shop. Such people were the priority. Everything had been prepared in advance. Ten years ago, after the autonomy of Kosovo was canceled, the paramilitaries developed some clout in Kosovo and they knew all the time who were the richest people. But their valuables were not taken then because they paid taxes and the Serbian administration in Kosovo received bribes from the Albanians. So the Albanians had no hindrances in opening gas stations and other businesses because everything benefited the state. When war broke out, we just carried out actions on people we had known about before."

Moving through the town, holding Albanians hostage until they paid up, was quick work. The state and the criminal world worked smoothly together.

"It's a state within a state. It's such a good organization. Better than the state, really."

Tony watched as the war seduced his colleagues. As a Serb from Pec whose family had to flee to Montenegro decades before because they were involved in a deadly blood feud with an Albanian family, Tony might have hated the Albanians, and taken pride in his own people. But his disdain for the paramilitaries was as great as it was for the KLA.

"These people had no heart, no feelings. A man's life didn't mean anything to them. It's a big mistake for the newspapers to say that the paramilitaries are patriotic nationalists, that we fought for the Serbs. That wasn't important to us. We don't give a damn about that. Even Serb houses didn't have a much better outcome regarding furniture and so on, especially if the owners were out of Kosovo. Anyway, it's astonishing how a man can turn into a beast in such a short time. I know a guy who was completely normal, who was there for the sake of business. He was ordered to execute one guy. He was told he was a member of the KLA but I doubt he was a member. After that this guy became a hard-core killer. I don't understand that. He used to tell me that the job was a real passion with him."

From Rozaje to Podgorica it is a three-hour drive along a twisty road that leads through mountain tunnels and deep limestone gorges. Cars with license plates beginning with the letters "PE" brought that road to a standstill on Sunday, Monday, and Tuesday. They had snaked up from Pec through the deep snow of Kula, their drivers paying off the Yugoslav border guards and soldiers at the checkpoints, then winding down into Rozaje. Some of the cars stayed in town, their occupants sheltering with friends or relatives or kindly strangers, but most of the first ones headed south. In that first exodus there were a good number of Mercedeses and BMWs, cars owned by Pec's wealthy Albanian merchants. Their homes and businesses had been targeted first by the savvy paramilitaries who levied a toll on the Albanians' lives. Deutsche marks and gold for survival. Most of the cars were not as expensive, though. They were Opels, made in Germany, or Zastavas or Yugos, made by the Yugoslavian state car manufacturer. They were small cars, often old and every single one seemed to be packed with at least five people. Most were grotesquely overloaded at the back, their rear ends only inches from the surface of the road. Trunks overflowed with bags and suitcases. Twine bound more luggage to the roofs. Every space in every car that wasn't filled by a human being was filled with clothes, diapers, food, shoes, and the occasional piece of furniture, a chair perhaps. Faces stared out of the car windows at Montenegro, a country that was the homeland of many of the armed men who had arrived in Pec over the past few weeks and had just hours earlier forced them out of their homes at gunpoint. As they entered Podgorica, groups of teenage boys stood at the side of the road waving Yugoslav flags and making the three-fingered Serbian hand signal at the Albanians as they drove past. It was no welcome. These people had left in terror and they arrived in fear. Unshaven, unwashed, robbed —the smoke from their homes rising into the clouds as they drove away from Pec—the tens of thousands of Albanians who poured into Montenegro, headed south to the seaside resort of Ulcinj.

For thousands of Kosovar Albanians, Ulcinj was their Fort Lauderdale, their Newport, their East Hampton. Every summer, Kosovo's affluent families and young people would drive over the mountains and down through Montenegro to the old beach town where many owned or rented summer homes. Here they walked along the promenade next to the beach and started holiday romances or sat under the canopies of restaurants on the main streets keeping one eye on the kids and the other on a dish of fresh fish that the restaurants cooked after buying the day's catch from the men who fished the Adriatic. Ulcinj is overwhelmingly an ethnic Albanian town. It is geographically close to Albania, too. If you stroll far enough east along the apparently endless sands at Ulcinj you will reach the border with the land most Kosovars dreamed of as they were growing up.

Every house, apartment, off-season hotel, and parking lot in Ulcinj suddenly filled up as if all the well-off types and middle classes in Western Kosovo had decided to take a weekend break at the same time.

Ulcinj was a place with good memories for Besim Mulliqi. I met him in a refugee registration center on the afternoon of Tuesday, March 30, as the first week of the war was nearing its end. Usually he and his family—he had a wife named Flora and three small children—rented a comfortable apartment near the sea but now they were spending their last remaining marks on an overpriced room with two single beds and enough space between the beds for a roll-up mattress.

The Mulliqis were luckier than many. They had smuggled out some money, at least. Those who could not afford rooms relied on charity. Most aid agencies had fled Montenegro for security reasons before NATO started bombing the country and so it was left to the cash-strapped Montenegrin government to provide tents in Ulcinj and food and medical care for the refugees, who in a matter of days had contributed to a more than 10 percent growth in the population of Montenegro. Its resources stretched, many of its people increasingly intolerant of the newcomers, the Montenegrin government issued warning after warning to the international powers: If this went on too long, a coup was likely and war would follow. The nightmare scenario of a spreading Balkan war would begin.

Besim had just left one war and hoped he would never see it again. He had built his own large, five-bedroom home just outside Pec. In the flower beds of the backyard were every type of rose Besim could lay his hands on in the nurseries of Kosovo. Trained at Pristina University as an agricultural engineer, he owned a shop in Pec that sold spare parts for household appliances. When he drove back from work in the evening in his silver Opel Kadett, he would head straight for the flower beds and before the sun went down through the leaves of the apple trees in his backyard he would practice jump shots and lay-ups in the basketball hoop behind the house. Besim was thirty-six and had the start of a belly but was still handsome. As he described his life he spoke in the present tense—"I go jogging every morning at seven"—as if his home had not been burned down two days earlier, on Sunday.

That day, with tanks, flames, and the sound of gunfire around them and with only enough time to grab a single bag of clothes, Besim unwittingly echoed the plot of the Roberto Benigni movie *Life Is Beautiful.* He tried to fool his three children into thinking they were going on vacation again.

"Veton understands everything," Besim said of his eight-year-old boy. "But I told the other two that this was just a military exercise. As we drove out of Kosovo I hid them from seeing things and listened to loud music so that they wouldn't hear the shelling. They thought it was kind of a game."

Two days after its start, the game was losing its appeal for Besim and Flora's two younger children. Two-year-old Mehmed kept asking to play with his neighbor from back home. Their wide-eyed five-year-old Vesa had started to ask her mom why the Serbs had done this to them. In the grass and gravel patch in front of the apartment building they were now sharing with dozens of other refugee families, Veton strolled around in silence with his hands in his jeans and his eyes examining the little stones that he kicked around with his shoes.

Still, Ulcinj was about as good as it gets for refugee destinations. The sun was shining and the locals, nearly all Albanians, tended to be generous and kind. No one starved and few lacked for medical care. Many young Albanians sat around in cafés all day.

In Rozaje, where Albanians continued to arrive after the brutal journey over the mountains, it was still cold and wet and the world had largely forgotten the town. I spent a night in one of the several derelict factories that were home to thousands of the poorest refugees, the villagers without cars or tractors, the sick, and the stubborn.

In the Kristal factory, workers used to make quality glassware, but although Tito still gazed down on the factory floor with a look of stern encouragement from a framed photograph hanging on a gable end wall, the last goblet had been cut there many years ago. Now it was home to about three thousand of the millions of people in the former Yugoslavia who have suffered the implosion of Tito's artificial country. In lines of hundreds, they slept on blankets on the concrete floor; babies in week-old diapers nursing at the exposed breasts of sleeping mothers; half a dozen siblings dozily squirming under one blanket, their breath turning to rimy vapor. One teenage girl had a makeshift bandage around her shoulder, which had been hit by part of a Serb shell as she fled through the mountain forest. Some people, men mostly, had to stay awake all night because there was no room for them on the floor. They would sleep when the sun came up. Violent, phlegmy coughs, the crying of babies, and the distant roar of NATO jets flying into and back from Serbia and Kosovo were the sounds of the night. The air smelled damp and used. There was no source of heating for the vast factory. Piles of excrement around the perimeter and inside some of the buildings told you all you needed to know about sanitation at Kristal. All night, people crowded around the two stoves that burned constantly in the paved courtyard outside the factory, boiling water and old diapers in large pans. Clothes hung on washing lines outside, sodden in the rain.

Through that rain and snow, up at Kula Pass, the last people from Pec were still coming into Montenegro. On Wednesday, March 31, one week after the war had started, I drove up there with Ibrahim's cousin Edin, another translator, Marko, and Colin Nickerson of the *Boston Globe,* who had replaced Charlie.

At the side of the road were shoulder-high walls of snow that led off into the steep mountainside of pines. Visibility was poor on account of the fog, and I could not see far up the mountains or far along the windy road with its potholes and muddy snow. People were coming by foot and perching on the backs of tractors. Staggering along the last few meters of Kosovo's territory before they reached the relative safety of Montenegro, they were desperate, the last to leave Pec and its surrounding villages, and they were exhausted, freezing, and terrified. Emerging from the fog, they were like ghosts. Some had slept out in the open after days of walking. Hour after hour, as they had done for days, many Montenegrins drove their cars up to the pass to pick up exhausted refugees. The drivers asked for nothing, set their passengers down in the bus station in Rozaje, and then drove back up to collect more.

On the road, two Yugoslav soldiers stood with their automatic weapons keeping the traffic moving out of Kosovo. They stopped and searched some cars but not others and not ours.

In dozens of interviews in Rozaje and Ulcinj, I had heard of killings and expulsions in Pec. I knew the names of neighborhoods and streets and dead people and I had asked people to draw me maps of the city, to show me where their homes were, where the Bistrica River ran through the town, where they had seen bodies, where they had been herded into the town square before being herded again into the town's basketball arena for one terrified night. The stragglers of Kula that day told me that there were hardly any Albanian families left in Pec, a town of a hundred thousand people, most of them Albanians. In cars, on tractors, in buses, on the backs of refrigeration trucks, on foot, nearly everyone had gone. The town was burning still, they said, but it was almost empty of Albanians.

But there were a few left. It amazed me. Why on earth would any Albanians stay behind in Pec? Many towns and cities in Kosovo were being cleared of their inhabitants but none seemed to be suffering the destruction that the Serbs were inflicting on Pec. Most people told me that only old people and invalids had been left behind. But I also heard that there were a handful of families hiding in their homes. No one mentioned Isa Bala, the butcher, but he was there.

Chapter 3

Staying Behind

There was not enough food in the house and so Isa had to go shopping. It was the morning after the bombing had started, March 25, and Isa woke early as he always did and walked to the bakery nearby. The sky was clear and it was a chilly and fine morning. But the mountain air was mixed with ash and smoke. Isa met friends along the way and they told him stories of what was happening around Pec. One told Isa that a mutual friend had been killed the previous evening. The man had received a phone call and was told to come to his front gate. As he stood there in the darkness someone shot and killed him.

Isa hurried on to the bakery. About thirty people stood in line, panic-buying. Most were Serbs, the Albanians in the neighborhood either too frightened to come out shopping or already making the journey to the borders. There was no bread left, only rolls.

"These rolls are too expensive for me," grumbled a Serb man who stood in front of Isa in the line.

"Just buy them," Isa told him. "Now's not the time to worry about money."

The line took forever and Isa left, impatient and increasingly uneasy. Nearby some Serbs had started to break into two Albanian-owned shops. The owner of the one of the stores stood there and begged them to leave his shop.

"This is a war," one of the looters said, laughing. "So don't worry about your shop any more."

Isa walked across Yugoslav People's Army bridge and into the center of the town to the Albanian commercial district of Haxhi Zeka, the old part of the city where jewelry shops and bookstores squeezed in together along narrow streets. He walked around and saw most of the jewelry stores burning. Only a few stood untouched. But now Serbs were kicking in their doors and windows and stuffing watches, necklaces, and rings into their pockets and into bags. Even the police were doing it. Hardly a car moved through the town. Those that did blared Serbian music from their stereos. Besides Isa, the only other Albanians were passing through the center toward the road to Montenegro. Adults carried babies and others pushed their old and sick parents in wheelbarrows. The police officers were taking money off them and then letting them go. In some Serb-owned cafés, young men sat and drank coffee, entertained by the spectacle of the Albanians' flight. Here too the Serbian music was loud and martial and it filled the street.

Cheese; Isa's wife and kids wanted cheese as well as bread. He had to get to the cheese market, near the train station. So far he had just bought dishwashing detergent in a Serb-owned shop.

"Hey, where are you going?" It was a Serb police officer.

"The cheese market," Isa said.

"Don't bother," the officer said. He wasn't aggressive but Isa sensed that the police wanted all Albanians off the streets. So he quickly started to walk home back over the Bistrica River. Isa saw houses with their front doors kicked in, family photographs littered on the grass of a front yard. He kept his head down and tried not to see who was burning the houses, afraid that he would be shot if the men saw him looking. As the merry arsonists started a new one, they would fire a burst of gunfire into the air to celebrate.

In the street on the way back, Isa met a Serb woman he knew, a woman whose late husband had been Albanian. "Shame on them for what they're doing," she said.

He met another Albanian man he knew wandering around, looking lost.

"Why are you crying?" Isa asked him.

"They killed my father and my son," the man said, stumbling on.

He overheard two Serb women in conversation. "The Serbs are used to war," one said. "This will be easy."

"I'm not afraid of the NATO pact bombing us," the other said. "We'll fight back and win."

There was the smell of burning furniture, wallpaper, plastic, and floorboards everywhere. Small patches of smoke drifted across the street. As Isa reached his shop on the way home he noticed that someone had scratched the name "Ivana" onto the front wall of his store. That was the name of a ten-year-old Serb girl who lived in one of the apartments upstairs from the shop.

He couldn't resist visiting his second home, the shop. He slipped the key into the keyhole and quietly let himself into the cool room with its smell of blood. In the back room of the store, which he usually used for storing equipment and unwanted pieces of cow, he had hidden the large slabs of beef he had expected to sell from behind the counter in the later days of March. His knife sliced through the flesh and a large chunk of meat was ready for his family in a plastic bag. Sausages still looped down from the hooks behind the counter and he pulled off a few of them and stuffed them into the bag. And then he left.

So far, apart from the meat and the detergent, he had found nothing on his mental shopping list. He had wanted to buy something to drink for his kids, some candles in case the power went off, and some dishwashing liquid, shampoo, soap. What kind of provider was he to come back empty-handed to his wife, mother, and four children? And there was his brother's family to feed also. The bakery was still open across the street from his shop. He scurried over, bought some cookies for the kids, and handed the Serb store owner sixty dinars.

"Wait, wait until I give you the change," the man told the quickly exiting Isa.

"No, it's no problem," the butcher called over his shoulder as he strode out of the shop.

Pec is emptying and still we haven't left, Isa thought. Everyone else is going.

Barely a house in the Albanian neighborhoods of Karagac, Kapesnica, and Zatre was undamaged by now. In the days to come, tanks would shell and then drive down the streets of Haxhi Zeka and the Long Quarter, ramming into the shopfronts on the south side of the main street in the commercial district, until all that was left of the row was a pile of rubble. The streets of Pec were already ruled by the Serb paramilitary groups—the Frenkis, *Munje,* the Black Hand—who had moved into Pec in the weeks and months leading up to the start of the bombing. They seemed to have it all planned, moving from house to house, street to street. Then forming people into columns and marching them out, or forcing them onto buses and trucks bound for the borders. They had not come down Dushan Mugosha Street yet, though. Aside from Isa, quite a few Serbs lived on the street. Perhaps that's why it had been spared. Or perhaps it was just a matter of the paramilitaries getting to it in due course.

Isa Bala didn't know what on earth he should do. Should he and his family get into his white Zastava pickup truck and join the exodus? He had lots of Serb neighbors and surely they would protect him from this. He was on good terms with everyone. Also, it would be hard to take his paralyzed mother, Mahie, out of the country. Several years before, his mother, now sixty-two, had been standing on a table at home painting the ceiling when she had fallen and broken her back. Now she spent her days lying on a mattress. Taking her on a long journey without a home at the other end would be hard.

Three days before the bombing had started, he and his brother Musa had stood in the shop discussing their options. Musa still had his car at that point, a light blue Mercedes A 190—it would be stolen two weeks later—and he too had the option of driving over the mountains with his wife Vjollca and their three children and then down to Ulcinj, where Vjollca's family had fled. Musa happened to have rented an apartment in the popular vacation town for a year and so he knew they would have somewhere to stay.

"You should go," Isa told Musa. "Go to Ulcinj." He could see that Musa was afraid even though the worst was yet to begin in Pec.

"No, no, it's too dangerous. Look, I'll come to your house. You've got lots of Serb neighbors. They know you and they won't touch us."

"I'm telling you," Isa said. "You'd be better off going now."

"No, we'll come to your place. You can't be sure on the roads anymore. There are bandits everywhere. We'll be round soon."

It was late afternoon. Musa left the shop, drove his car quickly through the backstreets to his house in Kapesnica, packed up his family, and by seven that evening he and his family were at Isa's house. There was plenty of room for them. But Isa thought his younger brother was making a big mistake.

Now, several days later, Isa was making his way back to his house and still wondered what to do. With the start of the bombing and the paramilitaries' campaign of evicting people from their homes at gunpoint, Musa's fear had overwhelmed him. He had become silent, barely ate, smoked his favorite L&M cigarettes constantly, and took the wind out of his racing thoughts with the scorching grape-liquor *raki* until he lost consciousness. When Isa looked at his brother's face he saw wide, unblinking eyes and cheeks still with fear.

Isa walked up the path to his front door and made his way inside. At the top of the pine stairway, his children stood wearing their hats, scarves, gloves, and winter coats. Halise was tucking their scarves inside their jackets, getting them ready to leave. She wanted out. She wanted to pass through the city center, meet the road to Montenegro, pass the Serb checkpoints, and push on over Kula Pass into Rozaje with the few Albanians still left in town, most of whom were leaving. They would walk in the snow if no one gave them a lift. Everyone else was doing it. From Rozaje, Halise planned to head south to Ulcinj. It was still Yugoslavia but it would be safe compared to the hell of gunfire and burning houses that surrounded them.

"No, absolutely not," her husband told her, shooing the kids back inside, telling them to take off their winter gear. "We're staying. I can't leave my mother here. Anyway, we have no enemies so it'll be fine."

The children were scared. "Daddy, send us to Montenegro or somewhere. They'll shoot us dead," his daughter Dardane told him. Isa's word was final. He had made his decision.

～

43

On the inside of Nebojsa Minic's lower lip is tattooed the word *Mrtvi*. That's Serbian for "Dead." He also has "Dead Man" in Serbian tattooed on his chest. *Mrtvi* is his nickname and he is very fond of it.

There are two slightly different versions of how he came by the name.

Minic was involved in a gunfight either during the Bosnian war or in one of the early battles with the KLA in 1998. One version, offered by a paramilitary who knows Minic, has him surrounded by the enemy. He has become separated from his comrades and back at base everyone thinks he is a lost cause. Minic is dead, they say. But Minic keeps fighting. Everyone, even those who now hate him, acknowledge that he is a brave and excellent fighter. For over a day he darts around the terrain, picking off one enemy soldier after another.

Another version, from another paramilitary colleague, has it that Minic is surrounded and isolated and he realizes he is in a cemetery. He wrenches off the top of a grave and hides inside for two days until the enemy has moved on.

Either way, Minic eventually returns to the base and everyone is amazed. We thought you were a dead man, they say. Minic likes that. He begins to call himself *Mrtvi*.

He was still Minic to his neighbors, though. The Ramajs had long since grown terrified of the man next door but they still called him by his childhood name. The first weekend of the war, their childhood playmate told them they had only a few moments to leave their home. "I won't kill you but someone else will," Minic said, standing at their front door, heavily armed.

He had started his own campaign of terror in his own neighborhood.

At four fifteen in the afternoon on March 27, Minic and some members of his gang leaped over the garden walls of his neighbor Ali Gashi's house. Gashi's now charred house is just around the corner from Minic's. Fifty-eight-year-old Gashi and a neighbor were the only men in the house, remembered his wife, Sherife, and their daughter Hidajete after the war. The women were outside.

Minic told the neighbor, who survived, that he would save the neighbor's life for a hundred marks but Gashi, Minic said, was a dead man. *Mrtvi*, just like Minic.

"I heard a gunshot and my husband screaming," said Sherife Gashi,

44

one afternoon a few weeks after the war, as she sat crying with her daughter in front of photographs of the man who killed Ali Gashi. "Then Minic shot again and killed him."

Minic inspired devotion in his close associates and hatred among some of his foot soldiers. "I'd split open his skull," said a former Minic recruit called Momo, who said after the war that he was left unpaid by the *Munje* leader.

By the time the war started on March 24, Vitomir Salipur, often known as Shalipuri, and Minic had assembled up to two hundred men in the Pec region, said Momo and Vladan, another disillusioned recruit. They were divided into groups of around fifteen to twenty men, living in houses in and around the city. All these groups fell under the control of either Minic or Shalipuri. Minic took over when Shalipuri was killed on April 8.

"He was our superior, at least one hundred of us," said Momo, a fidgety and well-built career criminal who wore dark glasses and claimed that he only ever "disabled" people with his gun while evicting Albanians from their homes during the war. "We were in smaller groups. Sometimes he would wear a colorful headband. He would address us as a group, coming to see us in a jeep, to see how we were doing. Where are you going? Who are you picking up today? That kind of thing."

Minic seemed driven by two things: money and killing.

"He was exterminating Albanians," said Vladan, a forty-year-old man who grew up in Pec. "He didn't like them. He was killing entire families. He didn't distinguish between women and children. There was a constant group of ten men with him. They were doing the executions. He was their leader."

"He had his executioners," echoed Momo. "He would order them. There was no need for him to do it. He had enough sick-minded people around him. Tough criminals."

The retired senior Yugoslav Army officer who served in the Pec region against the KLA also disdained the brutality of some paramilitaries. "Some didn't go to wage war but to hunt people," he said, his face thin and calm as he sipped cappuccino in a Podgorica café in August 1999. "Some experienced it as sport, manhunting. To some of them it was more important to butcher victims than anything else. They had trophies—a chain of fingers on a string, some put ears on a string. The parts of a human body that would remain in one piece for a while."

Momo is haunted by one particular memory of the bloodlust of Minic's hit squads. "There was one house we were supposed to rush into to pick up an Albanian. Inside I saw a naked woman massacred with the heads of two children on her stomach. I know the man who did it. It was Minic's executioners, the jerks who were doing the cleansing. A normal man would have just killed them."

Momo said the children were between six and eight years old.

As they ate a breakfast of cookies and soda and coffee on one early morning in the war, the Balas had to leave the double-glazed windows closed to keep the smoke out. Some of their neighbors' houses were burning. The children weren't meant to go near the windows anyway. The purple Venetian blinds were down and the house had to look deserted. And there was another reason to keep away from the windows. When the NATO bombs landed nearby, the house shook and a couple of the windows had cracked already. Perhaps a closer bomb would send shards of glass rushing into the rooms. So whenever the adults heard the sound of aircraft overhead they had started to send the children down to the basement. Bored, the children sat squirming with impatience on an old rug that lay on the concrete floor that hadn't been warm for months.

"Daddy, can we come up now?" they called up to Isa. "It's cold down here."

"Just a bit more," Isa called down merrily. "Just a bit more."

The house had started to fill with the smell of baking bread. With her strong forearms and hard-worked hands, Halise had started to knead the dough almost as soon as Isa had come back without bread from his first shopping trip and as soon as she had been told by her husband that they weren't going to leave Pec. If she couldn't take her children away, she would have to make sure they survived here. She had enough food for about a week—beans, potatoes, rice, and flour and oil for baking. And Isa had five hundred kilograms of onions in big orange net bags that he usually used for making sausages. They had enough tea for two weeks. But she was missing things. There was no cheese, no milk, no cans of Coke or fruit juice for the children. She had to speak to Isa again. She

needed to go out. This time he let her have her way. Halise would take
their only daughter, eleven-year-old Dardane, and together they would
make quick trips to the shops. Perhaps the paramilitaries were less likely
to hurt the two of them than they would Isa, a man walking alone
through the streets of a town known for its support of the KLA and
Kosovo's independence from Serbia.

Over the Yugoslav People's Army bridge again, on the same route Isa
had taken earlier, Halise and Dardane rushed through the bullet-ridden
afternoon to a minimarket near the Korzo, the town square. The looting,
the burning, the fleeing. It was all still going on. Halise, speaking Serbian
as ever, bought cheese, milk, jam, and canned goods and she and Dardane skipped back over the Bistrica at the end of the first of many trips
they would make into the heart of the nearly deserted Pec.

That night Halise cooked cheese pie. There was nothing that her oldest child, twelve-year-old Hajri, liked more. Hajri was a quiet boy and
often looked a little anxious and perhaps he wasn't as quick to smile as
the other children. A slight overbite gave him a fretful look, and he
would peer out from under his heavy eyebrows with wide, wondering
eyes. Like his little brother Veton, he was slim and wiry. Perhaps later in
life his body would become thick and strong like his father's. Right now,
Hajri was fidgety and aggrieved; his sense of justice was challenged by a
world that allowed only the Serb kids on the street to go out and ride
their bicycles and kick soccer balls around. He had to stay inside all the
time. They all did. So his mother cooked him his favorite food, cheese
pie, even though she knew that it would only improve things briefly for
her gentle oldest boy. What would really make him happy would be to
go back to his routine. Up at a quarter to seven in the morning with the
rest of the family for a breakfast of juice, cake, and fried *cebob*. And then,
later in the morning, to school. Like so many Albanian children, the Bala
kids went to school at different times because of the different shifts that
Albanian and Serb children operated on. Different teachers, different
students, different language, different history, different schedules. Hajri,
who did well in math and biology, went from half past twelve until four
in the afternoon. Veton went earlier, Dardane later. Agon was still too
young to go to school, although Halise had decided that he should begin
at the start of the next academic year.

Hajri never got into scraps with other kids. He wasn't that kind of twelve-year-old. His young choice of careers reflected his gentleness: When he grew up he wanted to be a *hoxha,* a holy man at the mosque. Every Friday morning he would go with Isa to the mosque and they would sit side by side and bow down together toward Mecca and even though he was young he seemed to remember prayers the first time he heard them.

You had to keep an eye on Hajri, though. Some things made him quite unhappy. At one point his parents had taken him and the other two out of the Vaso Pashe Shkourani school in Karagac. Isa was anxious about the walk to school. He wanted the kids to go to a nearer school so that they wouldn't have to cross so many roads. To see one of his children under a car. It was his, and every parent's, waking nightmare. The thought made him shiver. They meant everything to him.

Isa regretted having married late—at twenty-four—because by now he and Halise could have had more than four kids.

It was this perhaps slightly overprotective father who moved his three older ones to the nearer school so that they would not be run over. For Hajri, it was hellish. All his friends were still at the Karagac school and he sat in class with his mouth turned down like a slice of lemon. His grades started to suffer. He was sad and missed the hallways of Vaso Pashe Shkourani and the feeling that the school had, being opposite Karagac park and surrounded by only a few houses, that it was in a world of its own. His parents saw their quiet one growing quieter. The change didn't last long and soon the Bala kids were again walking to Karagac for their lessons. Hajri's smile reappeared.

Now, he had to stay away from school again. This time it was worse. Home was suddenly a prison to him and his siblings. If only they could take that familiar morning walk again to Karagac.

Being cooped up inside wasn't so easy for Isa either. Halise and Vjollca were used to staying indoors most of the time, like many Albanian wives and mothers. And Musa wouldn't have wanted to walk through the center of Pec as Halise and Isa had for anything in the world. But for Isa, besides his family and God, work was his life. Only once before had he been kept away from his shop. That was for a month, when the Serb health inspectors closed all the Albanian butchers down, including him. It was the time of the British scare over mad cow disease, or BSE. The Serb butchers in town were allowed to remain open.

Isa knew the Bosnian war had gone on for years and he wondered if he would be imprisoned in his home until some time in the next millennium. Best put our trust in God, Isa thought. He looks over us all.

"Thanks to Allah for the food we are to eat, for bringing all this goodness to us," Isa prayed aloud before dinner that night, with his hands flat in front of his face and his head bowed.

Hajri drank a soda with his pie and as the family ate they sat watching television on the two long sofas that curved around the walls at the corners of the living room, alternating the news with children's cartoons. Like nearly every home in Pec, the Bala house was crested by a white satellite dish that picked up channels from all over Europe. The satellites beamed down views of the outside world to the family that now knew little beyond the goings-on inside the four walls of their house. On the German and Albanian news channels they watched Jamie Shea, Madeleine Albright, Bill Clinton, Tony Blair, James Rubin, Javier Solana, and different men in uniform explain why and how they were bombing Serbia and Kosovo. On the Yugoslav channels they saw Slobodan Milosevic and footage of the damage that NATO planes were inflicting on the civilian population in Serbia. Bugs Bunny was of more importance to the kids.

That night was like many more that the adults would spend in the house, trying to pretend for the kids' sake that everything was fine but terrified that perhaps tonight their address would rise to the top of a paramilitary list.

Before bed, the younger kids and Hajri watched a famous Albanian comedian on videocassette while Dardane helped her mother and aunt Vjollca clean up. When she was finished she took her skipping rope and started to make fast, blurry circles around her body as she skipped up and down in low, controlled hops. Her uncle Musa drank glasses of clear *raki* in silence. Her grandmother Mahie lay on a mattress on the floor as she always did, her hair graying and her flesh loose with years of inactivity. Her father Isa couldn't sit still and busied himself with hiding the twelve thousand German marks he had in cash. One third went into a nook in the couch, a second found a home under a floorboard, and the third bundle of notes was to spend the rest of the war on top of the water tank in the bathroom. If they were robbed Isa would give the thieves one of the stashes and then hope they would go away satisfied.

The twelve people in the house slept on mattresses on the floors and in the beds in the bedrooms. Musa slept with his shoes beside his bed and a huge cleaver from the shop within reach. Isa sat at a window in the living room and kept watch throughout the night. In the morning, there would be even fewer Albanians in Pec. And the next day, fewer still. By the end of the week, the Balas wondered if they were the only Albanians left in town.

Chapter 4

The Serbian Canterbury

"Pec was a very good town to grow up in," Isa said one day after the war. No, what Isa said exactly is this: "Peja was a very good town to grow up in." Like most places in Kosovo, the city has two names. It is Peja (pronounced "peya") in Albanian, Pec ("petch") in Serbian.

For centuries, Pec was two towns in one. Under Ottoman rule when the League of Peja met in 1899, Pec became part of Montenegro in 1913 and then fell within the new Kingdom of Yugoslavia in 1918. But it didn't seem to matter which political power controlled Pec—its two identities never blended into one. Both names, Pec and Peja, survived. In 1999, the two towns were as separate as they had ever been.

For Albanians, it was one of the most vibrant cities of Kosovo. Believed to have been populated since the second century, by the nineteenth century Pec had become wealthy and politically central for the majority Albanian population; in 1899, it hosted the League of Peja, a meeting dedicated to uniting Albanians of the region and resisting Ottoman rule. It was a town where Islam was strong but not radical. The town's mosques sounded the call to prayer every day, the tinny loudspeaker chants of the *hoxhas* echoing over the red rooftops and bouncing off the Mountains of the Damned that rise around the town like pyramids from the desert.

At the same time, Pec had long been the spiritual heart of the Serbian Orthodox Church, not just for the minority Serbs in Pec or Kosovo, but to the ten million Serbs in the whole of Yugoslavia. Partly by chance, few other patches of Yugoslavia are more precious to the Serbs than Pec. "One factor only made Kosovo central to the Serbian Church: the location of the seat of the Archbishopric, and then Patriarchate, in Pec," writes Noel Malcolm in his *Kosovo: A Short History*. "This was largely the consequence of a chance attack on the monastery of Zica in the 1290s by a marauding force of Tatars and Cumans. Had those raiders taken another route, perhaps Kosovo would never have acquired the significance which it has gained for modern Serbs."

It was the mountains that drew the church fathers toward Pec after the assault on Zica. Both strategic and spiritual, the Mountains of the Damned would make it easier for the Serbs to defend their holiest site while also providing the priests with convenient access to the caves of Rugova. For many years, according to priests now in residence at the Patriarchate, Serb priests had made the journey to the holy caves that still glower out of the sheer, ashen rock faces of the gorge like dark eyes. Taking some food, water, a blanket, candles, some incense, and the Bible, priests climbed up alone to the caves for a few days to pray and be closer to God in the high mountains. There are still frescoes on the walls of two or three of the caves, the priests say.

The Patriarchate sits at the foot of the mountains, its walls enclosing an Eden of flowers, trickling water, honey bees, and their hives. Church workers tend nearby fields, shoo mice away from the sacks of flour in the mill room, feed the trout who thrash about in the concrete tanks behind the priest's dormitories, chop firewood, collect eggs from the chickens, and milk the cows. Priests float around the grounds and the complex's five churches in ankle-length black robes and tumbling waterfalls of beards. The tendrils of a sprawling old mulberry tree taken from Jerusalem many years ago lean across one of the main paths.

During and after the 1999 war, the priests remained within the high walls, debating among themselves the conduct of their people and where their political loyalties should lie. Once a great supporter of the Milosevic regime, the church had abandoned him by the end of the war. The few priests who visited the Patriarchate at this time were left with no parishioners and a lot of time to sit and serve visitors Twinings Earl Grey tea in the gardens.

"Pec is the Serbian Canterbury," explained Father Jovan Culibrk, a worldly young priest from Cetinje, Montenegro, who spent his time after the war as the church's representative at the heavily guarded Patriarchate. Italian soldiers, tanks, and barbed wire blocked all roads and tracks leading to the monastery. Culibrk is a man of surprises. Before he was a priest he was close to the prepunk German chanteuse Nico and is as passionate about Joy Division and the Berlin recordings of David Bowie as he is about the mystical insights offered by his church. Along with the Bible, his regular reading includes the British style magazines, *The Face* and *I.D.*

His analogy to the geographic heart of the Church of England only fails in that the English are not a people who generally consider their religion to be part of what makes them English. Soccer, for example, is a much greater national glue than the Church of England. The Serbian Orthodox Church, however, provides probably the strongest bond between the people and the land of Serbia. Practicing or not—and most are not—Serbs tend to see the church as a kind of spiritual constitution. As Branimir Anzulovic has argued in *Heavenly Serbia: From Myth to Genocide,* the Church and the land make them Serbs. Often defeated in battle, ruled over by others many times, deprived of their own nation for centuries, it is harder for the Serbs to take pride in a glorious history than it is for other, more established European nations. The only true constant in their history has been their church. So when Serb paramilitaries wore crosses around their necks and sprayed religious graffiti on the walls of burning Albanian homes during the war, they were not making a religious statement as much as a national one.

It wasn't primarily Islam that the paramilitaries hated about Kosovo's Albanians—for there were plenty of Catholic Albanians, fellow Christians, who were forced to join the fleeing masses out of Kosovo—it was the hatred of another tribe that had long competed with the Serbs of Kosovo for land, trade, and political power. Religion is what keeps the Serbs together culturally but the mystical faith that Culibrk lives for plays little role in the lives of most Serbs. Culibrk is the first to acknowledge that. Even after the fall of communism in Yugoslavia, church services in Serbia and Montenegro were poorly attended. And so, if anything, the Pec Patriarchate is the Serbian Buckingham Palace or the Serbian Lincoln Memorial. It is a national monument with the deepest cultural resonance.

For Tito, half-Slovene, half-Croat, absolutely secular and antinationalist, Pec was no Canterbury and no Buckingham Palace. It was not the center of the Serbian nation. Nor was the town the center of predominantly Muslim Albanian culture or the home of the Albanian solidarity movement as intended by the League of Peja. It was a town of a hundred thousand Yugoslavs who, Tito insisted, absolutely *would* live with each other productively and harmoniously under Tito's brand of beneficent self-deluding communism.

As the brutal wars of the 1990s bore out, neither the people of Kosovo nor the rest of Yugoslavia adopted Tito's official policy of denying ethnic differences. In the Balkans, spoken history is usually distilled into an inaccurate and exaggerated chronology of grievances and past wrongs with no mention of crimes committed by one's own people. Any visitor to the Balkans knows that to sit down for coffee or throat-rasping *raki* with a person from any ethnicity in the region is to risk a not so quick, uninterruptible, vitriolic five-hundred-year history lesson so skewed that it doesn't deserve the name of history. Those twisted histories were too important to the Serbs and Albanians of Kosovo to let go of, even after half a century of communism. To do so would be to weaken one's own national identity and to make one's tribe vulnerable to the neighboring tribe, which remained strongly bonded by its own histories and customs. History, many former Yugoslavs claim, fueled the wars of the 1990s. But real history has just about ceased to exist within Albanian and Serbian discourse. It has largely been replaced by monologues of myth and prejudice. It is now a weapon of survival.

Like all Yugoslavs old enough to remember, Isa knows exactly where he was and whom he was with when he heard that Tito had died. He was escorting a friend of his, a soldier in the Yugoslav People's Army, to the train station. They were walking through the streets of Pec when the news came over the radio. Someone told the two passing men. Isa doesn't cry but he felt like crying that night.

Tito was liked by many Albanians in Kosovo—but not because they felt any kinship with his nationless view of Yugoslavia. Quite the opposite. They liked him primarily because, in an attempt to balance ethnic rivalries, he had orchestrated the adoption in 1974 of a new constitution that gave Kosovo, at that point just a province of Serbia, status as an autonomous region inside Serbia. The northern Serbian province of Vojvodina was also given the same powers, which included having a separate central bank, police force, schools, courts, and regional assembly. Its leaders sat on the rotating federal presidency. All the two new regions lacked was the right to secede from Yugoslavia, something that no republic had ever realistically considered, and so the Albanians of Kosovo did not particularly feel its lack at the time.

While Albanians were delighted with the new constitution, the change fed Serbian anxiety. Allowing Kosovo and Vojvodina autonomy from Serbia essentially cut down the population of Serbia from ten million to six million. Until that point, Serbia had been by far the largest republic in Yugoslavia. Its capital, Belgrade, was Yugoslavia's federal capital. Until this point, Serbia had been the biggest bear in the crowded bed and when it rolled over, the other republics made room. Now nationalist resentment was growing all over Serbia and particularly inside Kosovo, where Serbs all of a sudden found themselves part of the minority, not part of the dominant majority.

From 1974 on, numbers dictated that Albanians would run Kosovo. The population was 90 percent Albanian. Sure that he had found the right politico-ethnic balance, Tito made little effort to relieve the anxiety of Kosovo's Serbs.

After Tito's death in 1980, the barely concealed Serb and Albanian nationalisms emerged rapidly. Only a year after Tito was laid to rest, Albanians in Kosovo organized street demonstrations, demanding full republic status and the right to secede. Tito's antinationalist legacy lived on in Belgrade where the new federal presidency ordered the security forces to quell the Albanian protests.

Although they failed, the demonstrations only confirmed the worst fears of Kosovo's Serbs. Autonomy was bad enough. Now they felt they were headed for complete separation from Serbia, their homeland. From the Serbian perspective, the Albanians, with their brutish ways and their dream of welding Kosovo onto Albania proper, would take over completely.

In Pec, perhaps the most precious corner of Kosovo to the Serbs, tensions were particularly high. Serbs still talk of attacks by Albanians on the Patriarchate. Even during the Tito years the majority Albanians, growing eventually to over 80 percent of the town's population, occupied most of the senior positions in town government and in state-owned industries like the local plant for making spare parts for Zastava cars, the battery factory, and the Pec Brewery. Without a doubt, during the 1980s, Albanians enjoyed an uncompromising dominance in Pec's workplaces, government offices, and on its streets. Serb men felt they could not even glance at young Albanian women without being threatened by Albanian men. Serb farmers complained of their crops being stolen by Albanians.

The Serbs of Pec and Kosovo made their feelings known by leaving Kosovo in a steady trickle for the rest of Serbia. Intimidated, scared, and struggling to find decent work, they sold their houses cheaply to Albanians and left for the comparative security of the north, in Serbia proper. Those Serbs who remained tended to be less compromising, more defiant. They began to organize themselves, held their own street protests, and made contact with the Serbian Communist Party in Belgrade. Some armed themselves.

Yugoslavia remained intact on the outside but it was beginning to rot like a dead animal from the inside. Earlier than most, Serbian Communist Party leader Slobodan Milosevic picked up the scent of his decaying country and realized that it was dead on its feet. That continual exodus of bitter and frightened Serbs was a warning flare to Milosevic. For him, the flare illuminated an opportunity for power.

With Tito gone and the country ruled by a weak federal presidency that rotated around the six constituent republics of Yugoslavia and the two autonomous regions of Vojvodina and Kosovo, Milosevic decided that it would not be long before the different nations in this federation wanted to rule themselves. Rather than wait, Milosevic hurried along the process. He had two main goals. He wanted a Serbia that included Kosovo and the substantial territories in Croatia and Bosnia-Hercegovina where Serbs were in the majority. And he wanted to rule this new Serbia. Kosovo was his ready-made catalyst.

On April 24, 1987, Milosevic addressed a gathering of angry Serbs in Kosovo Polje, the site of one of the Serbian nation's greatest battles in 1389. While his official line as a communist and a Yugoslav was that nationalism was abhorrent and the preservation of federal Yugoslavia was an inviolable ideal, Milosevic's speech that day played to the anxieties and aspirations of his audience on the ground and around Serbia. While he was meeting with local Serb leaders inside a government building in Kosovo Polje, outside Serb demonstrators were clashing with police, most of them Albanians. Milosevic came outside and addressed the crowd.

"No one should dare to beat you," he told the crowd, rather to the astonishment of the police. In that moment, he became the hero of Kosovo's Serbs. Later in the day he built on his explosive sentence:

> You should stay here. This is your land. These are your houses. Your meadows and gardens. Your memories. You shouldn't abandon your land just because it's difficult to live, because you are pressured by injustice and degradation. It was never part of the Serbian and Montenegrin character to give up in the face of obstacles, to demobilize when it's time to fight. ... You should stay here for the sake of your ancestors and descendants. Otherwise your ancestors would be defiled and descendants disappointed. But I don't suggest that you stay, endure, and tolerate a situation you're not satisfied with. On the contrary, you should change it with the rest of the progressive people here, in Serbia and in Yugoslavia. (quoted in Laura Silber and Allan Little's *The Death of Yugoslavia*)

Riding on the back of the Serbian fury he had picked up on that day in Kosovo Polje, Milosevic quickly outmaneuvered his mentor and the old communist guard to become the President of Serbia just a few months after his speech. In an ominous move for the Albanians of Kosovo, Milosevic orchestrated the stripping of peaceable Vojvodina's autonomy in late 1988. As he had throughout his rapid rise to power, Milosevic put the squeeze on Communist Party leaders to get his way. This time his target was the Kosovo regional Assembly. In March 1989, both the Kosovo Assembly in Pristina and the Serbian Assembly in Belgrade ratified a new constitution that stripped Kosovo of its right to and mechanisms of self-government. Dozens of Albanians died in clashes with the police and the army in Kosovo. In Belgrade, the party organized official events to celebrate the reunification of Serbia. Kosovo's Serbs were again the majority. It was a disaster for the Albanians.

Almost overnight, Pec was transformed. The town's Serbs, who had been fleeing the region for years, started to rule with a vengeful force.

Most Serbs will deny that they or their kin administered Kosovo unfairly. Father Jovan is more frank. "Yes, there was Serb totalitarianism in Kosovo for the last eight or nine years," he acknowledged, sitting in the Patriarchate garden just weeks after the war. "But there was Albanian terror here for fifty years."

Before 1989, Albanians filled most of the powerful positions in the town. They sat behind the commanders' desks at the three-story police station that stands on the road to Rozaje. They carried their briefcases in to work at the executive offices of the banks and main state employers in town. They staffed the library, local radio station, music school, and dance classes at the tall, monolithic cultural center, just north of the Korzo, the town square. And they filled most of the thinly carpeted offices on the three floors of Pec's Prefektura, the local government building, which stands opposite the Hotel Metohija in the Korzo.

"First the intellectuals were attacked," said Rexhep Nulhaxha, an economist by training who was working as Pec's director of planning until he was forced out of his job at the end of 1991. "Every professional Albanian was kicked out of his or her job and replaced with a local Serb. Lately you couldn't find a single Serb who didn't have a job."

Another local economist, Ali Dresha, also worked for the regional government of Pec. He would show up every day in his suit and tie, carrying his briefcase full of painstakingly neat chronicles of local economic minutiae. One day in early 1990 he arrived at work to find a Serb police officer at the door, standing between the two small poplars that sit in concrete boxes on either side of the inconspicuous entrance to the Prefektura. The policeman told him that he was no longer allowed into the building. Dresha stood there for a moment and then turned around and walked away. He knew there was probably a Serb economist sitting at his desk already.

Unusually, Dresha soon found another job as deputy director of a local bank. In September 1990, he joined in a large one-day strike held by Albanian workers. The next day tens of thousands were laid off. "They sent me a telegram to let me know that I was fired," he said. A Serb took that job too.

One man orchestrated this changing of the ethnic guard in Pec. And for the next ten years, Mile Ivanovic dominated the Pec Prefektura, which had authority over the towns of Istok, Klina, Decani and Djakovica and the surrounding villages. Ivanovic was governor of the Pec region when he died of natural causes a few days before the NATO bombardment began, but he had held several posts in local government throughout the decade. As the local boss of Milosevic's Socialist Party of Serbia, it didn't matter which particular job he held at any given time. Milosevic ruled Serbia. Ivanovic ruled Pec. A former doctor, he was known around Pec even before his political career as being unwilling to treat Albanian patients in the town's hospital, which sits just off the road to the Patriarchate. "He was a bigot and a nationalist," Dresha said.

Ivanovic had a right-hand man, another SPS loyalist named Zivojin "Ziva" Cvejic. Nulhaxha remembers watching Cvejic play soccer when both men were younger. Nulhaxha was a fan of the Serb. Cvejic was something of a local star in the days when it didn't much matter what nationality you were, as long as you could dribble and pass the ball well. Cvejic took a law degree and entered politics, becoming a Party man who couldn't always hide his Serb nationalist leanings. After 1989, Cvejic was appointed the top regional judge in the Pec region by Belgrade.

"He had extraordinary powers," said Adnan Zeka, an Albanian who was dismissed from his own position as a judge in Pec in 1989.

Albanians involved in the biggest Albanian party, the Democratic League of Kosovo (LDK), or any other political activity were frequently given long sentences by Kosovo's Serbian judges. Nulhaxha, who operated during the 1990s as the local financial director of the parallel Kosovar Albanian government's education program, got off comparatively lightly for his role. He received only a year in prison from his former soccer hero, who also died of natural causes in December 1998.

Rather like the South African regime during apartheid, Belgrade went to great lengths to use the official tools of the state to suppress the Albanian minority in Serbia rather than just killing or imprisoning them willy-nilly. Judges such as Cvejic were one part of the process. The police force was Milosevic's other main instrument.

Among those laid off in 1989 were most of Kosovo's Albanian police officers. Some of their Serb replacements came from outside Kosovo. Others were hired from the local population and were given the blue camouflage uniforms and heavy weaponry that gave Milosevic's police the look of a military or paramilitary organization rather than a civilian law enforcement force. In the early 1990s, some Albanians still called the police when they were the victims of normal crimes like burglary. At best, the police took down the details of the incident and nothing came of the matter. Later in the decade the mere suggestion of calling the police for help became laughable.

Long before paramilitaries came to Pec, it was fear of the police in their camouflaged trucks and armored personnel carriers that emptied the streets of Albanians in the afternoons and evenings. Cafés and bars like Café Pizzeria Mozart and Dolce Vita became the exclusive hangout of young Serbs. V, a gaudy disco on the ground floor of the cultural center, was a Serbs-only nightclub. The library in the same building became out of bounds, as were the dance and music classes and the radio station. While not destroyed, the library's Albanian books were pushed into a corner and ignored. The city's schools no longer taught in Albanian, nor did they educate most of the children who attended them about their culture and history. Very few Albanian teachers kept their jobs. To compensate, Nulhaxha and his colleagues in the LDK set up evening classes in the living rooms and basements of people's homes. (Later in the decade Albanian teachers were allowed to return to the schools to teach Albanian children only.) Matters were slightly better in Pec's hospital, but still the Albanians faced enough discrimination to conduct their own blood drives and start up their own storefront medical clinics, paid for by the parallel Kosovo Albanian government through its voluntary 3 percent tax on the earnings of Kosovo's Albanian émigrés.

Lemane Hatashi, an architect who practiced privately during the 1990s and took up a job as a city planner at the Prefektura after the war, explained why Pec's Albanians needed extra medical care. "Last year my brother had a car accident and was rushed to the hospital," she told me with an effortful calm. "The Serb doctors could have given him better first aid and then Med-evaced him to Belgrade or Skopje but they didn't. He died."

Kosovo's young Albanian men also had the army to fear. Throughout Tito's rule, the Yugoslav People's Army had been a strictly nonnationalist force. A year in the army was a rite of passage for any self-respecting Yugoslav man. On the forearm or upper arm of many older Albanian men—in fact, of men all over the former Yugoslavia—you can still find a proud and simple tattoo made up of the letters JNA followed by a date. JNA are the initials—in Serbian Cyrillic script it appears as JHA—for the Yugoslav People's Army. The dates pinpricked into thousands of Albanian men's skin marks the day each one started his national service. But with each successive war that Milosevic waged during the 1990s, the Yugoslav People's Army became ever more the Serbian army. Those soldiers who were not Serbs faced danger on two fronts: From the enemy they happened to be fighting at the time—usually Croats or Bosnian Muslims—and from their fellow Serb soldiers.

"If you sent your son to the army he'd be killed," Isa said one day after the war had ended. Hajri, born in 1986, was only a few years away from being called up when the NATO bombardment started and Isa had already been thinking of how to help his son escape military service.

During the years after 1989, young Albanians facing conscription into the army bolted to countries like Germany or Switzerland, fearing that they would be murdered by their Serb comrades in arms as increasing numbers of Albanian conscripts were. Their deaths were usually put down as accidental—car crashes, equipment malfunctions, training disasters, a misfiring gun. One Albanian man I know deserted in the middle of the night after he learned that some of his Serb comrades were coming that night to abduct him.

Young men of draftable age left Kosovo in their tens of thousands, staying as refugees and guest workers in Lausanne, Munich, Lucerne. It was a migration that unexpectedly helped the Albanians who remained in Kosovo. As the Yugoslav economy crumbled and Albanians found it hard to find work, thousands of their relatives were making good money in hard currency and almost without exception, the émigrés sent money back home. The self-proclaimed Government of Kosovo, led by Ibrahim Rugova, the leader of the nonviolent LDK, asked that every Kosovar Albanian working abroad pay 3 percent of his or her earnings to the government in a voluntary taxation system. How was this enforced? Gossip. Woe betide anyone's reputation around the neighborhoods of Kosovo if his wealthy brother in Berlin or Geneva was not contributing to the national cause.

The families left behind had to cope with unfairness in even the most mundane parts of life. These things were perhaps insignificant in the larger, more violent scheme of things but to the Albanians of Pec they were like mouthfuls of spit gobbed onto a beaten man. Albanian visitors to the town could no longer get rooms at the three now Serb-run hotels in Pec—the Hotel Metohija, the Hotel Karagac, and the Hotel Korzo. Garbage was left uncollected for days in Albanian neighborhoods but regularly collected in Serb quarters. And there were the roads. Albanians joke that if you wanted to find the Serb living in a village all you needed to do was to follow the asphalt to his front door. In Pec, the roads in Albanian neighborhoods like Kapesnica had no asphalt on them at all. They were dirt tracks at best, hazardous obstacles with deep potholes at worst. Take the road from Pec to the nearby Albanian village of Nabergan and the drive will last about half an hour. A trip by car from Pec to the Serb village of Gorazdevac, situated about the same distance away from the town as Nabergan, is a five-minute meander along a smooth road under a row of arching trees.

These things really nagged away at Albanian pride.

Then there was the extortion by the police on the roads and by the tax inspectors who showed up amazingly frequently to check the books of Albanian businesses and always seemed to find irregularities that incurred fines or excessive profits that begged heavy taxation. Serb businesses could go for two years without inspection.

Isa suffered both kinds of extortion. It was a routine that the Albanians of Pec grew to consider a completely normal part of their daily lives. If Isa wanted cows, he had to drive to Pristina. His Tuesday morning trips to the Pristina cattle market became expensive and dangerous.

"If I wanted to go from Pec to Pristina I would be stopped in as many as twenty places by the police. They would take money, sometimes thirty marks, not to mention beating and worse. On Monday evenings I was always thinking of how I should travel there, or if I should go at all. What if something happens to me, I would think."

Sometimes the police would stop by the shop before closing time. Isa made it a point to be friends with everyone but that didn't help him at those times. The drawer in the small wooden table on which his weighing scale sits would be full with the day's takings. Sides of beef still hung from the steel hooks in the window. The Serb police would take whatever they wanted, money or meat. Isa had to come out from behind his glass counter with a sharp knife in his right hand to slice off as much meat from the carcasses as the police wanted. As the years wore on, the police visits became daily events, the men collecting the precise amount and type of meat their wives had requested that day. They never paid.

"I had to give it to them, otherwise I would have been beaten."

One time a police officer insisted that Isa hand over his gun.

"I don't have a gun," Isa told the man, speaking truthfully.

"Rubbish. Fetch your gun and hand it over."

"I don't have a gun, I swear."

Isa paid the man four hundred marks to let the imaginary gun go uncollected.

"We paid so much in extra taxes, too," Isa says. "The inspectors came by all the time. They lived off us. Every single time they fined us. In so many ways they tried to push us out of Kosovo, hoping they would tax me until I closed down and left. I had to give the tax inspectors bribes. They bought sports cars and shops with our money."

When the KLA started its war with the Serb police in 1998, the daily harassment and extortion of the previous eight years began to seem like the good old days to the Albanians of Pec. Isa once had to take a long way home just to avoid three drunken fifteen-year-old Serb boys who were picking fights with Albanians in the street. "We had our heads in the mouth of the wolf," Isa recalls.

Serbian criminals like Nebojsa Minic were recruited by the police, even as they continued their criminal enterprises and coalesced into paramilitary groups under the ultimate leadership of the Interior Ministry.

Starting in the Drenica region between Pec and Pristina, the KLA soon took the battle to other parts of the region, including territory around Pec. For long periods, the KLA controlled several areas around the town, including the nearby Rugova valley, villages like Loxhe and the town of Decani. The countryside became a guerilla war zone, with the Albanian rebels ambushing police vehicles and Serb helicopters and tanks rocketing and shelling KLA strongholds. The road between Pec and Djakovica became very hazardous for the police.

Both sides reached an uneasy truce in late 1998. But that agreement was shattered on January 15, 1999, when Serb police massacred forty-five Albanian civilians in the Western Kosovo village of Racak. All bets were off. After a failed attempt to reach an agreement in February at the French chateau of Rambouillet, just outside Paris, a full-scale war seemed likely.

By this time, the people of Pec had noticed an influx of Serb men who wore a variety of military-looking uniforms but were clearly not soldiers in the regular army, the VJ. Some were locals—bus drivers, judo coaches, bar owners, farmers. Others were strangers from Serbia and Montenegro. They formed groups with colorful names like the Black Hand, the Wolves, the Tulips, the Hawks, Black Star. Even members of those groups lost track of who was who. But everyone knew that there were two groups in the Pec region whose names and identities were unforgettable. One of those was the Frenkis, or Frenki Boys, the disciplined and well-equipped men who wore Australian outback or cowboy hats with the flaps turned up on one side.

While the Frenkis were newcomers to town, the other group that everyone knew about was made up mainly of locals and men who had been in Pec for some years. This was *Munje*. In the days leading up to the NATO bombing, local Albanians would see the members of *Munje* sitting in cafés in the morning until about ten o'clock. After breakfast, they and the Frenkis and the other more organized groups—some paramilitaries were less disciplined part-timers or entirely unidealogical businessmen looking forward to the easy looting they hoped would come in Kosovo—would head out to fight the KLA.

When they returned in the evening, they liked to pick fights with Albanians in cafés, loot Albanian stores, and demand instant protection money from the Albanian money changers who stood on the street corners of downtown Pec, trading marks for dinars. They moved around town as if they owned it and everyone there. But they were more menacing than anything else. People around town thought that the paramilitaries looked like they were waiting for something.

Chapter 5

The Friendly Lion and the KLA

Through the center of Pec flows the glassy Bistrica River, its water so translucent that every bouncing pebble is visible on the riverbed. "Bistrica" means "clear" in Serbian. Before the Serbs changed its name, the Albanians called it the "Lumbardhi," the White River. During the war the Serb officers living in the town's central building, the Hotel Metohija—a confused mixture of Romanesque stone arches, Swiss chalet-style wooden balconies, and lifeless communist symmetry—could look out from their back windows and see it sweeping past and on through Western Kosovo, its currents rumbling in a constant and calming drone. In the early days of the war, according to people who were fleeing the city, the soldiers would throw the bodies of Albanians whose throats they had slit into the river, streaming threads of dark red giving some brief color to the transparent water that flows into the White Drin River, through Southern Kosovo, over the border with Albania, through the town of Kukes, and west to the turquoise Adriatic.

Upstream a couple of miles, the Bistrica flows past the Patriarchate of Pec. The nearby spring of Saint Nicodemus bubbles up from the earth and provides the Patriarchate with its water, flowing through the trout tanks and beautiful gardens that hide behind the high stone walls, and then pouring out into the varnished Bistrica. At times, the gurgle of the spring water is the only sound to be heard in the grounds.

On the other side of the Patriarchate a narrow asphalt road runs parallel with the river, bordered by the oak and chestnut trees that populate the lowest slopes of the Mountains of the Damned. Side by side, the road and the river cut a path between the suddenly steep mountains and lead into a region of sheer rock faces, deep caves, and Albanian peasant villages known as Rugova. The glacially carved valley is the ancestral home of Ibrahim Rugova, the leader of the Democratic League of Kosovo.

Once the road has crossed over the river two or three times on solid stone and wood bridges it narrows and the asphalt turns to a shingly dirt. By this time the Bistrica is flowing along the bottom of a plummeting gorge far below the level of the road, cutting right through some of the world's oldest mountains, the gray rock from the Mesozoic and Paleozoic eras parting for the Bistrica, the descendant of hundreds of millions of years of persistent ice and water flows. When these mountains were first formed, mammals were about three hundred million years in the future. Glaciers squeezed and ripped at the new, smooth rock during the ice ages, turning the gentle horizons into violent, serrated peaks and reshaping the Mountains of the Damned and Rugova forever. The creeping tidal waves of ice slashed knife-sharp gorges into the mountains, scooped out lakes high up on the peaks and left bowl-shaped valleys—glacial cirques—on the upper slopes. The ice also carved out U-shaped gullies to collect the water that now tumbles down the mountains into the Bistrica.

Above the river, the ancient cliffs of the gorge rise sheer for hundreds, maybe thousands of feet, turning Rugova into a European Yosemite. You have to tilt your head right back to see the top of the cliffs as they tower over you, the silhouette of small pines standing out on their jagged crests. As the road winds and twists into Rugova, breaking up so badly in spots that the horses and carts that some farmers still drive along it have difficulty making progress, it remains enclosed by the rock and at times has to worm its way through unlit tunnels.

Several miles upstream from the monastery, on the north bank of the river, stand four burned-out buildings. One was the local post office. The largest was an agricultural warehouse, owned by the state. For a few months after the war, a chalkboard sat a few feet from the end of a long dining table in the old warehouse. Officers used to map out strategy on the board after dinner as their soldiers sat on the benches next to the table. For the first month of the war, these buildings were the headquarters of the 136th Brigade of the Kosovo Liberation Army. Up here, a few miles from Serb-controlled Pec, the Bistrica belonged to the Kosovar Albanian guerrillas.

I made my trip into Rugova with two colleagues from the *Daily Telegraph* in London.

Mick Smith was a reporter who had once served in the British Army's intelligence services. Mick likes secrets and he likes uncovering them. He writes books about spies in wartime. We met at the Hotel Crna Gora in Podgorica. He and I realized over breakfast one morning that we both wanted to go into Kosovo to take a look at the war zone that Milosevic was so keen to keep reporters away from. The war was three weeks old and we wanted to see Kosovo from the inside. The place was more or less invisible to the outside world. It was hard to find out what was really going on in there. We decided to go together. I had contacts with people who could guide us in to see the KLA. He had his own savviness—and Heathcliff O'Malley, whose images I could use in *Newsday*. Heathcliff is the hippest war photographer one is ever likely to meet. Brought up in the Notting Hill area of London, he was more used to shooting thin-armed catwalk models at the shows in Paris and Milan than heavily armed Albanian guerrillas.

In the predominantly Muslim town of Rozaje near the Kosovo border we met up with my contacts, Ibrahim and Anna. Ibrahim knew the right people and spoke Serbian and Albanian. Anna spoke Serbian and English.

Ibrahim and Anna are not their real names. They both still live in Montenegro and could face reprisals from the federal Yugoslav authorities for helping Western journalists cross into Kosovo during the war. Crossing into Kosovo without visas or permission from the Yugoslav authorities amounted to illegally crossing a border and spying.

The five of us left Rozaje in the early afternoon of Wednesday, April 14, knowing we had left too late to make it all the way over the mountains before night fell. Ibrahim had shown us our route on a map. We would hike over a pass beside a mountain called Hajlla and from there into Rugova.

To our surprise and delight—just to reach the foot of Hajlla would take hours of tough walking through the woods—Ibrahim had arranged a taxi for us. It was an old tractor stitched together and it pulled us up a steep and windy forest track beside sunny riverbanks of snowdrops and blue crocuses. Spring was beginning here but we were lumbering up into winter. Our trailer filled up with villagers as we chugged along the track.

The driver of the tractor pulled us over rickety bridges made of logs lying perpendicular on top of other logs, through snow drifts and along narrow stretches of the track that ran beside steep drops. After an hour the snow became impassably deep even for the tractor and so we jumped out and walked the final few hundred yards to a tiny village of wood huts, haystacks, and pathways of mud. An old orange BMW with Pec license plates sat marooned in the snow. It was the first clue that the villagers had strong links to Kosovo. We were in an Albanian village.

Along Montenegro's border with Kosovo are several similar villages, all home to ethnic Albanians. Again, it wouldn't be right to name this place. It too was to suffer during the next few weeks. It too remains inside Yugoslavia.

Our old host, a man who used to go climbing on Hajlla with Ibrahim's late father, guided us through the quagmire that led right up to his front door. As we took off our caked boots we could see Hajlla sweeping into the clouds ahead of us. The light was fading and the mountain looked unwelcoming.

In a large square room, with nothing but thin, hand-hewn walls of pine between us and the brutal wind outside, we passed around triangles of Toblerone and accepted cigarettes, dinner, and the comfort of the foam mattresses that lined the edges of the room, folded so that one half was a cushion against the wall while the other lay on the rugs of the floor. An old wood-burning stove did its best to keep the entire family and us warm. Besides the old man and his wife, half a dozen kids and several young men and women—his grandchildren, children, and their spouses, I guessed—filled up the mattresses. They didn't usually live there. The village was only a vacation spot. They were refugees from Pec.

Before going to bed, Gani, one of our guides from the village, explained that we would have to leave early in the morning because at that time of day the surface of the snow was still frozen and we would be able to walk along the crust of the powder that lay up to two and three yards deep. If the snow melted too much, passing into Kosovo would be impossible.

We all slept on the foam mattresses laid out on the floor. Lying side by side like the logs on the wobbly bridges down the track, we listened to the wind whistling through the cracks in the walls until we fell asleep in our clothes.

It was shots of clear, brutal *raki* for breakfast at seven in the morning.

"It wakes you up, gives you energy," said Ibrahim, smiling as ever. I knew that it was extremely impolite to decline a man's *raki* when you were a guest in his house. I drank.

Gani and another of the young men of the village led us out of the village along another path. A few clouds passed overhead but it was a clear sunny day, the crest of Hajlla slicing a sharp line into the blue sky more than seven thousand feet up. Soon we cut into the woods and started climbing up a steep gradient, stomping through snow that went up to our thighs. The snow this far down on the mountain had already softened. Gani and the other guide strolled ahead as if over a mildly sloping croquet lawn. We sweated and silently wondered how on earth this journey was going to be possible when this was only the beginning.

"I didn't think I was going to make it after that first bit," Mick told me later. He was forty-seven and his years of basic training must have seemed like a thing of the past. He wasn't the only one to feel that way.

As we came out of the trees we reached an open plain of snow that reflected the sun so brightly I had to close my eyes to bare slits.

With the mountain to our right, we pushed on in single file up the white slope. Gani was right this time. The surface was frozen and my black boots only sank in two or three inches. Every now and then we would pass the tops of small pine trees poking out from under the several feet of snow below us. A wind that was whipping surface snow from the flinty backbone of Hajlla's long summit kept us cool.

Around the side of the mountain we could see two untenanted shepherds' summer huts known as *stane* in Albanian. They were almost completely buried under snowdrifts.

"Matchew, Kosovo," Ibrahim told me, pointing at the huts.

As we approached the border at about half past ten, a group of human figures appeared over the horizon. Terrified and shivering children pushed through the snow, holding the hands of their exhausted parents. For much of our route, candy wrappers and abandoned clothes had littered the snow. This was a back door to Pec for the Albanians. As the refugees stopped to pass on news of what was happening inside Kosovo and to ask of the conditions and welcome they might face in Montenegro, where thousands of Yugoslav Army soldiers roamed the roads, the deep boom of a Yugoslav shell bounced off the rock faces of Hajlla. The refugees didn't flinch. The Serbs had been shelling Rugova a bit, they said, but not very much. These people didn't want to take any risks and they had decided to leave. We went in our opposite directions.

At the border we could see a conical concrete monument poking out of the snow. On its flattened top was a small red metal star. It was the communist Partisans' memorial to those who had lost their lives in the mountains when fighting against the Italian occupiers in World War II.

We were in Kosovo.

Once over the crest of the mountain we could look down at Rugova. In late winter—and in the mountains of Kosovo, April is a winter month—a snow line appears, allowing the more than a dozen villages further down the valleys their first break from the barrage of ice and snow that starts in October.

We pushed on down the mountain and met a group of refugees, mostly young men, sheltering under a tree and eating snow. Their faces gaunt and sunburned, they told us they had walked from beyond Pec.

"I'm from a village near Decani," twenty-eight-year-old Bashkim Sokolaj told me as he pushed snow between his cracked lips. Decani is south of Pec. "I passed through Decani and into the forest. I saw people who had been killed there. Their throats had been slit, cut with a knife. Five of them."

Bashkim had hurried on past the bodies and now he was nearly out of Kosovo.

Shortly before we reached the snow line, with the snow now slushy and treacherously deep, we spotted a group of young men with guns standing next to a haystack and staring at us. It was the KLA.

At the gateway of a wooden fence that surrounded a sloping field stood eight KLA soldiers in mismatched uniforms, carrying old Chinese rifles. Somewhere on their uniforms they had all stitched on the KLA's red, black, and gold badge, showing a black double-headed eagle at its center. Gani strode ahead to pave our way. The soldiers on guard at the checkpoint were clearly surprised to see us. Nearly everyone the young soldier in the brown leather jacket noted down in his logbook was going in the other direction, fleeing the Serbs. As we arrived, another few dozen refugees walked past on the way to Montenegro.

Sheltering next to the haystack, the younger of the soldiers—a teenager who had just started shaving and wore an Adidas running suit, a blue jacket, and black Wellington boots—talked shyly with Ibrahim. Over his shoulder was an M-47 rifle, made in China, brought into Kosovo from Albania, once a client state of China. Etched into its metalwork was the year of its manufacture—1950.

We had not been invited into the KLA's area of control and we had not told them we were coming. So Gani and the older soldier left us at the haystack while they walked downhill to the small farmhouse at the end of the field where Gani would negotiate permission for us to proceed. When they returned and we set off again, our other guide from the village inside Montenegro was not allowed to go on with us. I asked Ibrahim why.

"They don't trust him," Ibrahim said. That didn't seem to ring true to me at the time—the man was clearly an Albanian who had been to Rugova many times before—but it was the first sign of a trait I came to recognize in many parts of the KLA. In a bid to appear like a real army, they had developed an excessive sense of secrecy and paranoia.

What they had not managed to develop was a rudimentary communications network. I imagined Gani and the KLA soldier had been down in the farmhouse radioing ahead to the next KLA checkpoint. But when we arrived there, the special forces soldiers who greeted us were as surprised as the previous group had been.

With pistols stuck down the back of their black knock-off Calvin Klein and Versace pants and chickens running around their feet, the special forces men looked like Mussolini's Blackshirts lost on the set of *The Sound of Music*. The KLA's inclination toward all-black outfits—the special forces and military police units particularly liked the look—gave them this unfortunate echo of their grandfathers' actions during World War II when some Kosovar Albanians, seizing the opportunity to take revenge on the local Serbs after years of oppression, collaborated with their fascist Italian occupiers to deal brutally with the anti-Axis Powers Serb population. As Chris Hedges of the *New York Times* has noted ("Kosovo's Next Masters," *Foreign Affairs,* May–June 1999), an early tendency of the KLA to use a clenched fist salute did not do anything to dispel this fascist image. By the time the NATO bombing campaign began, the KLA's senior commanders, understanding the importance of public relations in modern warfare, had successfully discouraged this way of greeting a superior officer.

We were exhausted and sat on a pile of logs just outside the farm compound. A young soldier rode around us on his pony, showing off a little, too bashful to get off and chat. The senior soldier listened to our explanations of who we were and ordered someone to bring us water and food. Soon we were eating strong, delicious sheep's cheese, pulling chunks off a large, warm round loaf of bread, and passing around a plastic cup that a soldier had filled with stream water from a red jug he carried.

Further down muddy paths and grass slopes saturated with running water, we passed a tiny village, Reka Allage. Children stood by an old stone house staring at us and then waving. We were nearly there, nearly in Drelaj, our destination in Rugova. We could see its houses dotted around the slopes of the village, smoke coming from their chimneys, goats grazing in the fields that separated them.

A shot rang out. I crabbed sideways toward a boulder but the rifle crack had come from the towering cliff above us and I realized the rock would be no good for cover. I guessed that again, the parts of the KLA who knew we were coming had not managed to communicate with the parts that did not. Bang. Another shot, its retort echoing around the cliffs and hillsides. Gani ran toward the village, his friend-not-foe smile almost as wide as his arms. He called out something to someone and waved to us to move on. There were no more shots.

~

Mick positioned his sodden boots and socks in front of the stove and lay back on the mattresses. An old British army trick: Learn to grab a few moments' sleep whenever you can. Heathcliff lit a cigarette and exhaled into the warmth of the living room. I closed my eyes and listened to the Albanian and Serbian chatter of Ibrahim, Anna, Gani, and our hosts, a civilian family. Gani went out of the house we had been taken to and came back with a new toy and a grin. It was a heavy chunk of mangled metal, its edges sharp and jagged. It was part of a Serbian shell that had landed next to a house just up the hill several days before.

Sunlight angled into the room, hitting the scarlet carpet, and we closed our eyes again.

An hour later a middle-aged soldier with a gold wedding band on his finger, a deep voice, and a drooping moustache came into the room. He laid down his Kalashnikov, an extra magazine attached by masking tape to the one already inserted in the gun. Sitting cross-legged on the floor, the officer, who introduced himself as Selmon Lajqi, the local brigade's information officer, examined our passports and credentials, asked us why we had come and what we wanted to see. He had some practice in dealing with journalists: It turned out that some French journalists had also made the journey in recent days.

He was formal and kindly but not exactly chummy. And he was well schooled in the KLA's art of excessive secrecy.

"How many men are there in Rugova?"

"That's a military secret."

"Where do your arms come from?"

"That too is a military secret."

And on it went.

I never did find out who the top commander of the KLA's 136th Brigade was. I suspect it was Salih Lajqi, Selmon's brother and a former engineering teacher. He joined us in the room soon after Selmon arrived. But with everyone from the Western equivalent of a lance corporal to a five star general being dubbed a "commander," it was never easy to locate where true authority in the KLA lay.

What had become clear, and was unknown to most of the rest of the world at this point, was that the KLA controlled this rather large section of Western Kosovo just up the river from Pec. It looked like these rag-tag guerrillas had held back the third largest army in Europe.

Is the NATO campaign helping the KLA at all?

"There's not much impact," Selmon said, opening up a little. "The Serbs are a little too well hidden in the mountains. If NATO ground troops did come, though, it would not be difficult to fight the Serbs."

Have you made contact with NATO to let them know of Serbian positions or your own?

"No."

Mick and I had a list of things we wanted to do. On top of the list was "See Pec," if only from a distance.

"You might be able to see it from the top of a mountain," Selmon said. "It's a long way away and it depends on the fighting. The Serb snipers are very dangerous."

After our meeting, we were led to another house further up a flooded path that passed for Main Street, Drelaj. We passed through the gate, took our boots off at the wooden deck, climbed up the outdoor wooden staircase above the sheep pen, minded our heads on the low door frame, and walked through a short corridor and into the main room. With thin mattresses lining the edges, the room was of the same wide, low-ceilinged dimensions as the two other Albanian living rooms we had visited. A garish rug depicting Mecca during the hajj hung on one wall. Two guns dangled from their straps on hooks on the opposite wall. Our host was an old man who kept a pistol tucked down the back of his pants. It was a quick stop, to drop our bags off, and soon we were out to visit the local military hospital.

Around Drelaj goat kids sucked on the teats of their mothers, human kids played leapfrog in a field, and the clucking, crowing, mooing, bleating, and barking of the village's animals filled the still mountain air. Men slammed axes into logs. Smoke rose from the roughly sixty roofs of the village.

The hospital was a small house in the center of the village. We took our boots off and walked in over a ropy old carpet through one small room where an elderly man sat stoking a stove. In the next room, a dozen young men lay on foam mattresses. Blankets hid most of the bandages.

One had been blasted by a shell on April 3, his arm broken and lacerated. Others had been shot as the Serbs drove the KLA back in the first days of the war. In this hospital ward there were no doctors or nurses, no medical equipment whatsoever, no books or televisions, no cups of coffee, no magazines.

Lying in the far corner of the room was Sabit Bytyqi, his bandaged knee only visible when he pulled aside the gray blanket that kept him warm. He was nineteen and said he had been in the KLA for seven and a half months. He was a farmer and wanted to rid his land of the Serbs, he said. He had had the standard one month of military training before going on active duty. His wide brown eyes, blond hair, and rosy skin made him look about sixteen.

"I was shot after five days of fighting in the front line near Jablanica. It was a sniper, a Serb sniper. I was crawling around, trying to hide, when I was hit. I was saved by my friends. They came and pulled me out. I felt the pain in my leg but I didn't shout."

The bullet had passed under the knee and out the other side. He said he would be up and ready to rejoin the battle in two or three days. I wondered if he was afraid of dying. "No, I'm not afraid. If I do get killed I won't really die. It's for our country and they'll remember me. People will remember me and what I did."

Selmon hurried us out of the hospital. He didn't want to tire the soldiers.

Outside in the sunshine our group had grown bigger. We talked with the soldiers who milled around. Drelaj was a place where soldiers were sent for rest, training, and in the case of the injured, convalescence. We talked to a new recruit called Gani Lajqi—no relation to Selmon and Salih—whose father, brother and uncle had had their throats slit by paramilitaries in Pec. He never wanted to fight in any war. But after that, he joined up. And then there was the quiet Luan Shala. He had his own reasons for becoming a soldier.

As he walked along the path he had a noticeable lack of swagger in his gait. KLA soldiers, most of them teenagers or in their early twenties with almost no military training or experience, often reacted the way most young men with a Kalashnikov strapped across their chest would react. "Hey, me Clint Eastwood," some would say, grinning. "Stallone, boom

boom," others said, holding their guns in mock readiness, their English exhausted. Usually, that attitude faded after the young men saw combat for the first time. Only twenty-five, Luan had seen combat long before the NATO bombardment began.

"I am called Luan," he said. "Like a lion. It's our word for lion."

If Luan was a lion, he was a friendly one. About five foot six and with the blond hair, blue eyes, and rosy skin common to many Albanians, he spoke quietly, almost stuttering at times. A former English student in Pristina, he was determinedly polite. A damaged left eye—the pupil was lodged in the top corner of his blue iris—made him look even less fearsome. He wore gray corduroy pants, a camouflage jacket, and a khaki military cap with the red, gold, and black KLA badge sewn onto it. Slung over his right shoulder was an old Chinese semiautomatic rifle.

Many weeks later, when we met up again after the war, he reminded my translator, Enver Doda, of a family legend.

"There was a man called Gjumshit who lived seventy years ago in my mother's village," Enver said. "He was the leader of a group of Albanians who fought against Serbs in the village of Marec, near Pristina, in the hills. One guy from Prizren went to Marec to meet Gjumshit. He went in the room, the *oda*—in every Albanian house they used to have such a room, just for men, to stay and talk during the day—it's an Albanian tradition. And the man was expecting to meet Gjumshit. After a while he asked someone when Gjumshit was going to come back. One of the men in the *oda* told him by pointing that the small man—everyone says he was one meter sixty-five and skinny—was Gjumshit. When the man looked at him he was expecting someone tall and strong and big and he saw only a thin, short guy. He was surprised and he said, 'You are Gjumshit?' So Gjumshit just grabbed his gun and pointed it at the visitor. He said to him, "I may not fill up your eye but I can fill up your asshole.'"

Luan preferred to talk about E. M. Forster than to boast about his ability to kill Serbs. "My favorite book is *A Passage to India*," he said. "The way the main Indian character—I really can't remember his name, I have no time to think about these things these days, I'm losing all those names—the way he understands his British rulers is just extraordinary. It reminds me of how we should understand and outsmart the Serbs. It corresponds to our situation." He was days away from his final exams in English literature when the KLA's war against the Serb police interrupted his studies in June 1998. He had hoped to go on to a doctorate.

Luan's family home was in Loxhe, a village outside Pec, just off the road south to Djakovica. He had six brothers and three sisters. Months before the NATO bombing campaign, it was a KLA stronghold. Tensions around the area were high. The Serb police knew the KLA was strong in the village and held off. On June 19, Luan and his younger brother Skender, who was seventeen at the time, set off by bicycle to Pec on a much-needed shopping trip. On their shopping list were intestines, salt, peppers. The family had a calf they wanted to slaughter and these were the other ingredients needed for making veal sausages. It was a terrible risk even to leave Loxhe but the Shalas decided that Skender's youth would help the brothers look innocent and harmless if they were caught.

The brothers pedaled along the back road to Pec. Luan had decided it would be safer that way. All was quiet. And then, at about nine o'clock, a white Zastava car appeared along the road, coming toward them. Luan felt his stomach tighten but they rode on toward the car. When the Zastava was fifteen yards away it slowed down and three men in their forties leaned out of the window, pointing two small Scorpion machine guns at the brothers. "Stop," they shouted. "Get your hands up."

Skender turned pale and started to cry. The men, who wore civilian clothes, got out of the car.

"Let's take them both," one of the men said.

"Leave him, he's nothing," Luan said, gesturing to his brother.

"OK, let him go," the leader of the men said. "We'll take this one."

Tears falling down his cheeks, Skender raced back home to tell his family that Luan had been taken. In the white car, Luan was already answering questions and trying to get his lies straight in his head so that he wouldn't be caught out. Luan had been working in a primary school as an English teacher. The Serbs didn't like teachers—or any Albanian intellectuals—so he had to remember to leave that out of his curriculum vitae at the interviews he was about to face. Worse, Luan did happen to know some of the people in Loxhe who owned guns and what the KLA were up to there. His own family owned a rifle.

The men drove him to the police station in Pec, marched him up the concrete steps to its front door, across the marble floor, and upstairs to an interrogation room on the third floor, the top floor of the building. The men who had abducted him were police officers. Luan sat on a chair in the room and two of the men who had captured him began asking him questions.

"Tell us everything you know about the KLA in Loxhe," his interrogators asked him. "Who has weapons? What kind do they have? How many KLA terrorists are there in the village?"

"I live in Pristina," Luan told them. "I don't know that stuff."

"Try again. Who owns a gun in Loxhe, Luan?"

"I'm telling you, I don't know."

"Who owns a gun, Luan?"

Over and over the men pressed him.

"I don't know. I don't even like the people in my village."

"What kind of weapons do your brothers have?"

"They have no weapons."

"You're kidding with us. Don't mess around with us, Luan. You know, no one will know you're here."

Another man came into the room. "Is he talking yet?" he asked.

"No, but he will."

The first blow was a surprise to Luan. The men started to hit him with their fists and their billy clubs.

Luan guessed he would be in the police station for five hours. That imagined deadline came and went.

The police changed tactics. They came into the room with what seemed like a pistol with an electrical wire leading from it. Some kind of stun gun. Pressing it against Luan's body, they shocked him until he stood up wailing in pain.

Later he heard screams from other rooms along the corridor.

"No, my God, no," came the shouts.

"You hear them?" a police officer asked Luan, who guessed that the screams were faked—Serb police officers trying to scare him.

"Yes."

"It'll happen to you, too."

"If I have to lie, I will, to save my life. I'll say anything you want but it's not true."

Another tack. An officer came in with the ID card of an Albanian neighbor of Luan's. "You know him?"

"Yes."

"He's saying you have an AK-47 and lots of bullets. What kind of gun does he have, Luan?"

"I don't have a gun. He's lying."

At around three in the afternoon, they seemed to give up and forget about him, handcuffing him to a hot water pipe connected to a radiator in another room. No one came to see him for twelve hours. Eventually, an officer came and Luan begged to be allowed to go to the cells. On Sunday night they took him, handcuffed behind his back, to a cell in the basement. He remembers it as being number thirty-six. "Do not look to either side," said one of the men who took him downstairs.

Luan was famished. It was Sunday night and he had not eaten since breakfast on Saturday morning, apart from a small piece of cake one of the police officers had bought for him with Luan's money. But Luan had missed the evening meal round.

There were six beds in the room—three bunks—and a putrid toilet in one corner. The rules were strict: Get up at six in the morning; no lying down on the beds; do exactly what you are told. Some of the other prisoners in the cells tapped on the walls, trying to communicate. Luan was terrified that the cells were bugged.

Twice the police came and took him to the court building that adjoins the police station. In the parking lot outside, a group of other police officers tried to hit Luan as the guards rushed him over to court. "Hey, you KLA fuck. Yeah, you, you fuck." The guard protected him.

In court, the Serb judge was very fair.

"Did you give this evidence?" he asked Luan, after reading out words of confession and information Luan had never spoken or seen written.

"No," Luan said, and the judge dismissed him.

Luan was held for three nights. He was released on Tuesday, at two thirty in the afternoon. Without warning, they told him he could go home. He thought they were joking. They weren't. Only, they wanted a favor from him. They arranged to meet him at the Hotel Metohija on July 13 so that he could have a few weeks to gather information about the KLA's activities in Loxhe and then report back to them.

"I'll be there on the thirteenth," Luan told them. "I can't stand those KLA guys, the way they kill policemen. Don't worry. I'll be there."

One of the men who had tortured him asked him one more question before he left: "Luan, you want a ride? If you want I can take you home in my car."

"No, thanks very much," Luan said. "You're most kind. Thanks."

They didn't even see him out of the building. Luan walked down the stairs to the front door where the men who had tortured him had said he could pick up his personal belongings. They had taken his coat, his shoelaces, his belt, his watch, a pencil, his ID card, and fifty deutsche marks. He made his way to the front desk, too scared to leave the building without some kind of official send off. He didn't want to be shot for escaping. Besides, his jeans were too wide at the waist and he had to keep them up with one hand. But there was no one behind the front desk. Luan found another officer. "You'll have to come back in five days," the officer said.

"But I need my ID card."

"OK, what's your name?"

"Luan Shala."

"Wait here."

Five minutes later the officer returned with his ID card.

"What about the other things?" Luan asked.

"Like I said, come back in five days."

Luan walked to his sister's house in Pec. They were overjoyed to see him. He was very shaken. "Could I have some rope for my jeans?" he asked. And then he walked back home, the rope holding up his pants.

At home, he didn't find the nights easy. In perfect detail he remembered the faces of the men who had tortured him. They came to him at night and began the questions and the torture again. He woke up exhausted, wondering why they had done such things to him, longing for revenge on the men.

He didn't show up to claim his other possessions five days later. And he broke his promise to his torturers: He didn't keep his appointment at the Hotel Metohija on July 13. A couple of weeks later he was at the heart of a fierce battle around Loxhe. The Serbs had decided that Loxhe had to be taken, that the KLA could not be allowed to control a village so close to Pec. It was mid-1998 and although much of the world was not look-ing, the crisis that resulted in the 1999 war between NATO and Yu-goslavia was brewing fast. The Serb police were waging an increasingly violent war with the increasingly strong KLA. In the Drenica region of Central Kosovo and around Pec, thousands of Albanians were beginning to flee their homes in a preview of the mass exodus of 1999. Loxhe was one of the key battlegrounds.

First the Serb infantry attacked but the KLA repelled the assault. And then started a long period of shelling from artillery. Tanks circled the vil-lage and their guns began to fire. Yugoslav air force jets bombed Loxhe and helicopter gunships pummeled the town's houses.

At 7 P.M. on August 15, Luan said, the shelling and air attack stopped. The Serbs relaunched their troops. Luan, who had not yet joined the KLA but was in the village's civilian defense group, was placed in the front line outside the nearby village of Graboc. With him were relatives, including his brother Ymer. While Luan sheltered in a bunker the vil-lagers had dug, firing at the Serb troops, the shelling started again.

"My position was attacked by everything. At 5:55 A.M. they started using planes and helicopters. We were near the street where the buses usually go, under the walnut trees. They had detected us and shelled us right in those places. Luckily I was hidden in the bunker. The dust and stones and wind from the shells went right over our heads. There were about ten shells right on target. The blast was so strong from one of the shells that hit the bunker that I couldn't breathe. It pressed the air around me against my chest."

The attack from the artillery and infantry was relentless. At around five o'clock in the afternoon on August 16, Luan and his fellow villagers decided to abandon the bunker. They alerted the other villagers and KLA members in Loxhe and started to cut through woodland paths to the village of Strellc, five kilometers away.

At seven o'clock, the last Albanian left Loxhe.

Safe in Strellc, Luan looked out across the fields toward Loxhe. "I could see all the houses burning. We could see the flames in the night. Everything was being burned. It really was terrible. The only thing I thought about was our books and pictures. Pictures of us as small boys, the family. And I had left my passport."

The sight of his village confirmed for Luan what he had been thinking for a while. "It was at that point that I decided to join the army."

Early in 1999, Luan was posted to Rugova.

His job was to keep an eye on the enemy. He was a member of a reconnaissance unit that would go out into the hills on the front line, trying to avoid direct firefights with the Serbs. With their binoculars and the telescopic sight on the Mauser sniper rifle one of his colleagues carried, they would watch the Serb soldiers eat and move about, taking note of their movements so that they could report back to the KLA commanders. Sometimes the Serbs would spot them and the two groups would watch each other through binoculars. Only occasionally would the soldiers on either side decide it was worth attempting a long-distance potshot.

Now he was having a brief period of rest in Drelaj before returning to the mountainside with his unit. His time in Drelaj was up that same afternoon. He had been good company and I was sad to see him go. He said goodbye and I promised to send him a copy of *Howard's End* once the war was over.

It was Albanian home cooking—some ingredients coming from bags of humanitarian aid—for dinner that night. One of the soldiers pulled down the round pine table that hung on a hook on the wall. Its surface was about a foot and a half off the ground. A young woman, silent and unthanked by the Albanian men as ever, came into the room carrying a bowl and a jug of water. She moved around the room, pouring cold water over the outstretched hands of the guests, who then dried their hands on the towel hanging over her forearm.

There was no electricity in Rugova, the Serbs having cut it off from Pec at the start of the war. So we ate meat stew, warm bread, cheese, and jam by candlelight. We passed around a single glass of water, refilled from a jug.

After dinner we listened to the radio and talked of NATO's tactics and lost families who were now, hopefully, in refugee camps somewhere in Montenegro, Macedonia, or Albania. Better in a camp, awful as they were, than still inside Kosovo.

~

Friday in Drelaj was a spring day full of life, sunshine, and the sound of shelling and rifle fire in the distance. Mick and I wanted to see Pec and we had been told we could go to the front, to the mountain that overlooked Pec. But as we walked down the valley toward the town, our guide, an English-speaking soldier called Tony, told us that the trip was off.

"It's too dangerous at the front right now," he said. On cue, boom, the explosion of a shell bounced around the walls of the valley.

We walked down the road that leads to Pec, beside the Bistrica and past the brigade headquarters on the other side of the river, where soldiers rested on the grass and drank from the water fountain outside the old agricultural plant. From the roof flew the Albanian flag, red with a black two-headed eagle. Over the front of the main building was a painted sign: "Brigada 136 Rugova UCK." A makeshift wooden guard hut stood at the end of the small bridge. Soldiers came and went over the bridge, some heavily armed with two Kalashnikovs apiece and knives, pistols, and grenades hanging off their uniforms. Further down the road we met others returning from the front, exhausted but happy that their turn was briefly over.

I asked Tony a question I had asked Luan and Selmon. Why don't the Serbs just drive up this road from Pec and take Rugova? I got much the same answer.

"Look at these hills, these caves. We can hide in them forever. And the first tank that comes up this road, boom, we hit it with a rocket-propelled grenade or a missile and it's out. Then the others can't get past and that's the end of that."

Far down the valley, we came to a track that led up to a group of farmhouses. The property was surrounded by immaculate wooden fences. The fields between the road and the houses glowed with the new green of spring. This tiny place was Big Shtupeq. Selmon was already there. We found him inside one of the houses with a young woman from Finland whom we had heard about in Drelaj. She was a volunteer, a soldier of conscience. Grenades hanging from her black cotton jacket even while we drank coffee and fresh creamy milk and ate yellow Turkish delight, this young blue-eyed, blonde-haired, Finnish woman called Joanna Carlsson said she could not tell us much about herself without permission from "upstairs." I guessed that she did not want to make a big deal out of her unusual situation. So all I could really think of asking her was what on earth her parents thought of her becoming a KLA soldier.

"They're worried," she said in sing-song English. "But they know I've fallen in love with this country. I'll never go back. This is a fight for freedom, it's a fight for justice."

Outside, another shell exploded in the distance. The walls of the house we were sitting in had been blasted by a shell in a previous Serb attack in 1998. Plastic sheeting had replaced the glass in the windows. Before we left, the people who owned the farm, the Nikqi family, brought us plates of stove-warm *petlla*— delicious, light doughnuts that we rolled around in a plate of icing sugar. Gunfire sounded in the distance, echoing through Rugova from the front, from near Pec.

On the road back to Drelaj we met a military policeman who only gave his name as Selim. He was twenty-three and carried his left arm in a sling. I asked him how he had been wounded. He was shot on a reconnaissance mission to Pec, he said.

"What did you see?"

"Houses burning, the police going into houses. There are no people there. Sixty to seventy percent of the houses are destroyed. They're taking trucks full of valuables. TVs, fridges, videos, cameras."

The rain fell hard on Saturday. Rivulets formed in the pathways that wound through Drelaj. Water ran down the hillsides of the village. Holed up inside the house, we were impatient to get going. But the skies were dark and Gani suggested we give up the plan to leave that day and stay the extra night, leaving on Sunday morning. Keen to make it back to Montenegro so that I could file my story, I grumbled that I would rather walk through the rain than stay another day. I wanted to file the piece and ask the office in New York to send out a photographer with all the right equipment that would enable us to send our stories and photographs from inside Rugova for the rest of the war.

In the late morning, the rain eased. We took the opportunity and left.

Soaked within minutes, we stopped for coffee in Reka Allage in the same stone house I had seen on our way down to Drelaj. The renewed rain pounded outside.

The journey seemed harder on the way back and when we got to the village inside Montenegro, we sat on a log in silence. I felt nauseous with exhaustion. We said good-bye to Gani. He was grinning as ever. For him, it had been just another casual stroll over the hills.

Back in Podgorica on Saturday evening I filed my story and made my request to the office. "There's a KLA pocket inside Kosovo and I want to spend the rest of the war there," I told my editor. I asked him if the paper could send a photographer and every gadget needed to run my laptop and satellite phone and all his equipment off the car batteries that the KLA had in Rugova. I would get some rest, buy some of the things I realized I needed for a long stay in Rugova, and then make my way back to Drelaj, leaving directions for the photographer.

On Monday morning the front cover of *Newsday* featured one of Heathcliff's photographs of two KLA special forces soldiers near the brigade headquarters and a headline, "Rebels Hang On." The subheadline was a quote from Selmon's musings in the house in Big Shtupeq: "We will fight until the last man." He had said those words on Friday afternoon between sips of coffee and mouthfuls of Turkish delight.

By the time most people read that line in New York on Monday morning, Selmon was dead.

Less than twenty-four hours after we had left, the Serbs had launched a surprise offensive against Rugova. Selmon was shot by Serb troops near the concrete memorial to the fallen Partisans, his Kalashnikov with its taped magazine at his side, warm with use. He and a handful of other soldiers had been trying to defend Rugova from the surprise attack that had come from the route we had taken into and out of Rugova. No one had expected an attack from Montenegro.

Ibrahim got the message to me by phone. He had been speaking with the family we had stayed with in the Albanian village in Montenegro. Along with Albanians from two other villages in Montenegro, they had been forced from their homes by Yugoslav troops. In clearing out these villages of their occupants, the troops had shot six Kosovar refugees who happened to be passing by. Our hosts were suddenly refugees again. A few days later in Rozaje, I met our old host. He was hanging around the UNHCR building looking for humanitarian aid. He smiled, his white moustache spreading across his broad face, and gripped my hand as he had done when we showed up at his house. He and his family were sheltering in a local mosque.

The Serb forces had attacked from Montenegro and from Pec, up the supposedly impassable road that snaked beside the Bistrica. The villagers in Rugova were caught in a terrible trap.

My trip back into Kosovo was over before it had begun. It was impossible even to approach the Albanian villages on the Montenegrin side. The heavily armed Montenegrin police could not travel safely up those tracks. Representatives of the Montenegrin government had to negotiate with the Yugoslav Army to gain brief access to the villages, which were legally under Montenegrin control.

From Rozaje, in the days that followed, I looked up at the mountains and wondered what was happening on the other side to Luan and the others I had met there. Later in the war, in hotel bars in Tirana and at KLA border positions in Albania, I asked KLA soldiers if they knew what had happened to Luan. Most officers knew that Selmon had been killed. But with thousands of young men now in the KLA, no one knew Luan's fate. No one even knew who he was.

Chapter 6

In the Trunk of a
Gray BMW

"Of course the orders came from the top." Tony, the former Tiger paramilitary, laughed at the question: Did Milosevic control the ebb and flow of refugees?

"That was his order, obviously. He played a game with the West. When the bombing started he ordered the police and others to make the Albanians leave their homes. He hoped he would win the game that way. Then he started taking refugees back into Kosovo, closing the borders, making them walk along highways to cause NATO to kill them by accident, causing a negative reaction among Western public opinion. I saw large streams of refugees and beside them were army trucks."

Suddenly, the refugees stopped coming. For days, the world had watched the columns of people, cars, and tractors moving as if through molasses toward the border crossings in Albania and Macedonia and Montenegro, but in the second week of the war the exodus stopped. It didn't make much sense to those on the outside. If Milosevic was intent on clearing Kosovo of Albanians, as the actions of his forces during the first week of the war seemed to imply, why didn't he just keep up the pace?

Isa Bala first learned of the change in the policy from another Albanian who had stayed in Pec. But he only really believed it when confirmation came from Ranko Stojkovic, a Serb neighbor and retired police officer in his early fifties who had a son in a senior position in the Pec police. Each day during the first week of the war, the week that saw Pec become an almost Albanian-free zone, Isa ventured out of the house and strolled around on the sidewalk in front of the building to survey the street for a few minutes and talk with the Serb neighbors he hoped would protect him and his family. Isa and Ranko developed a mutual respect. They wouldn't have called each other real friends but there was no hatred involved—and at this time that meant something. Ranko's house was just fifty meters away and so they saw each other almost every day. Sometimes Ranko would bring over a bottle of *raki* for Musa, a goodwill token that Isa reluctantly passed on to his brother.

One afternoon in early May, Ranko's younger brother Slavko knocked on Isa's door.

"Hey, sorry to bother you, Isa," Slavko said, "but I've got this calf I bought in a village. Could you help me?"

"Sure," Isa said, happy to be given a chance to work. And he went back inside the house to get his knives and then walked with Slavko to his house.

When the calf was cut into veal steaks and legs and ribs, not a fleck of meat wasted, Slavko thanked the butcher and insisted on giving him cans of soda and cookies for the Bala kids.

Shortly after that, Ranko came over, asking Isa over to kill a calf he had bought. Payment came in two ways this time. First, the meat. "Isa, take some of this meat to your kids. They're used to it, aren't they? Growing up the kids of a butcher. Their tummies need meat."

But perhaps the second payment, which came later, was more important. It was the next morning and Ranko bumped into Isa as Isa hung around as usual outside his house.

"Listen, Isa," the Serb said, a little conspiratorially. "My son told me something. They've changed the policy. Don't worry and don't leave. The government has decided that the Albanians who stay won't be touched."

Milosevic was embarrassed, Ranko said. The government had realized that it was losing the public relations battle by feeding foreign journalists at the borders with endless new stories of brutality and killing and house burning. The refugees made incredible television. So there were to be no more expulsions from Kosovo. For the time being. Albanians trying to flee would be sent back. In fact, it was now against the law for Albanians to leave Kosovo, Ranko said. The only way to get out now was to go to the military police base in town, where they issued travel permits to Albanians.

It seemed too easy to Isa. The expulsions and killings and burning over? Just go to the army and ask for a permit to leave? Other friendly Serbs on his street were still telling him not to venture into town. Smoke was still rising from all corners of the city. Then again, Ranko's son was a captain in the police and he should know. Why would Ranko lie to him?

"Thanks, Ranko, you've given me hope," Isa said, trying to believe him but knowing he wouldn't go.

The news jerked Musa out of his stupor. It was May 11. The Serbs were letting people leave, officially? He could already see himself staying at his rented apartment in Ulcinj, scrunching his toes into the sand of the beach as his kids paddled around at the lip of the Adriatic. And then the fear set in again. And he started to drink, wrestling motionlessly on the sofa with his dilemma. He tossed coins in his mind, pulled the petals off a thousand imagined daisies—we should go, we should stay—and ignored every random answer the coins and daisies offered him. And then he made up his mind, for once. He gathered up his, Vjollca's, and his kids' identification documents, left the house for the first time, and walked to the military base to apply for permission to visit Montenegro.

A couple of hours later Musa came back with the permit. It was a piece of paper with the names of all the members of his family and an army stamp over them. "Valid for travel for three days," it said. Musa had tried to give the military police a thousand marks for their trouble but they wouldn't take it. All they needed to see was the ID cards.

Musa and Vjollca packed a big black suitcase with T-shirts, shorts, jeans, and as many clothes for the kids as they could cram in and they told the kids they were going on a bus journey to visit grandma in Ulcinj.

In one of the unlikely twists of war, a bus continued to carry passengers from Pec to Rozaje and then to Ulcinj nearly every day at the same time—eight o'clock in the evening—as it had always done.

For once, though, the war had interrupted normal service. For three evenings, Musa and Vjollca and their three children stood on the sidewalk platform at the bus station and waited for the bus that was due in from Djakovica and would take them over the mountains to Rozaje, south to Podgorica, and on to sunny Ulcinj. The children grew tired and cried and each night the bus didn't come. After the third evening, Musa gave up. It wasn't going to come. They were stuck in Pec. He went home and poured himself some *raki*.

A regular bus during wartime, plying its route as if a massive air war and guerrilla war were not being waged around it. Serbs giving Albanians written permission to leave Kosovo after forcing hundreds of thousands of them out at gunpoint. Sometimes war does not make much sense.

"In war you have many absurdities, like in life, in history," explained Tony. "You have some men who haven't done anything wrong but who end up getting killed. I remember in one village, where the KLA had been very strong and well supported, the police had gone in and captured three hundred prisoners. You can recognize soldiers really easily even if they're in regular clothes. They have marks on their shoulders where the gun strap has been. They are tanned because they've been outside so much. And their fingernails have very specific marks underneath from the discharge bullets give off. All these men were soldiers. There were three hundred of them, sitting on the grass, surrounded. I was expecting the order to shoot. But they let them go, under an order over the radio. I saw this. It's absurd.

"And then there was another village. It was quiet. There were not really any extreme Albanians there. But they killed fifty or sixty people."

The weeks passed. Every now and then, members of the family would stretch their legs outside. Isa hung out on the sidewalk. Vjollca popped outside once or twice. And Halise and Dardane went on their raiding-like trips to the shops across the river where the Serbs were still selling food and dishwashing liquid and shampoo and toilet paper. Those who most wanted to get outside, the children, were the ones who were kept inside. They would make too much noise in the street. Dardane was the only exception and her trips outside weren't exactly fun. They were dangerous, even more than they realized. Sometimes Halise and Dardane would go to the stores next to the towering red brick and concrete complex of apartment buildings called Soliter, not perhaps the name a thoughtful town planner would give to a thirteen-story collection of box-homes where graffiti covered the walls of the stairwells and the elevators hadn't worked for years. At least one member of *Munje* lived there. Opposite Soliter was the police station. This was where the KLA's Luan Shala had been tortured and where convicted criminal Nebojsa Minic worked as a police officer. Unknowingly, by shopping around the corner from the police station, Halise was taking her daughter to the haunts of the man who would end Dardane's life.

Dardane seemed old for her age. At eleven, she was already taller than her aunt Vjollca. Her face borrowed heavily from her parents' genetic repertoire—the same giving, solicitous smile as her mother. She pulled her lips slightly down to the left when she was anxious or sad, just as Halise did. From Isa she had inherited the strong Bala nose and his big, flat ears. She had her mother's wavy hair and her father's patience. She was tall and serious, grave even. But perhaps that was just the responsibility that fell on her once the bombing started. Although Hajri was older, Dardane was the unofficial boss-entertainment manager-morale booster for the children. Her charges were loud and many. There was Hajri, her older brother by one year, and her two little brothers, eight-year-old Veton—or Tony, to his dad—and wee Agon, who was six. People called him little Isa because he already had Isa's fleshy features and thick neck. He was naughty, adorable. Her cousins were all much younger than she was. Rina, the oldest, was six. Next came another girl, Nita, who was five. These two were in kindergarten, although Rina was about to start school for the first time.

At the end of the line of Bala kids, Isa's and Musa's, was Roni. Sometimes Roni would open his dark eyes wide and silent and then his confusion would overflow in tears down his cheeks. He was four years old and he clung to his mother, Vjollca, more than his older sisters. Of all of them, he understood the least of what was happening and it was beyond him to understand why he couldn't go outside and play as he usually did.

Physically, he was the smallest child in the house—something that would forever affect his life—but his needs were great. And Dardane often held him, and often sat with him on the pine floor throwing a rubber ball toward him and playing with the few toys he had brought with him from his own house in Kapesnica.

She did that with all the kids, ad-libbing living room soap operas for Rina's and Nita's dolls, rewinding the video cassettes of the Albanian comedians Cima and Qumili, even when she knew the jokes backwards and didn't find them funny any more. And when she felt she couldn't control her young and growing body's urge to play hopscotch for two hours or chase her absent friends around the playground in a game of tag, she reached for her skipping rope and fixed her eyes straight ahead and bounced up and down for as long as she could with the whirring of the rope making her feel like she was running outside with the wind rushing past her slightly too-large ears.

Chores were never in short supply for her. So many children locked up inside make a big mess. She swept the floors and mopped them and she took the piles of dirty clothes and washed them by hand and hung them up to dry and ironed them when they were ready. To Halise and Vjollca, she was almost an equal partner. She was learning the job of wife and mother even before they had.

Every now and then Dardane and her mother would see another Albanian family who were hiding on Dushan Mugosha Street just two doors down. Former judge Riza Loci and his wife Servete had sent their grown children to Montenegro but had decided to stay in their home with four others—two neighbors and some in-laws. Riza believed the war would be over soon and that staying behind was a risk worth taking. He spent much of his time keeping a diary during the war.

Cautiously, the two families started to visit each other, slipping through openings in the iron grille fences between the backyards of their homes. Fifty-five-year-old Riza and his family had been hiding more carefully than Isa's. Now they could drink tea together and feel that little bit more connected with the outside world. There was a union between the families, who had previously not been close. When a NATO bomb damaged the water mains and for some reason the Locis had water but the Balas didn't for four days, the Locis supplied the Balas with water.

For Isa, who got little in the way of male companionship from his brother these days, Riza was a godsend. The two men played dominoes for hours and hours, remembering to keep their voices down when they won. In Riza's living room, they kept only the sound of the TV on, so that no one passing would notice the flicker of a TV screen. Like anyone cut off from the world, they were hungry for stories, to hear them and to tell them. They discussed what they had seen or heard on the television, conducting their domino diplomacy and news analysis just as millions of others around the world were doing. When would Milosevic give in? Why wasn't NATO using those Apache helicopters that were sitting in Albania? And ground troops—why weren't they amassing ground troops in Macedonia and Albania? Was the worst over in Pec? How safe was it out there? Isa liked to discuss these things. But ultimately, if he came across something puzzling like the refusal by the Western powers to use ground troops, he would put it down to God's will. God is protecting us, he thought. And every day that the family survived, he became firmer in his conviction.

Toward the end of May, the relative quiet of Pec came to an end.

On May 22, Riza noted in his diary, the large house between his and Isa's erupted in flames and burned for two hours. Its flames licked close to Isa's house. It was a tense day. Isa had come round in the morning, saying his satellite receiver had stopped working. He was extremely anxious.

The next day, the house opposite Riza's began to burn.

On May 27, Musa came round to Riza's for the first time. He was drunk when he arrived but brought along some *raki* anyway. And then, on May 28, Riza noted in his diary that at last the terrified Musa had found a way out of Pec. He was happy for the man.

That morning, at about ten o'clock, Musa received a letter. It was from his sister-in-law in Ulcinj, Vjollca's sister, and it was delivered by two Montenegrin men who had driven into the war zone to deliver it by hand. With them was Zarko Backovic, a Serb and a former police officer who lived in one of the manila brick apartments upstairs from Isa's shop on Yugoslav People's Army Street.

With their dominoes, skipping ropes, dolls, cartoons, food to buy, meals to cook, clothes to wash, and scraps of street news to pick up, the

Balas had filled up the days. Musa had remained frozen ever since he had changed his mind about leaving Pec. Now his in-laws, the Trakaniqi family, were taking charge from afar.

"We thought he had gone on ahead of us because he had rent paid on an apartment in Ulcinj for a year," remembered Vjollca's brother, Vllaznim Trakaniqi, after the war. "But when we got there he wasn't there. We got another apartment in Ulcinj and all the time we went to check his place but they never arrived."

In early May, the Trakaniqis heard from someone who had left Pec that Vjollca and her family were alive and still inside Pec. Vjollca's sister and mother decided that the family had to be rescued. They had heard about Montenegrins who were driving into Pec and smuggling the remaining Albanians out, for a price. Vllaznim, who was unsure about the safety of the plan, found an old friend from Pec called Ilir who said he could help. Ilir had been in the cigarette smuggling business and one of his suppliers from Podgorica was a short, thin, ugly Montenegrin man named Nikola. The Montenegrin had found a new business in wartime —smuggling Albanians.

Ilir arranged a meeting between Nikola and the Trakaniqi family in the apartment. They made a deal: Nikola would fetch Musa, Vjollca, and the three kids for a price of three thousand marks, which Musa would pay. They gave Nikola a letter to give to Musa.

"Dear Musa," wrote Vjollca's sister Esma, as Isa remembers it, "I've sent this man to get you and the family. I want you and Vjollca and my nieces and nephew out of Pec. Why didn't you come earlier with all the others? You must come now. We have agreed on a price of three thousand marks."

For verification, the letter came with a photocopy of Vjollca's other brother Baskim's ID card.

The letter was like a shot of adrenaline to Musa. The Montenegrin men—somehow there were now two of them and Backovic had become involved—said they would travel in two cars. Musa was delighted. They would go now, for sure. And they would be safe. His original travel permit had long since expired but he went back to the military police base and secured another one. The two Montenegrins were eager to leave, as was Backovic.

Isa didn't like the plan. He was playing dominoes with Riza when Veton came in and told him that Uncle Musa was leaving with Mr. Backovic and two other men from Montenegro. Isa knew Backovic and didn't trust him. The Serb had never done anything bad to Isa but he was the kind of guy who hung out with guys an Albanian wouldn't want to find himself alone with. He was a Serb nationalist. But worse, perhaps, he was more concerned with his own well-being than with that of his nation. And then there were the two Montnegrins. Who were these men Vjollca's family had sent? Musa was going to entrust his own safety and that of his family to them and Backovic, to people whose neighbors and countrymen were the ones torching Albanian houses. He didn't like it and he told Musa that afternoon.

"I'm going to leave tonight with them," Musa said.

"Look, just take the bus," Isa told his younger brother. "You have your passes. Just get on the bus and go with other people."

"No, it'll be safer with these guys," Musa said.

"I'm telling you, if you're going to go, then get the bus because then you can just blend in with the rest of the passengers. You can't go paying people to take you out of Kosovo. That's illegal. But there's no problem on the bus if you have the right documents. Which you do. And anyway, there will be fifty other people on the bus with you, fifty witnesses to see if something bad happens to you. If you go by car there'll be no one there to see."

Isa was wasting his breath. Musa had made up his mind and told the Montenegrins and Backovic that the deal was on and he would see them that evening.

The cars showed up at Isa's house at six. The Balas could tell that it was the start of a cold night and it would only get colder as the sun went down further and they went up further into the high mountains. The family wanted to take a large bag of warm clothes but Backovic, the driver of the gray BMW, told Musa that the bag was too big. They left it behind.

This is how they had arranged it: Backovic would drive round to the track behind Isa's house, between the wall of the backyard and the perimeter of a small sports stadium. Musa would go alone in this car. At thirty, he was a relatively young man, young enough to fight for the

KLA, for sure, and so he was the kind of Albanian man of whom the Serb authorities would be suspicious. What was he doing in the Pec region if not helping the "terrorists"? So he made a risky calculation: He curled up in the trunk and prayed that the police and the military police, who controlled the border, wouldn't check the car. If they did, he would be in even bigger trouble than if they had just taken a dislike to his face in the passenger seat. But this way, they would hopefully never even see his face.

He kissed his wife and children inside the house and strode over the grass in the backyard, through the gate, and climbed quickly into the trunk of the BMW.

At the front of the house, the Montenegrins pulled up with a Zastava with Podgorica license plates. Vjollca and her three children got into the car and they set off.

It was not a well-conceived plan. Musa was taking an incredible risk by hiding. Surely they would shoot him if they found him. Worse, he had accidentally taken all the permits with him in the trunk of the car, even though his own permit was now of extremely limited use given his decision to hide. He was thinking like a man only just off a two-month *raki* binge. And he had sent his wife and children off toward Serb checkpoints without documentation at a time when it was illegal to try to leave Kosovo without permission.

It was dark and hot and bumpy in the trunk. It was disorienting. But Musa knew the road well. First the long, flat drive out of Pec. The car stopped soon and Musa heard Serbian spoken. It was the first checkpoint, just outside Pec. The car moved on again. Relieved, Musa felt the road continue straight for a few kilometers. They must be passing Novo Selo about now. Then the fork to the left. And then, just before the road really started to climb, they pulled over at the side of the road to wait for the Zastava and the rest of Musa's family. Nearby was the village of Radvac, now emptied of Albanians and home to a paramilitary group. Backovic opened the trunk and Musa climbed out and stretched his legs. It was working. They were only a few minutes away from the checkpoint up the mountain on Savine Vode. In a minute the Zastava would appear and then they would all push on to the final stretch through the mountains.

At the side of the road they waited. Five minutes passed. Musa knew that the engine of a Zastava, especially one laden down with two adults and three kids, wouldn't make it as quickly along the road as their powerful BMW had. Another five minutes passed. And another. And as much as he wished it to come chugging around the corner, the Zastava did not appear. This can't be happening, Musa thought. They should be here by now.

Without papers, Vjollca and the kids had made it as far as one of the first checkpoints outside Pec. The Serb military policemen at the checkpoint could see at a glance what was going on. These were Montenegrins on the make, trying to pull in some easy money by smuggling Albanians out of Kosovo. And this lot didn't even have the permits. They would have to be questioned. With two military police as their guard, the occupants of the Zastava turned around and drove back to Pec, to the military police headquarters.

Musa couldn't stand it anymore. He told Backovic they would have to go back. He couldn't leave his family behind. He couldn't show up in Ulcinj without the daughter and grandchildren of the woman who had arranged the escape. It would be hard to explain. Backovic wasn't amused —who knew what kind of trouble lay behind them?—but he agreed to drive back to Pec. There would be no refunds, he told Musa, who climbed back into the trunk. Hajri saw Musa arrive outside the house.

"Daddy, Uncle Musa's back," Hajri told Isa, as he stared out of the window into the street.

"No, that's impossible," Isa said.

Musa came running in.

"Are the children here? Is Vjollca here? Where are they? No, I can't bear it. I've lost my wife, my kids, three thousand marks. I've lost everything."

Isa couldn't comfort him. Only a drink could. "Where are they?" he asked, over and over.

An hour later, he had his answer. Two military police officers knocked at the door and took him away in a black car. Half an hour after that, the military police came for Halise and Isa.

"Why are you taking us?" Isa asked the two Serbs who took them to the base. "We don't know anything about this."

It took Isa and Halise two hours to convince his interrogators that he was telling the truth, that he wasn't involved in the illegal escape attempt.

"Who arranged this?" they asked. To Isa's surprise, they had been taken to one of the undamaged Albanian homes in Karagac. Apparently fearing NATO attacks on military, civil, and police buildings, the military police had requisitioned the house as their base. Although still in one piece, the house had been looted and trashed. Odd shoes lay about the floor. Furniture was smashed up.

"Who took Musa out of Pec?" the men asked. "How much were they paid?" And on it went. It was relatively civilized, like a regular police interview. The men weren't particularly angry, just doing their job. Isa told the men that Backovic and the two Montenegrins had been paid five hundred marks for smuggling Musa and his family out of Kosovo. The men seemed satisfied with this explanation.

Once the interview was over, the military police drove Isa and Halise home. But the others remained at the house, Vjollca and the kids in one room, the men in another. The military police weren't as gentle with Musa as they had been with his brother. They punched and slapped him. A senior officer arrived at the room and played good cop, supplying him with *raki*.

In the afternoon of May 29, the military police released Vjollca and the children. The four men were taken to the cells at the police station. Musa ate the bad food and lived for days without a sip of *raki* or a single cigarette. The guards beat him. Musa knew that sometimes people didn't come out of the Pec police station alive. The military police at the house had told him that he would be facing a trial, along with the three other men. But Musa found it hard to believe that during a war like this one the authorities would hold a criminal trial for an Albanian and a Serb and two Montenegrins.

On June 2, the trial began.

Musa and Backovic were brought from the cells to the home of an absent Albanian, which was doubling as a courthouse. Isa and Halise were picked up by military police and driven to the trial where they were to be called as witnesses. The court had decided to deal with the two Montenegrins in a later hearing.

The trial began at eleven in the morning and lasted for three hours. Behind a table, sitting on simple chairs, were two judges, both men, both Serbs. They were dressed in civilian clothes, in pants and shirts open at the neck. A stenographer kept a record of the proceedings. Musa didn't have a lawyer but Backovic did.

As he stood in the hallway of the house waiting for the proceedings to begin, Isa overheard two police officers talking over cups of coffee in lowered voices. These men, armed with pistols, had escorted Musa and Backovic from the jail. Isa heard them talk about him and he did his best to look like he couldn't hear them.

"What's that guy doing here?" one of the men asked his colleague.

"Waiting for a trial."

"He's Albanian?"

"Yeah."

"Right, let's kick him out of town."

"No, no. We can't do that. We have orders from them upstairs to protect everyone."

Isa was surprised. It seemed to fit with what Ranko had told him but it didn't fit with what was still happening in Pec. Just that day a neighbor had told him that another Albanian man had been murdered by Serb paramilitaries the previous night. Isa felt that animals had more rights and safety in Pec than Albanians did right now.

When the trial began Musa was the first to be called to the witness's seat. The judges were the prosecutors and they began a line of questioning familiar to Isa from his interview with the military police.

"How much did you pay these men?" one of the judges asked.

"Three thousand marks," Musa replied, and Backovic, who was in the room, glared at him from under his dark eyebrows. Isa winced as Musa continued with his truth-telling. It was a mistake to make an enemy of Backovic, Isa felt. The man was a former police officer and by his mid-thirties was already bitter. While serving in the Yugoslav Army, he had been standing at a checkpoint a couple of years earlier when someone, perhaps a very early KLA unit, lobbed a hand grenade toward him. It exploded next to him and caused great damage to his thigh and genitals. Backovic was impotent. He couldn't have children and didn't appear to like children at all. His wife had left him. Isa knew all this because the

Luan Shala, former KLA fighter, in a café in Pec in August 1999. Photo by Matthew McAllester.

The house in Rugova in August 1999 where the author stayed. It was destroyed by Serb forces shortly after. Photo by Matthew McAllester.

Father Jovan Culibrk in the gardens of the Pec Patriarchate, August 1999. Photo by Matthew McAllester.

Isa Bala in his shop, August 1999. Photo by Matthew McAllester.

Members of *Munje* in an undated photograph. In the back row on the right is Minic. Shalipuri, now dead, is next to him in the center.

Zejnepe and Haki Zekaj in Zejnepe's hut in the mountains in April 1999. Behind are other family members. Photo by Viorel Florescu. © 1999 by *Newsday*.

Members of the Zekaj family pay their respects to their dead, including Zejnepe, in Jablanica, August 1999. The mountains they sheltered in are visible. Photo by Matthew McAllester.

Nebojsa Minic, on the left, in an undated photograph found in Pec after the war.

Isa Bala with Veton on the left and Roni on his lap, June 1999. Photo by Julian Simmonds.

Isa Bala in his shop after the war. Photo by Julian Simmonds.

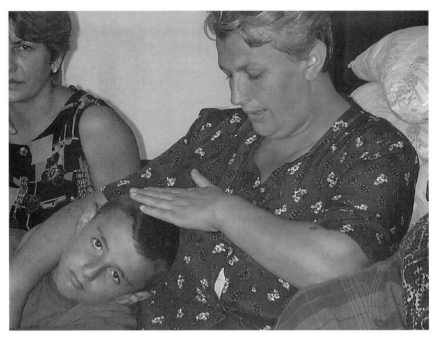

Veton Bala and his mother Halise at home, August 1999. Photo by Matthew McAllester.

A resident of Pec starting to repair his home, August 1999. The Mountains of the Damned are in the background. Photo by Matthew McAllester.

Serb had lived above Isa's shop for years. People talk. Even paramilitaries working in Pec at the time had heard about Backovic's injury. It made Backovic testy. Isa knew that if Musa was smart, he wouldn't incriminate a man like Backovic in his testimony. But that's exactly what Musa was doing.

"How did you set off in the two cars?" the judges asked.

"I went in the BMW and my family went in the Zastava," Musa replied.

"How did you get into the trunk?"

"I climbed in and Mr. Backovic, the driver, closed the trunk door on me."

Backovic's face rumpled in anger.

After Musa's testimony, Isa was called to the stand. He proclaimed to know very little about anything. Vjollca was next. Then Halise. And finally Backovic.

After the hearing the judges adjourned for a day to discuss their decision. The Balas were disappointed—they had hoped that the authorities would release Musa the same day. Vjollca and Halise had prepared a meal made from the last of two goats that Musa had recently bought and butchered.

The next day, the judges went easy on the men. Musa was found not guilty of trying to leave Kosovo illegally—he had the permits, after all. But Backovic was found guilty of accepting a bribe to smuggle an Albanian out of Kosovo and the judges sentenced him to a week in jail, suspended. A doctor in the court recommended immediate release for Backovic on account of his medical condition. Musa went up to Backovic when it was all over and offered his hand.

"Fuck you," Backovic said. "Get away from me."

On June 8, Musa again testified, this time against the two Montenegrins. Again, the men were convicted and immediately released.

That day, Musa left the court relieved. When he arrived at his brother's house on Dushan Mugosha Street, he was in the happiest mood anyone had seen him in for months. But it did not last. Riza noted in his diary that Isa and Musa had a row in the early afternoon. If Riza had not intervened, it could have become physical.

Backovic had left the court in fury. Later that day, Backovic bumped into an Albanian friend of Isa's, Rama Gashi. The Serb felt betrayed, Rama could see that. At some personal risk, Backovic had tried to help the Balas, albeit for a price. And what had Musa done? He had grassed him out. Every last detail. And Backovic, a Serb and former police officer, had spent time in jail and had then been found guilty by Serbian judges while Musa had been acquitted.

"I'm going to kill all the members of that fucking family," he told Isa's friend, Rama, one of the only other Albanians living in Pec. Rama was an elderly man who lived with his family around the corner from Isa's shop and Zarko Backovic's apartment. He knew them both. "And we're going to kill Musa with knives, not bullets. I have people here to do it. And I have people in Montenegro."

Back in Montenegro, the Trakaniqi family could not believe it. After all that planning, Vjollca and her family had still not arrived. Ilir called Nikola and for a few days there was no answer. Eventually Nikola picked up the phone at his place in Podgorica and he was not happy to hear from his former cigarette smuggling partner. He had spent time in jail, he told Ilir. The military police had confiscated his car and the court had fined him ten thousand marks. He hung up the phone on Ilir.

Chapter 7

Coffee with Zejnepe

M usa Zekaj was coming home. Usually, he loved his twice yearly, two-week-long trips back to Pec to see his wife Zejnepe and his grown children and young grandchildren. It was tough being away from his wife, even after all these years in Switzerland and now Germany. He had first gone away to earn a decent living for the family in 1971. He was sixty-eight now, still working as a handyman in the town of Memmingen. Perhaps he would have liked to stop working in Germany soon and come home for good. Only, if he did that, he would lose out on his German pension. So he would probably stay for more years to come like so many Kosovars who paid for their families' education, homes, and cars with their hard-earned hard currency.

It was a long journey. The bus took him through Austria, Hungary, Serbia, and down to Kosovo. He was tired and worried. As he got off the bus in Pec's bus station at about eight in the evening he was a taxi ride away from the meal that would be waiting for him, the comforting hubbub that his grandchildren would make, and the warmth of Zejnepe's body, wiry and old and familiar. Journeying home and being treated like a king when he got there was his reward for self-imposed exile. This time, though, he wasn't just back for home cooking and kisses. It was late

February, a month before the NATO bombing campaign began. Musa knew that the peace talks between the Yugoslav government and the Kosovo Liberation Army were making little progress at Rambouillet. Slobodan Milosevic and his police in Kosovo were showing no sign of backing down from what they considered their right to fight back against the KLA, a conflict that had already led to the killing of many Albanian civilians and the exodus of thousands. NATO leaders were threatening massive military retaliation. Every Albanian in Kosovo worried about how the Serbs would react under a NATO bombing campaign. They had seen Milosevic's version of war in Croatia and Bosnia. They knew that nothing angered the Serbs more than the idea of having Kosovo pulled away from Serbia. They knew what the Serb men in irregular military uniforms, with their crew cuts and cartoonish names for their groups, had come to Kosovo to do. Musa had watched the news closely in Germany until he could sit there no longer. He had packed, put thirteen hundred deutsche marks in his wallet, and headed back to Pec to protect his family.

At the bus station, Musa looked around for a cab. A tall, well-built man with short black hair, a large nose, and dark skin caught his eye. "Hey there, we'll take you home," the man said. The man, who had a friend with him, said he was a taxi driver. Musa assumed from his dark looks that the driver was Albanian. He spoke perfect Albanian.

Musa accepted the ride and jumped in the back of the metallic gray Opel Ascona with two extra halogen headlamps attached to the front, giving his address in the northern part of Pec. The man who offered Musa a ride sat in the passenger seat while his friend drove. The man was polite and friendly and asked Musa about his trip and why he was coming back to Pec. Musa told the man that he was just back from Germany, where he worked. The man nodded in recognition of Musa's predicament. It was a familiar story among Albanians in Pec.

The three men drove past the main square, the Korzo, and up toward the northern part of town until they reached the single-lane track that led up to Musa's house, the house he had paid for with the marks he sent back home as often as he could. Perched on top of a small hill and surrounded by a large yard, it was bigger than most in Pec. Musa had been working hard and long. It marked the family out as slightly better off than most Albanians.

Musa paid his cab driver, exchanged good-byes with the two men in the Ascona, opened the metal gate, and walked up to the front door of his four-bedroom, two-story house. Home at last. Behind him, the driver reversed back down the hill, the pebbles on the track crunching under the wheels. Musa's son Naim wondered why the taxi driver had put his high beams on when the rest of the family came out. The glare made it impossible to see the two men inside.

There was a rush of small arms and legs as Musa's grandchildren threw themselves around him and he fell into a long week of being fussed over.

It was a week later when the police came to visit the Zekaj home. At five minutes to eight one evening at least three men in blue camouflage police uniforms, sporting police insignia and wearing balaclavas over their heads, drove up the track to the Zekaj house. The armed men burst into the house. Five members of the family were at home at the time, including Musa. The Serb police officers spoke very little, communicating to each other with hand signals. One stood in the living room. One stayed outside. Another searched the house. From outside came the voice of a fourth man: "We have information that someone here came from Germany."

Musa immediately thought he recognized the voice of the man who had driven him home from the station, the man he had thought was a sympathetic Albanian cab driver.

Inside the living room, where the men had entered and the family was gathered, one of the police officers approached Musa.

"You brought a thousand marks in counterfeit bills from Germany. That's all we want."

Musa didn't move so the man took him upstairs and beat him until he agreed to hand over his thirteen hundred marks. The police officer also found a box that contained some of the family's gold jewelry.

It was all over quickly. The Zekajs stayed inside and listened to the heavy steps of the men and the rumble of the car as it drove away.

Sometimes there is no logic to an oppressive regime. A Serb neighbor heard about the robbery and he was so outraged on the Zekaj behalf that he went to the police station to complain. Over several days, agents from the State Security Service took statements from the family and appeared to be investigating the case thoroughly. The weeks went by and, perhaps unsurprisingly, the police did not charge anyone with the robbery and assault. But during that time, Musa asked around to see if anyone knew who the big police officer with the dark hair, big nose, and leathery skin was. He drives a metallic gray Ascona, Musa said. You might think he was even Albanian. People knew who the policeman was. These people were mainly from the other side of town, where Isa Bala lived. The man's name was Nebojsa or Nena and his nickname was *Mrtvi*.

Minic, it seems, was not finished with the Zekaj family. It was two days after the start of the NATO campaign—Friday, March 26—and Pec was full of tension, day and night. More than ever, Albanians stayed in their homes, trying to avoid the police and the paramilitaries who had appeared in ever increasing numbers over the past month. Some faces were familiar to the Albanians of Pec. Some belonged to newcomers.

Musa and his son Naim were keeping watch on the house that night. From Kapesnica they heard heavy shelling and shooting and orange flames tore into the black velvet of the sky. They took turns standing at the front gate. Some of their neighbors were doing the same. Best to keep an eye out in case anyone turns up in the middle of the night—not that Musa or anyone could do much against armed Serbs.

At about midnight, Naim, a quick-eyed, warm young man of thirty who could probably look after himself quite well in a brawl, came inside after keeping watch at the front gate. It was painfully cold outside and besides, there was no sign of trouble. He heard only the chaos from the other side of town. About an hour after Naim went to bed, Musa got up and made his way out onto the balcony on the second floor of the house. He had been woken up by the headlights of a car that was now parked outside his house. Moving quietly through the house he crept downstairs, out of the front door, and out toward the gate to see who it was who had shown up so late.

Zejnepe was still in bed when the sound of gunshots filled the bedroom. First came automatic fire. Then two more separate shots. Some of the bullets Zejnepe heard hit the wall of the neighbors' house. Some hit her husband. Outside, Musa lay dead in the freezing night, two bullet wounds in his head, his killers driving rapidly back down the hill. On their way, they passed by the house of Tefik Krasniqi, another Albanian who was keeping an eye out for trouble that night. He had heard the shots and, in the darkness, watched as two vehicles drove quickly past the wall at the end of his front garden. The drivers had kept the lights of the vehicles turned off and Krasniqi, unseen, could make out that the occupants of the vehicles were wearing police uniforms. The first vehicle to go past was a white minivan, known in the Balkans as a *combi*. The second vehicle was an Opel Ascona. It was too dark for Krasniqi to make out the color.

Zejnepe wanted her husband buried in his home village of Big Jablanica, which lies about ten kilometers to the north of Pec at the foot of the Mountains of the Damned as they arc around the Dukagjin plain. The family owned a house there. At about ten in the morning, the whole family packed and drove to Jablanica, where the villagers buried Musa in a tiny graveyard next to the road leading into the village. Honoring the family, the residents of Jablanica dug a quick grave for Musa Zekaj, piling up a mound of earth over his coffin and ramming a simple wooden marker into the frozen ground at the head of the grave.

For over three weeks the family sheltered in the large house in Jablanica. War was all around them and although the paramilitaries hadn't reached Jablanica the stories they heard from Pec's refugees and the towers of smoke they saw rising over the Dukagjin plain from Albanian homes were all they needed to know that they couldn't stay in the village forever. At the end of the first two weeks of the war, Haki and Naim told their small, skinny fifty-eight-year-old mother that it was time to make the journey over the mountains, through the snow and the Yugoslav Army lines to Montenegro. Haki and Naim had wives and young children to look after and they couldn't risk staying inside Kosovo, no matter how brutal the journey would be.

"I'm not going to Montenegro," Zejnepe told her sons. "They killed my husband, they're pushing me out of my home in Jablanica. But I'm not leaving Kosovo."

And that is how Zejnepe Zekaj came to live in the single room of a shepherd's hut high above the snow line in the Mountains of the

Damned, just inside Kosovo. "I'm not leaving this place until they burn it down," she told Haki and Naim before they left for Montenegro. "I'm not leaving Kosovo."

In the media age, curiosity has great power. Before the war, it was the institutionalized curiosity of the Organization for Security and Co-operation in Europe (OSCE) observers, patrolling Kosovo in their Land Rovers, peering at the movements of the Serb police through their binoculars, reporting what they saw, that kept Milosevic's men comparatively restrained. Now that the battle had started for good, now that Europe was experiencing its largest war since 1945, people around the world were genuinely curious about Kosovo. For most, the memory has since dimmed. But at the time the war fascinated many people—for about two weeks. Then the curiosity began to fade. The public's information diet of NATO briefings and interviews with refugees in Kukes quickly grew familiar and unsatisfying.

Part of the problem was that although few in the West doubted the refugees' accounts of the violence inside Kosovo, there were almost no witnesses to that violence other than the refugees themselves. Videos of exploding bridges in Baghdad may have thrilled in their newness in 1991 but the grainy spy-plane images of possible mass graves that were displayed at NATO briefings just didn't cut it any more. Independent eyewitness proof of Serbian violence barely existed. I certainly hadn't seen much live evidence of the ethnic violence when I had been inside Kosovo, apart from the sounds of gunfire, shelling, and bombing. I hadn't seen houses burning and I hadn't seen Serbs committing crimes.

Philip Sherwell and Julian Simmonds were still curious too. In the same hotel restaurant in Podgorica, over another terrible breakfast, this reporter and photographer team from the *Sunday Telegraph* and I started to plan another trip into Kosovo. I had met Phil a couple of weeks earlier when he was in Podgorica. He had taken a trip to Macedonia and was back. Mick Smith had suggested to his colleague Phil that he get in touch with me when he arrived in Podgorica. I was pleased. Phil and I had spent one fun evening together in the same restaurant earlier in the war. One thing I had learned when in Kosovo was that I did not want to go back in alone. Julian was Phil's unflappable "lensman," as he jokingly calls himself. I do not think I have ever met such a well-suited reporter and photographer pair.

We drove up to Rozaje on Thursday, April 22, and I told Ibrahim I wanted to go back into Kosovo, this time with Phil and Julian and, if the timing worked out, *Newsday*'s photographer, Viorel Florescu, who was on his way. "No, Matchew, no," Ibrahim said, exhausting his English but making his point rather forcefully. "No, Kosovo, no." Through our translator, whom I'll call Marko, he said that since the Serbs had attacked Rugova, it had become impossible even to approach the border. To do so would almost certainly entail getting shot, he said. Phil and I suggested alternatives but Ibrahim, usually the most accommodating of persons, was insistent. You try to get into Kosovo, you die. We drank some more coffee and looked at our maps, hoping new routes would suddenly materialize on the paper.

"What about this place?" I asked Ibrahim, pointing to a village called Balotici, north of Rozaje and very close to the border. All the army action that we knew of had taken place around the road from Pec and south of there.

"Matchew, no," Ibrahim said. Still, it was worth a look, so we ordered a *combi* and headed for Balotici.

Made up of houses perched on two steep facing slopes of a valley on the Montenegro side of the mountains, the village of Balotici is mainly Slavic Muslim. It had become home to a number of Albanian refugee families who received a sympathetic welcome from their fellow Muslims. But in recent days, the ethnic cleansing had spilled over from Kosovo into two Albanian villages inside Montenegro and so many of the houses in Balotici were empty of their Muslim owners and the refugees who had been sheltering there since the start of the war. The Albanians had seen what the Serbs were capable of in Kosovo and the Muslims had watched throughout the previous war in Bosnia as their brethren were slaughtered by the Serbs. The Albanians and Muslims were natural, if temporary, allies, and naturally afraid. One old Muslim man we met there carried an old silver-colored pistol tucked into his pants and pointed to the jagged ridge crested with pine trees that rose several hundred meters up the slope. That's the way to Kosovo, he said. The area behind there is called Giljo Polje. That's where the Yugoslav

Army reservists are. They recently burned some shepherds' huts. They look down on the valley with binoculars and the other day they passed through the village. Don't go up there, he said. They're real Chetniks, he said, referring to the Serb nationalist fighters of World War II. They'll kill you.

We stared at the ridge but couldn't see anything, so we moved up the slope to talk with another family. Three young men were standing next to a tractor. Marko, our translator, told them we were looking for Albanians who had come over from Kosovo. One of them ran to a nearby house and came out with a man in his thirties who wore two V-neck sweaters and stood in the mud on the heels of his sneakers as if they were slippers. As he shook hands, his eyes darted around, as if he was on the lookout for something. He didn't smile and kept dipping his head of curly brown hair down to look at the ground when he spoke. He said his name was Haki. He was thirty-five years old.

Although Marko translated at first, Haki asked if we spoke German. Like his father, he said, he had worked in Germany as a *gastarbeiter*, a guest worker. I could understand most of his German but Phil, who had once lived in Berlin, did the talking. Haki had come from Pec with his family after his father had been shot and killed by Serbs. Haki's wife and children were inside the house, which belonged to a Muslim. His brother Naim was in Rozaje at the moment.

"Do you think it's possible to cross the mountains from here into Kosovo?" Phil asked.

"I know it is," Haki said. "My mother's living in a hut in the mountains and I go to visit her to check that she's alright. She's there with some other members of the family."

"Why on earth don't you bring her to Montenegro? What are they still doing inside?"

"She refuses to leave Kosovo," Haki said, a tiny, brief smile appearing on his thin lips for the first time.

In Podgorica, we waited for Viorel to arrive and prepared for the trip. On Sunday, April 25, with the war almost a month old, we drove back up to Rozaje, spent the night in the town's only hotel—one of the most disgusting I have ever stayed in—and set off the next morning for Balotici.

Marko came with us. Haki was making one of his trips to see his mother and had agreed to take us along, so we were six.

More details had come out in talk with Haki. The reservists randomly but rarely patrolled the area we would be traveling through. In recent days, some other Albanian men had made the journey back into Kosovo from Balotici. Some had disappeared. One had had his throat slit by the reservists, Haki said. But he said we would be alright.

We drove along the winding single-lane track to Balotici and stared at the rain hammering against the windows of the *combi*. Once we arrived at Haki's house we could see that a thick fog hid the peaks of the mountains. The surface snow was slippery and I knew from experience in Rugova that the rain would have softened up the deep snow, making it incredibly hard to walk through. There would be no icy crust to skip along today. Still, we went, and it was a mistake.

We were hit by two blows. First, Viorel, as tough as they come and an old hand in inhospitable environments around the world, nevertheless hurt his leg in two places. One injury was a muscle strain and the other came when his leg disappeared in the snow up to the thigh, wrenching his knee in the process. The pain slowed him down. The second problem only became obvious gradually. As we walked through the conifer forests of ancient white, black, and Heldreich pines, scrambling through the thick wet snow, I started to wonder if we were going in the right direction. I wasn't the only one quietly wondering this. My unease came partly from observing Haki's apparent indecision about which pathway to take through the trees. Everything looked the same to all of us—snow, trees, rain—the view never changed. We couldn't see the mountains because of the fog and so we had no way of orienting ourselves. We had a couple of compasses but none of us had thought of taking our bearings when we set off. It was one thing to be lost in the woods but to be lost in the woods frequented by Yugoslav Army reservists and to be soaked to the bone, our feet becoming numb and then jaggedly painful with the cold, was something else. There were other residents of the woods we did not want to meet: The Mountains of the Damned are well populated by gray bear, wolves, and wild boar. A bear's tracks in the snow were the only other sign of life we had seen up there. That was not a great comfort.

Marko quietly told me that he was sure Haki was lost. This became rather clear when we came across human tracks. If it was Serbs, we were in big trouble, because the tracks were fresh. I was sure, however, that we had come across our own tracks, having described a circle around another clump of trees and deep snow. We followed the tracks until we agreed that they were, without doubt, our own. Haki had been reluctant to admit that he didn't know where he was going. It was time to give up and go back.

Marko and I slept at Ibrahim's, where his mother dried all our clothes overnight. The other three drew the short straws and slept in the hotel again. There had been talk of spending the night in a *combi* because it might be cleaner.

After we had staggered back to Balotici, we had persuaded two other Albanian refugees who were absolutely sure they knew the way through the forest to Kosovo to take us to the border the next day for a hundred dollars each. They were at Haki's house when we arrived there on Tuesday morning, April 27, a bright and dry day, and cold enough to harden the snow up a little bit. The going was easier, although still incredibly tough. At least we knew we were going in the right direction.

From the start, it was clear that Viorel's leg had not healed overnight. If anything, it was worse. Viorel, who had escaped Ceaucescu's Romania with his family, was not keen to turn back. He had come halfway across the world for this. So we pushed on through the drifts and up the slopes, our guides effortlessly strolling ahead, at times telling us to stop so that they could gaze down at Giljo Polje, where the reservists were meant to be based. We saw no one. After about two hours we reached open ground and walked toward the border, exposed on all sides, silhouetted on the field of silver, the sun ricocheting off the snow to roast our faces. Half an hour later, we stopped at the border. We were on a snow-covered alpine meadow bordered by the beleaguered-looking bushes of the mountain pine. In a few weeks, this snow would melt and the meadow would burst into life with its long grass and delicate, hardy wild flowers like alpine star and wulfenia. For now, it was a smooth dune of white.

Viorel arrived. It was time to make a decision. Was it safe to continue at this pace inside Serb-controlled Kosovo? What if we were attacked and had to make a run for it? Eventually, we concluded that Viorel should continue but only as far as the hut that Haki's mother was living in. Beyond that, where Haki had told us there were more refugees further inside Kosovo, down on the Dukagjin plain, Viorel would not go. We paid our two guides, said good-bye to them and watched them go back the way they had led us. I never knew their names but in weeks to come their faces would force their way uninvited into my thoughts.

Inside Kosovo we felt surprisingly safe, safe enough to spend ten minutes rolling huge snowballs down the side of a hill, safe enough to rest for ten minutes in an empty shepherd's hut. Further on we reached a slope that was almost vertical and thick with snow. Beyond that lay a small plateau on top of the hill where most of the snow had blown off and the little remaining had partially melted in the sunshine so that the heads of purple crocuses were appearing in the tough, grassy spots. It was an incongruous preview of the lush spring to come, even as winter held on firmly.

From the plateau, we could see a shepherd's hut that was clearly inhabited. A couple of figures moved about, laundry hung out to dry, and smoke came from a metal flue poking through the roof. A young man came up to chat with us and said he had seen the army moving about near the spot where we had been pushing and throwing snowballs. After a rest, next to the crocuses, we made the final push for the shack that Haki's mother now called home.

It was dark inside, and draughty, but warm as a country kitchen compared to the swirl outside. Light sliced in through the gaps between the thin timbers of the walls. The floor was just the topsoil of the mountainside, pressed solid by shepherds over the decades, but the hut's residents kept it clean of garbage. In the center of the only room in the hut, which was no more than five meters wide and ten meters long, sat a rusty old iron stove on four legs that rested on two planks of wood. Unpeeled potatoes sat on one corner of the stove's rectangular surface, just next to the flue. Piled up around the hot metal tube were freshly hewn pieces of wood, drying out so that they could be used for fuel. Shelves on the walls held bags of sugar, vegetable oil, flour, an empty bottle of Johnnie Walker Red Label, pans filled with melting snow, empty plastic bottles, packets of cigarettes, and some tins of meat. Nails poked out from the shelves and walls, acting as hooks for jackets, tea towels, and plastic mugs. On the right side of the hut was a low platform, about two feet off the ground, which the family used for a bed. Lying on it was an old man, covered in blankets. Besides Zejnepe and the old man, who was Haki's seventy-one-year-old uncle, Xhafer Zekaj, the occupants of the hut were Xhafer's wife, Shahe, sixty-eight years old, dressed entirely in black; Haki's cousin Jeton; Jeton's mother, Vasfie, and Jeton's young wife, Merita; and an old woman, a neighbor called Xhylsyme. As he did every day, Jeton was on a special mission and was away from the hut. The hard wooden platform was the bed for these seven adults. There was nowhere to wash inside and the toilet was a rickety wooden outhouse with a couple of planks to stand on in front of a gap that led to a shallow hole in the ground.

Zejnepe was not at home when we arrived. She was out collecting bits of firewood.

Shahe and Merita led us to the platform bed, where we sat and took off our freezing cold socks and piled them up like a soggy house of cards on the wood around the flue. They put a pot of Turkish coffee on the surface of the stove and fired it up with fresh wood, after which we engaged in the small pleasantries and thanks and welcomes common to guests and hosts sitting in any living room in the world. Merita, her face pale but calm, her long blonde hair hanging straight down over her red synthetic sports jacket, wore a gold wedding band. She had been married just a few months.

It wasn't the time for joyful reunifications and when Zejnepe opened the creaky door of the hut and walked in, Haki didn't even get up to kiss her. He knew she was still alive and that's all her undemonstrative son needed to know.

Zejnepe was so small she barely needed to stoop to get in through the door of the hut. She said hello to her uninvited guests but barely smiled, her pink mouth curving down at the ends, a slight furrow of grief on her brow. We had had our coffee by now and as it heated our insides we started to talk to the tiny old lady with the white scarf wrapped around her head whom we had come to see.

"My son went to sleep and my husband went out a couple of times but there was nothing there," said Zejnepe, her eyes narrowing with tears. "Then we heard two shots. He never did any evil to anyone. He never did any wrong."

She was quiet and sad. But when we asked her why she did not escape over the mountains to safety, she looked up and her voice rose, and she told us what she had told her sons: "I will not leave unless I see them burning this house."

Our home for the next two nights was to be another hut, further down the mountain inside Kosovo. It was empty except for a stove and a twelve-foot long, four-foot wide platform that was to be our bed.

From the door of the hut we could see the Dukagjin plain. And there they were, the plumes of smoke and darts of flame coming from the miniature houses we could see in the distance. The smoke rose and then leveled off into plateaux of dirty clouds above the silent plain, the tiny burned particles of another Albanian family's home floating in the sky before the gentle breeze dispersed it around the atmosphere. Below the clouds, there were living rooms, kitchens, bedrooms, family photographs, places where babies had been conceived and born, where grandparents had died, all blazing and crackling and smoldering after being stripped of their valuable possessions. Who knew if the same houses contained the bodies of their owners? The homes were too far away to see the men who were torching them.

Before we settled down for the first night, Phil, Julian, Marko, and I went further down the mountainside with Haki, through the leafless trees, and over the loose earth and rocks that covered the steep forest floor, to take a better look at the plain and the burning. On the other side of the ridge we were walking below was a full view of the winding mountain road of Savine Vode that led first to a Serb checkpoint and then to Montenegro. So it was unwise to cross over that ridge. We crawled up to some rocks and poked our heads over. A white bus was crawling up the hill. Cars were stopped at the checkpoint. Julian took out his three hundred-millimeter lens and shot the houses that were burning nearby. There were between fifteen and twenty different fires at any one time, most of them quite some distance from each other.

From the ridge we looked down on Big Jablanica. Haki pointed out his house.

"You see the minaret on the mosque? My house is the big one opposite it." We could see the red tiles of Haki's roof. It had not yet been burned. Only a handful of houses in his village seemed damaged by fire. I wondered if the Serbs had decided that the village was not worth the effort or if they just had not gotten around to destroying the place yet. It takes a lot of work to loot and burn down the homes of hundreds of thousands of people.

Haki named the villages where smoke was rising. Studenica. Vrela. Novo Selo. And there in the distance, half a dozen miles to the south, partly hidden by the horn of one of the mountains, was Pec. It had taken on a kind of mythological existence in my mind and so to see it now, just a town with a few distinguishable large industrial buildings, was in a sense disappointing. And yet, a moment after the anticlimax, I felt drawn to the place like never before and asked Haki, as I would ask several people, if it would be possible to cross the Serb-controlled road at night and hike down the mountain range to a ridge that overlooked Pec. The answer was invariably "no." What drew me to Pec most of all was what I could see at that moment. A month after the war had started, the Serbs were still burning the town, determinedly laying waste to a place that was now almost empty of its detested Albanian residents. The burning was not to frighten everyone away. The Serbs had already done that in a matter of a few days. They were burning the place because they hated the idea that Albanians could ever live there again. They wanted to destroy the lives of Pec's Albanians for good.

We watched as the blanket of smoke hovered over Pec, constantly fed by fresh fires.

After about an hour we decided to head back to the hut. As we started to walk down the hill, a shot rang out. Immediately, we scurried down the hill. We were at the top of the slope, where there were no trees. We were completely exposed on one side. Another mountain loomed over us and anyone hidden there would have a clear sight of us. The shot echoed around the quiet rock faces. Seconds later, another rifle crack. As we ran I thought of the Albanian refugees tramping slowly through the snow who, according to other refugees, had been randomly sniped at by

Serb soldiers. My foot slipped on a rock in the dash for the trees. Once under cover, we heard no more shots and made our way back to our new home for the night.

Zejnepe sent down some blankets with Haki and we curled up in the freezing night on the painful boards, waking each other up every hour to do stove duty, keeping the sticks and branches we had collected outside in the snow drying on the surface of the stove and then burning inside. Sleeping was so uncomfortable that stove duty was a welcome pleasure.

"I've never slept on a shelf before," came Julian's voice in the dark.

Chapter 8

Burning

It was a different season on the Dukagjin plain of Western Kosovo. Down there, the untended fields were shedding their wintry spinach color for the newborn green of spring. On the lower slopes of the Mountains of the Damned the sun was conjuring buds out of the snow-shocked trees. We had slept on our shelf in the hut, surrounded by ice and wind, snoring and shivering throughout the short night, digesting the hunks of bread and fried sausage Zejnepe had sent down to us the night before. Our sodden boots and socks jockeyed for position around the stove, which we kept stoking all night in shifts. And when we had woken up and proceeded single-file down further into Kosovo, through the icy gully that fell between the slopes that we had scurried from when the shots rang out the previous afternoon, we were walking out of winter and into spring.

Striding over the frozen boulders of snow in the opposite direction was a young man with a two-liter plastic bottle of milk in his hand and a pistol tucked into his pants. Binoculars hung from his stubbly neck. Mud covered his boots.

"This is my cousin Jeton," Haki said, and we shook hands.

Jeton lived in Zejnepe's hut with his wife Merita. He smiled broadly with a mild overbite. Several days' stubble covered his face.

"Where did you get the milk?" I asked.

"My father is down in the valley and he has a cow," Jeton said. "Every day I go down and fill up the bottle."

This was where he had been when we had showed up at his home the day before. Like all the Albanian men who crossed the mountains, Jeton was unbelievably fit and this daily stroll from the peaks of the mountains to the plain below didn't seem to trouble him. To us, the journey down and back up the mountain to our hut would be so brutal that at one point later on I wondered if we would make it back to the hut that night.

Jeton, who was thirty, sat on a rock and we stood around asking him questions. Apart from the milk, what did he and his family eat and drink?

"At night, I go back into the village to our house," he said. "I was there last night, for thirty minutes. I watch with my binoculars for two or three hours to see if there are any Serbs there and then I crawl across the fields. Once I was shot at but it's always nighttime so they couldn't really see me. We have between ten and twenty kilos of flour in the house and other food in the refrigerator. The last time I went back all the food in the refrigerator was gone, but there are still bags of flour there. I carry some back with me each time. And oil, I bring back oil too."

What state is the village in?

"The Serbs have stolen nearly everything, but most of the houses are okay."

Isn't it a terrible risk to go back into the village for a bag of flour?

"We have to eat," Jeton said. And I realized that the bread we had eaten the night before and for breakfast, turned into chocolate sandwiches with the bars we had stuffed into our bags in Montenegro, had been baked with the flour that Jeton risked his life to pilfer from his own house. It was the food the family were counting on to keep them alive for the remainder of the war, however long the bombing and killing went on.

Jeton said that two men who had recently gone to the nearby village of Radvac had not returned. That village, which we could see, had recently become a home for paramilitaries.

"When are you next going into Jablanica?" I asked him. "I'd like to go with you."

I wanted to see what the village was like, cleared of its inhabitants, some of its houses burned. I wanted to go with Jeton as he fetched his oil and flour.

"Not for a few days," Jeton said. And so that was the end of that, or so I thought.

"What's the pistol for?"

"Safety," Jeton grinned, his upper teeth showing like dentures in a bedside glass of water.

And then the question that could have no logical answer, only an emotional one. "Why are you and Merita still here?"

"I have the money to leave, I have everything, but I don't want to leave. I'll die here if necessary. I was born here and I'll die here."

Jeton strode up the hill and we crept down further into Kosovo. Suddenly the mountainside became very steep and so Haki led us diagonally along a pathway until we could look down perhaps a thousand feet to the floor of the little valley that stood on the margin of the wide plain. We seemed to be directly over the hidden glen, gazing down as if from an airplane. Dotted among the trees and grass of the valley were the roofs of dozens of red and white tractors, parked at different angles, some driven into the woods. Among them were the tents of white sheet plastic that people had set up at the base of the mountain. They appeared to have been abandoned. There was no one there. It was like looking down at a meticulously designed train set, with its tiny, well-ordered trees and houses and its cars waiting forever at a level crossing, except that these miniature trees and tractors had been chaotically assembled and quickly abandoned and there were no little human figures to be seen.

The descent to the encampment was almost sheer. We grabbed at branches to prevent free falls and slid down the loose earth of the decline.

"I have no fucking idea how we're ever going to get back up here," Phil remarked.

When we came out at the bottom we were suddenly among people. It was not the tent village we had seen from above but another one nearby, one that was full of people. Perhaps fifty, perhaps more. A short old man in slippers and a felt hat shook our hands and stood in the grassy clearing, welcoming us in Albanian. Other men, many old, stood around in Wellington boots. Nearby, women and children peered out from under the white plastic covering of their tents, the frames made from sawn-off branches, twisted over into an arc. Other branches rested on the outside of the plastic sheeting, weighing it down against the wind when it gusted up the valley. Four tractors lay abandoned in the undergrowth. Wet laundered clothes hung from the bushes, drying in the spring sunshine. Other tents stood empty, their occupants now on the other side of the mountains in Montenegro. Inside their forsaken and temporary homes lay mattresses, blankets, pots, stoves, knives, forks, dolls, empty cigarette packets. The trickle of a spring was broken only by the overhead roar of NATO jets and the distant boom as their bombs and missiles landed further inside Kosovo.

It was strangely idyllic there. Hens and their chicks hopped between the feet of the tent dwellers. Fresh green nettles poked up nearby, their young leaves handy for baking in pies. Butterflies shimmied in the air and bumblebees swooped around us as we drank from the spring and sat on a blanket that the courtly refugees laid out for us on the ground, as if we were guests at a country picnic. Not five minutes passed before we were sipping hot Turkish coffee out of patterned bone china cups.

As we lay on the blanket and talked, a woman came to each one of us and poured cold water from a red plastic jug over our hands as we rubbed them clean. We dried our hands on the towel hanging over her forearm. She and other women returned to bring us plates of warm bread with cheese and jam. We ate sausage and warm cheese pie and they poured us as much sweet coffee as we could drink. I'm sure we were all uneasy at taking their food but it would have been rude to decline. Less honorably, we were also poorly prepared, didn't have enough food of our own, and had come to look on anything edible as crucial fuel in the bid to get over the next hill and through the next few hours.

The men were proud that we had eaten their food and been their guests. Kosovar hospitality, Albanian and Serb, is a powerful obligation for a host and it creates a strong semiformal bond between host and guest. For Albanians, that bond springs from part of a centuries-old tradition of social laws that require a man to treat a stranger as his king and brother once the stranger has stepped through his front door. The host has given his guest *besa*, a vow of honor, and he must be prepared to die to protect the guest. In return, the guest must suggest through thanks and reciprocal offers of hospitality that he is aware of the respect being shown him. For Sali Demaj and his friends, the blanket was their home.

"They were shelling my house and I'm afraid here just as I was there," said Demaj, a retired doctor who was all alone in the camp. His family had gone to Montenegro with the rest of the refugees. "I had no place left to stay, though. But I have hope that everyone will come back. I'm seventy-five and I was born in Jablanica and I don't want to leave here."

I am not sure if, at his age, Sali Demaj could have made it over the mountains even if he had wanted to. We asked him if he thought the Serbs nearby knew whether there were people still in the camp. He paused and his face fell flat in powerlessness. "Probably not," he said. "Probably they don't know. But I'm not sure."

Sali Demaj was living on a probability that was really a self-deception. And days later, he would have to face the truth.

The sound of a shell exploded through the still air as we finished eating. It was close, but on the other side of the abutment. That's where the Serbs were. Less than a mile away. No one seemed to flinch. They were used to the sound of shelling and the valley itself had been pounded by artillery. Everyone there had learned to differentiate a shell from a bomb from a hand grenade from an antiaircraft round. For many of the camp's original residents, that lesson had been too frightening. That was why there were so many abandoned tents, so many mattresses, stoves, pots, pans, T-shirts, odd socks, forks, pacifiers, manual coffee grinders, and tractors scattered around the valley. This place had been home to hundreds of residents from the five or six nearest villages and most had fled.

As we walked further down the valley and past dozens more tents, sheltering under trees or out in the open, most of them empty, I wondered why those people had had the common sense to leave but not their stubborn, hospitable neighbors with whom we had just eaten. For sure, some were too sick to make the climb that Phil had so appropriately remarked upon as we came down to the valley and some were too defiant to accept leaving Kosovo. But it seemed to me that others were just in total denial. They were like the Pec families who saw and heard what was happening all around them, who had even spent nights lying on the floors of their living rooms while men outside sprayed automatic machine gun fire into their homes, but didn't think of packing their belongings or hiding their valuables and money until the men burst into their homes and told them they had five minutes to leave or be killed. These valley people wouldn't leave, I suspected, until those same men bothered to drive or march up the valley and burn down these flimsy branch and plastic homes just as they had torched the cinder block and tile homes further inside Kosovo.

Further down the valley a young medical student in Wellington boots who carried a pistol but no stethoscope led us to the sickest people in the tent city. Besnik Ibraj, from the neighboring village of Novo Selo, had been in his fifth and last year of medical school in Pristina when the war broke out. Without any medication to help them or even ease their pain, Besnik and his four and a half years at school were useless to the dying men around him and it was taking a toll on his pride and his temper.

"What's wrong with him?" I asked, as we stood in front of a living skeleton who said his name was Selmon Sabani and that his age was eighty-two. The old man's knees poked up in his mustard wool pants like apples on sticks. His dark skin flopping in folds from his arms resembled cowhides hung out to dry in the sun on a fence. He leaned against a pillow nestled between his bony back and a tractor, prone under the hot sun. He wore a *plis,* the traditional white conical felt hat of Albanian men, and it now looked a couple of sizes too big for his shrunken head.

Besnik gazed at me dismissively. "He's weak and old," he said in English, frustrated at my question and, I suspect, his powerlessness. "He has a headache. Lack of nutrition. I have no medicine to help him."

A few feet away was eighty-three-year-old Ahmet Smajl Groci, more animated than the barely moving Selmon Sabani but supported by a young man. "I was in Tito's prisons and this is worse than that," he said. "But then I was young and I could resist. Now I'm too old."

Through some more of the briar alleyways of the camp was Jeton's father, Emrush. He sat on a stool outside his tent smoking a cigarette under his gray moustache. A stove coughed out thin smoke into the air. If Selmon and Ahmet were the sick, here was the defiant. "They are more scared than I am," said Emrush, referring to the people who had gone to Montenegro. "I am not scared at all. They can shell as much as they want but I'm not scared. There's no place to go. I'm not going to live over there. If they come and force me out of here I'll go. They got what they wanted. They took our houses and they burned them. But they don't like to walk and they'd have to walk up the valley, but if they burn what I have made here I'll just go up the mountain and live in a cave. I am fifty-two years old and I have lived here for so many years. I may have left my home but I'll never leave my land. Never."

Although he lived in the Zekaj family home in Jablanica, the house we had looked down on with Haki the night before, Emrush had made his living at the now closed battery factory in Pec. In spite of his gray hair, he was still an energetic fifty-two-year-old. He had the aggressive self-as-surance of Besnik but it came with the calm of age. To leave his homeland would somehow make him less of a man, I suspected. Like his son, he had felt the pull of his home and, ten days before, had visited it during the night.

"I just went once to see what's happening," Emrush said, his cigarette smoke darting out of his mouth as he spoke. "They've broken the doors. We have a big metal door. I crawled there, over the hill and then in the village I had to go from house to house, from wall to wall, sneaking around. It was a dark night with no moon and I took a small torch. It was about nine in the evening. But there was no one there, just cows and sheep. It took an hour, an hour and a half, something like that. I opened the main door and tried to fix it with wire so that it would be closed. I had to be really quiet. You know, we have a cow and a calf still at the house. My son went to check on them twice."

That's what Emrush was all about. Fixing his front door. He desperately wanted to avoid being just a face in the hordes of a refugee camp, yet another wiry, unshaven Albanian man in an old suit, stripped of his home by the Serbs and reliant on the aid agencies and the Montenegrin government for his bread, his soap, and his mattress. Someone had damaged his front door and he wanted to go and fix it, even if the same people were to come back and burn down the house in a few days. Even if he was shot as he crawled through the fields and crept through the dirt track roads of his village.

As Emrush spoke, his son showed up. Jeton had made his milk delivery and was back. He had been mulling something over.

"Listen, if you want to go to Jablanica tonight, we'll go," he said. "I wasn't going to go for a few days but we could go tonight. What do you think?"

Phil, Marko, Julian, and I fell silent. Marko obviously didn't have to go. Jeton spoke enough German, having also worked in Germany for some years, for Phil and I to get by on our own. Besides, it would be a silent journey.

Without making a decision we went with Emrush to see his cow, which was tethered under a small roof further down the valley. Dozens of flies swarmed around the pen and its piles of dung. Next to the cow's shelter were two huts, slightly bigger than Zejnepe's. Primary school-teacher Isuf Sejfi Maksutaj, from Novo Selo, explained that his family and another one had been thinking ahead ever since the KLA started its campaign against the Serb police in 1998. When things started to get tough, Isuf said, the families suspected that the day might come when they would need to leave their homes and hide. So they had built the huts.

In the darkness of the larger hut lay Zek Hasanaj, who was eighty-five. He was stretched out under a pile of gray blankets on a wooden platform for a bed and looked up to see who had come to visit. His wife Rabe began to cry as she told us that her husband was dying. Besnik explained that Zek had high blood pressure and heart disease that was worsening. Zek's medication had run out.

"If this lasts any longer there will be no need for anyone to come and kill these people," Besnik said. "They'll be dead anyway."

Running up the center of the lower portion of the tent city, where we were, was a long grassy clearing. It was here that Phil, Julian, and I stretched out in the sunshine to consider Jeton's offer. Around us were the empty and tattered shelters, more red tractors, and a carefully locked, new-looking black Audi. The Albanians perhaps sensed that we needed to talk and so, aside from bringing us more cups of Turkish coffee, they left us alone. It was a conversation of few words and long pauses. We could talk about the risks and benefits of going but we all knew it was a choice each of us would have to make on our own. Julian made his decision quickly. He has a wife and two daughters, and besides, it would be dark when we went to Jablanica, so there was no practical point in a photographer going.

Phil and I lay on our backs and sipped coffee and continued our monosyllabic conversation. We had had these talks before and would have them again. They were always tense. The issue was always the same: As journalists, there was nothing more we could want than to witness up close an ethnically cleansed Albanian village that was frequented by Serbs. On the other hand, we could get killed. Although we knew that we were already in some danger by being inside Serb-controlled Kosovo, we had all made our own private calculations and then shared the results and decided together to cross the mountains into Kosovo. We had decided that this was an acceptable risk. Crawling into Jablanica at night seemed much closer to being an unacceptable risk. Given that hopefully there would be no one in the village to talk to except Emrush's cows, we would have no one to interview. Was the story worth it? And given that we were all already exhausted and still facing that impossibly long and steep journey back to the hut for the night, how on earth would we make it back there if we had spent the previous six or so hours out in the open, crawling to Jablanica and back?

As ever on my trips over the mountains, one factor more than anything influenced my decision. I believed that I had a moral duty to chronicle what was going on inside Kosovo, to offer evidence of the destruction and violence that the Serbs were wreaking on the Albanian population. To see that destruction up close was something I could not turn down, in spite of the risks. I believed then and believe now that it was simply worth the danger. I know that some people, including some colleagues, would consider my decisions ill-advised, perhaps stupid. But it is a personal choice. To me, the story had to be told.

My decision to go with Jeton brought an end to the conversation, leaving Phil to sit there in sunny silence making his own calculations. And after perhaps another twenty minutes he decided to go too.

Jeton wanted to leave much later, as the sun was going down, so we lay listening to the roar of the NATO jets somewhere overhead for a couple of hours. At around six o'clock, as the evening was starting to filter the day's light, Phil, Julian, Marko, Jeton, and I started the climb back up the mountain, although this time we took a route that led us south to an escarpment with a view of Jablanica. It was further down the mountain from the spot where we had gazed at Savine Vode the previous evening.

The view of the villages on the plain and the sprawl of Pec was better from here. At the butt of the escarpment was a low wall of boulders and as we walked through the woods toward the rocks Jeton signaled to us to crouch and then wait. He and Julian crawled forward and peeped over the rocks. This was Jeton's lookout spot. This is where we would be for the next two or three hours until he decided that Jablanica was indeed empty, that there were no paramilitaries dozing in one of the houses waiting to be surprised by nighttime visitors.

Jeton gazed through his binoculars, which hung around his neck at all times. Julian pulled out his long tube of a three hundred millimeter lens and the clicking of his shutter started. From behind them, by gazing into the sky above the Dukagjin plain, I could see that there must be at least a dozen fires burning and I knew this was what Julian was shooting. This time I had brought Viorel's camera and his own massive lens so that I could photograph what I had missed the previous evening.

We stayed and watched for about twenty minutes, taking turns to peer over the ridge, crawling back and forth from the hidden path. The Serb soldiers at Savine Vode were still within view and Marko warned us that if they saw us through their own binoculars, perhaps after glimpsing a reflection off our lenses or binoculars, we could expect trouble. During the earlier Balkan wars, Marko had been drafted into the Yugoslav Army and his job then had been to operate and fire Praga antiaircraft batteries. (Throughout the war in Kosovo, Marko fought a tireless and ultimately successful battle to avoid being redrafted. His skills were wanted for the battle against the KLA. But Marko, a fierce Montenegrin nationalist whose family deeply disliked Serbs, was in no mood to fight for them. Instead, he wanted them to relinquish control of Montenegro.) Most of the time, he said, the army used Pragas as lethally powerful ground weapons. Against modern jets they were pretty useless, but targeted at people on the ground they were accurate over great distances and had devastating effects. Over the past twenty-four hours Marko had heard a familiar sound in the mountain air, the deep crack of a Praga, and he worried that the Serbs had a position nearby.

Gingerly, Phil and I gazed down at Jablanica. Nothing moved except the small river running alongside the main road of the village and the dozens of stray cows that grazed in the flat fields of the village as if life continued as normal around them. The red-tiled roofs and stone walls of the village's houses were unpeopled and, with a few exceptions, undamaged. The Zekaj house was much clearer from here. The worrying thing about our view of this calm hamlet was the smoke billowing out from a house on the outskirts of the village. Clearly, Serb forces had been down there within the last few hours, maybe more recently.

Soon we had the answer to that question. As if out of nowhere, a small red car, perhaps a Zastava, appeared from the vicinity of the burning house, slowly winding its way toward the center of the village. It stopped outside a house near the center of the village. "That's Abdul Muca's house," Jeton later explained, identifying the owner, who had fled to Montenegro with his large family. Two men in camouflage uniform got out of the car and entered the house. Fifteen minutes later, three men left the building, carrying rifles across their chests and wearing dark uniforms. In the small red car, they drove back toward the burning house, vanishing behind some other buildings for a few minutes. By the time they wound their way back to the absent Abdul Muca's home several minutes later, another white, red-roofed house had started to spew smoke and flames out of a side window.

It barely needed to be said but someone said it anyway: "There goes our trip into Jablanica."

It was dark when we reached the hut. By the time we staggered back in, Phil had sprained a muscle in his leg and we were all almost speechless with exhaustion and hunger. The stove in the hut was lit but only barely, the fire finding it hard to catch on to the wet branches we had collected from the snowy and muddy mountainside. Outside, down on the plain, the orange fires of burning houses pierced the darkness.

More welcome than a waiter at the Ritz, Haki showed up from Zejnepe's hut with cheese, bread, a pan containing oil, and some slices of sausage, and a request.

"My mother wants to know if she can use your satellite phone," Haki asked me. "She wants to speak to my sisters in Switzerland."

Zejnepe had, in fact, asked us almost immediately after we had met her if we had a satellite phone. I told her that I did and that she was welcome to use it. Oh God, why now? I thought. But I put my wet boots back on, grabbed my handheld Iridium sat phone, and walked with Haki up the gully, over the moonlit ice and snow. In broken German I discussed Northern Ireland, the European Union, ethnic differences, and love with Haki on the trudge up to the house. Inquisitive and bright, Haki was also shy and introspective. He hardly ever smiled, often looking at the ground or scanning his surroundings when speaking or listening. This was him at his most loquacious, high up on the mountain in the icy moonlight.

To get a good reception, I asked Zejnepe to step out of her hut into the freezing air. She handed me a scrap of paper with long numbers written in blue ballpoint. I dialed and as soon as I heard it ring I handed it to her. It rang and rang and no one picked up. She looked at me and shrugged bravely, handing the phone back. I tried the second number on the piece of paper. The tiny woman held the clunky phone to her ear and remained still for several seconds. And then her face creased into a smile and she began a conversation with her daughter Rukmane in Switzerland that was, in its particulars, entirely lost to me in the stream of Albanian. But it was not hard to tell what they were saying to each other.

Zejnepe didn't cry. When she had finished she handed the phone back to me and said simply, *faleminderit*—thank you.

Back at our hut dinner was about to be served. Besnik, the doctor, and some other young men came to watch us eat and to talk. They had unpleasant news. That day one of them had seen Yugoslav soldiers, the reservists probably, moving around the area we had passed through on the way to Zejnepe's hut. And so again, we started one of those tense monosyllabic conversations about when we should leave.

"If we left now it would probably be safer," Phil said, as he and I stood outside the hut staring at the mountainside. "We could walk in this moonlight."

"Yeah," I said.

"I'm so fucked," he said.

"I'm so fucked," I said.

"We could leave early."

"Yeah."

We talked it over with the others. We would leave early. When the sun came up. Reservists or no reservists, we simply could not walk back over the mountains in the night without sleep. We would have to chance it in the morning. Not that we slept much that night. As I tried to doze off, the elephantine snores of my shelf-mates, the cold, and the fact that I had ended up on the only three-foot wide part of the four-foot wide shelf prompted me to reminisce fondly about the putrid hotel room in Rozaje.

At first light, we left. In a hurry. People say the journey back is always quicker and in this case it was true. Even though we were drained, we walked faster over the snow and up the hills and through the trees than we had at any time before. We walked in silence, Haki and Marko pushing ahead when we reached the trees, holding up their arms in a signal for us to stop so that they could scan the terrain for movement. Together we had decided to avoid the easier tracks that we had taken into Kosovo. If our dining companion of the previous evening was right, we might happen upon reservists along those paths. So instead, we struggled through the heart of the forest, over fallen trees and into deep drifts. At times, the whispered discussions we had between us about whether we were going in the right direction were not entirely gentlemanly.

Well before noon we emerged from the forest inside Montenegro and found the track back to Balotici.

Although the Yugoslav Army had free rein in Montenegro, we felt safe now that we were out of the war zone. The sun came out and as we walked down the track to the house Haki had been living in, Phil picked up a signal on his mobile phone and we called Ibrahim who promised to come and pick us up in a *combi*. Soon we would eat pizza and drink the Montenegrin red wine, Vranac, in Rozaje. Soon we would be showering and sleeping in Podgorica. Phil and Julian would leave for a break, taking a rest on the way in the heaven of Dubrovnik, the most beautiful city on the Adriatic. I saw Haki sitting on the grass near his house talking with other Albanian men who had come out to meet us. His head was down and he was silent and I thought he was doing his quiet Haki thing, thinking and resting and staring at the ground when he could. I went up to him and smiled and said: "Haki, we're back. We did it." He looked up at me with a completely blank face and his gaze quickly flicked away.

"Matt," Marko said. "Those two guys who took us to the border. They didn't come back."

We had given each of them a one hundred dollar bill. They had grabbed our hands and grinned widely, showing their bad teeth. And then they had turned back and strolled easily through the glaring snow toward Montenegro. We were the flounderers. They were the experts. They knew the way. It didn't occur to me to worry that they would be caught by the reservists. After all, we had made it through there without seeing any sign of the Yugoslav Army.

Still, they had not come back. For them, it was a walk that would take an hour and a half. This was over two days later.

We wondered quietly, as we sat on benches in the sunshine drinking glasses of water, if the men could somehow have gotten lost. It seemed impossible.

Ibrahim came with a *combi*. His face fell at the news. He would ask his police friends, he said. He knew a man whose brother was an army reservist. He would ask him. And Julian, Phil, Viorel, and I looked at each other and wondered in silence how much responsibility we bore for the safety of these two men, these two fathers and husbands.

Chapter 9

Agreements

What was fueling the destruction of Pec? No other major town in Kosovo was facing such violence. Prizren remained amazingly intact. Most of Pristina survived unburned. Parts of Mitrovica and Djakovica were laid waste but not quite on the scale of Pec. Many villages were utterly destroyed—especially in the Pec region—but Pec was the only major town whose Albanian quarters and homes the Serbs appeared determined to devastate completely.

There are a number of different possible explanations; some of them have the scent of revenge.

One is that the KLA was strong around Pec, and the town and its outlying villages had supplied a good number of recruits. There was the 1998 battle at Loxhe to avenge, a fight that cost several Serb police officers their lives. And there were the deaths of six young Serb men to avenge, the victims of an apparent KLA gun attack on a café in Pec in December 1998. The Serbs considered the KLA to be terrorists and their families to be the protectors of terrorists. Targeted and overwhelming retaliation, therefore, could have followed as it did in the central Drenica region in 1998 and early 1999, where the KLA was born. Dragan, the middle-aged paramilitary of the Pit Bull Terrier group, said after the war that for every soldier or paramilitary who died in action against the KLA, the Serbs would compensate by killing several Albanian civilians.

There was also a tradition of personal revenge in the area. In the Pec region there was a strong history of revenge killings between—and *among*—the two peoples, fueled in part by the northern Albanian traditions or laws known the *Kanun Lek Dukagjin,* part of which demands blood for blood. A number of ethnic Montenegrin and Serb families, like Tony's, fled the Pec region over the years to Montenegro or Serbia as the only way to avoid Albanian retribution in a blood feud.

From the personal to the collective revenge: Many Albanians there were wealthy. To steal from them and destroy their homes is to enact a certain kind of economic and social payback for centuries of perceived Albanian dominance.

Revenge may be only part of the explanation. Perhaps stripping Pec of its Albanians and their homes was a perverse kind of defense of national identity.

"In Pec and around the Pec area there are the most sacred Serb shrines and the strongest national feeling," a member of Minic's inner circle told me in November 2000. "So in Pec there was the biggest hatred toward Albanians."

I asked him why he and his colleagues had destroyed so much of Pec, so many homes and shops, instead of just taking them over and profiting from them in the new Serbian-controlled Kosovo? "For the same reason that they burned our homes when we left at the end of the war," the man said. In other words, each side wanted to wipe out all traces of the other, to make sure they had no homes to come back to.

Some paramilitaries have suggested a more strategic reason why Milosevic chose Pec as the target for such destruction and almost immediately emptied it of its Albanian population. Part of his early goal in the war was to destabilize the Balkans, causing a larger war that could cause the NATO alliance to fracture and Serbia's ally Russia to involve herself directly in the conflict. Flushing seventy thousand Albanians out of Kosovo in a few days and into Montenegro, already quivering on the edge of civil war, did nothing to help stability in that republic. Montenegro was the last reluctant partner of Serbia in what was left of Yugoslavia.

There could be also a less conspiratorial, almost ahistorical explanation, for the singling out of Pec. Perhaps Milosevic had simply decided to make an example of a town to demonstrate his strength and scare other Albanians. And so he randomly picked Pec out of a hat that held the names of Kosovo's larger towns. If so, he might have been continuing a military strategy that has been in use for centuries, perhaps millennia.

The strategy is one of utter, overwhelming brutality. It originates in ancient peoples wiping out whole families to avenge a single death and scare their surviving enemies into giving up on continuing the cycle of retaliation, and it ends with the nuclear deterrent philosophy of the Cold War and the present. It has shades of the gangster: If you cross me, I'll kill you, your friends, your wife, and your children and I'll burn your house down.

In his book on the Middle East, *From Beirut to Jerusalem,* Thomas L. Friedman calls the strategy "Hama Rules," so-named after a town in Syria where the late President Hafez al-Assad literally flattened a considerable part of Hama in order to crush an incipient rebellion. He killed twenty thousand people in the process, a deliberate act of excess designed to send a message to any future challengers.

It is not just gangsters and Third World autocrats who adopt the strategy. In 1932, addressing the House of Commons, the conservative British politician Stanley Baldwin was surprising in his warrior honesty: "The only defense is in offence, which means that you have to kill more women and children more quickly than the enemy if you want to save yourselves."

That Baldwin could say this in public only fourteen years after Britain had lost a generation of its young men in World War I, the war that changed the meaning of the word, speaks to how quickly we become acclimatized to the escalations of war even when we think it cannot get more brutal and pointless. If ever a public signs on to a deterrent theory of war, as the West did in the Cold War with nuclear weapons and continues to do by having such overwhelming conventional military might in the shape of NATO, it signs on to hating the other side. It signs on to Hama Rules. If you threaten the worst, you must be prepared to deliver the worst. You must be prepared to butcher the innocent and to consider that butchery to be entirely necessary.

So perhaps it was this: It was in Pec that the Yugoslav Army, police, and paramilitaries conformed to timeless military strategy. They showed what they could do. They showed how omnipotent they could be in a certain place and for a certain period of time, how, to borrow from Baldwin, they were prepared to kill women and children more quickly than the enemy in order to save themselves.

NATO had the skies and, to begin with, it played more or less honorably. As a result it was not taken as seriously by its enemy as it had hoped. NATO's strategic weakness was that it did not hate its enemy. It did not rush to destroy its enemy and to quickly kill women and children. It was above that sort of behavior, morally and legally. But in the end, crushing the enemy was what brought about the end of the war—as many of NATO's senior generals had believed all along. After more than two months of war, NATO planes began to take out the electric grid. Babies in suddenly unplugged incubators in Serbian hospitals found their lives threatened by the war. Hundreds of Serb civilians died in bombing raids. NATO's political leaders, with visible reluctance, had chosen to play by a version of Pec Rules.

The mountains were no longer white and dark from the snow and rock. On its yearly orbit, the tilted earth had begun to show its western hemisphere to the sun and now the grass, flowers, and trees of the Mountains of the Damned were sucking up the long hours of light. One account holds that the peaks were so named by the people of Northern Albania because their part of the range is barren and dry. In Kosovo and Montenegro, however, the Mountains of the Damned do not deserve their name in the summer. In the warm months they teem with wildlife. Gray rock partridges with their white chins and red beaks seek out the south-facing slopes, and black and white, dark-beaked peregrine falcons share the high air with the smaller kestrels, both scanning the long grass hundreds of feet below for mice and other small furry dinners. Sometimes a snake will lie flattened on a road. Climbing higher as the snow line evaporates, wild goats, roebuck, foxes, pine martens, stone martens, and capercaillie stretch their legs and wings for these few luxuriously green months. Water tumbles over the rocks and through the valleys and there's good trout fishing in many of the rivers, including the see-through

Bistrica. The villagers who live between the peaks take full advantage of the lushness of the season to pick apples and pears, to harvest honey-combs from beehives, to let newborn lambs and kids feed on long, fresh grass. It's not much of a region for late summer sunsets because of the vast rock screen that the mountains form between Western Kosovo and the falling pink sun in the west, but the evening air is clean and mild and at times you can taste the pine needles and honey on the breeze.

The mountains' highest point, a peak of 2,382 meters, sits almost directly between Pec and Rozaje. It hangs there in the sky, like the sheer crags of the Rugova valley, overlooking Western Kosovo and its people. It is permanent and predictably inhospitable to all people, Serb or Albanian. As the dramas of Kosovo unfold down below, the mountains undergo their seasonal change, year after year, millenium after millenium, oblivious and uncaring. And yet they are important to the people of the town. Every resident of Pec has a different reason to love the mountains. They are reassuring in their size and beauty, one man says. A reminder of permanence, an older woman says. For others, they offer an almost instant escape from the worries of daily urban life to alpine space and quiet. For young couples, they offer the Rugova valley road, one long lover's lane where kids can get away from the traditional sexual mores of Albanian society. And for nearly all of Pec's Albanians, during the war the mountains had also become a painful barrier.

As the war ended, people prepared to cross the mountains again.

The end of the war had the feel of the final lap of a long-distance race or the fifteenth round of a title fight. There was a renewed energy, a burst of enthusiasm mixed with desperation. It was dangerous, unpredictable. All sorts of things could happen. The one thing that was certain was that change was on its way.

People were preparing to move. American, British, Italian, French, German and other troops were checking their weapons, poring over maps, and taking their orders as they sat in Macedonia and Albania, waiting for the order they knew would eventually come: Cross over into Kosovo.

From bases in Northern Albania, the KLA was pushing hard against the Yugoslav Army just inside Kosovo, testing the army as the KLA had not really done before. Refugees in Montenegro, Albania, and Macedonia dared to start believing that they could be home within days. Some Serb civilians were also thinking of packing, and some were also celebrating. Their side was losing, but no more war, no more war.

Zharko Djordjevic was at church in the Pec Patriarchate when another parishioner told him the news on June 3. The war was over. Milosevic had agreed to a peace deal. Djordjevic, an official for the local basketball team, was a religious man and he felt his prayers had been answered. Like a physical current, he could feel the world change in him and about him. That night he and his family and their neighbors—including three Albanian families—set off fireworks and hugged each other. The ascetic and lean Djordjevic treated himself to a double-sized coffee and he bought some meat at one of the Serb butcher shops and his wife grilled it for the family. He could not stop grabbing his wife and his seven-year-old son and hugging them. It had not yet sunk in but like nearly every Serb in Pec, Djordjevic was spending his last few days in his hometown.

His countrymen in the paramilitary units in town were initially stunned and then furious and they found a new energy. The Bala children felt the change too. They had been becoming increasingly stir-crazy and this just made them worse. Halise worried about what this imprisonment, these bombs, this fear had been doing to the kids' insides, whether they would go back to normal when it was all over. One day, near the end of the war, Agon found a toy gun in the grass in front of a nearby burned-out house and claimed it as his own. The boy whose gun it was had left his house along with the rest of his family weeks ago. The boy wouldn't miss it, at least for now. Agon needed it. He walked back along the street, pushed his front gate open, walked into his house and up the stairs to where his mother was preparing lunch.

"Mommy," said the six-year-old who sometimes took swings at his quiet brother Hajri, twice his age. "I have a gun. I'm going to kill all the Serbs. If I can, I'm going to help you."

Halise smiled and said he should stay mostly inside for just a bit longer. It was a few days before Milosevic was to sign the peace agreement and Isa and Halise had begun to relax a little, sure that the war was nearly over, and so Agon and the others were allowed out now and then for short walks along the street and, with their mothers, into town for quick shopping trips. Sometimes Halise thought it was a mistake, giving the kids a taste of their old freedom. Hajri would moan and beg to be allowed to go outside all the time. It was tough for him. Out in the street, Serb boys his age were racing around on bicycles, playing in the burned-out houses, and he had to stay inside and perform his allotted chores, the worst of which was changing the plastic bags that his paralyzed grandmother had urinated into. That really was no fun. Please can I go out, he would ask.

"No, Hajri," Halise told him one time, when her fears had flowed back strongly. Those fears came and went. "It's still very dangerous. But when we all have freedom then we'll go on picnics and we'll go all over."

There was other worrying behavior.

One day, for example, Halise came back from one of her quick shopping trips. It wasn't quick enough for Agon, who was waiting at the foot of the steps inside the front door when she came back. He was crying and saying over and over, "They killed my mother, they killed my mother."

When Agon slept, he pulled the sheet up over his head.

Just hang on, Halise thought. It'll be over soon. No more NATO bombs, no more burning houses, no more paramilitaries like Nebojsa Minic driving past in their camouflaged jeeps and black cars with streaks of pink or silver lightning on the doors. Adding to the oddness of the Balas' existence in these last days was the occasional unexpected intrusion of normal life.

On one of the first days in June, as the war appeared to be nearing its end, three of the military police officers from the nearby base knocked on Isa's door at eleven in the morning. It was a routine visit, they said, something they did every few years, to register which members of a family had identity cards and papers. They were polite and chatty. Isa asked them in for coffee and they sat on the two large sofas in the living room. None of them were strangers. Throughout the war, Isa had made a point of befriending these men and even though he didn't smoke he always tried to make sure he had a packet of cigarettes on him when he went outside. Here, take one, he would tell the military police whenever they passed by. His Serb neighbors got the same treatment.

The soldiers sipped from the small cups and accepted a few bits of

Negro candy that Vjollca had bought from a Serb-owned shop near the bridge that morning. It was a short visit, fifteen minutes, and when they left they shook Isa's hand and one of them said, "I just hope the situation will get better very soon."

"God willing," Isa said, and the soldiers went on their way, leaving Isa with a feeling that things really were going to be alright if this was the way the Serb authorities were treating Albanians now—politely and normally. Even the police officers who passed the house when he was outside were becoming more civil.

Inside the house, spirits were high one minute, tense the next. During this time, the family had to deal with Musa's escape attempt, incarceration, and trial. And while that drama played itself out, the children still had to be fed and clothed.

One morning Halise went into town and came back with a few cheap pairs of shorts for the kids.

"Why did you get these cheap shorts?" Isa asked her, gently teasing her in front of the children. "The war is almost finished and when it is I'm going to buy expensive ones for them and everything they want."

The kids were delighted.

"Look what else I got," Halise said, showing Isa a fancy clock she had bought for fifty dinars, a pittance. Isa lost his smile.

"You shouldn't have bought that," he told her. "It's probably stolen. They just rob and sell, you know."

"But I bought it in the market."

"It doesn't matter. In the street or in the market, it's still stolen."

Halise told her husband that she had seen almost no civilians in town, just police and the villagers who had come in to the market to sell their produce—eggs, yogurt, cheese, milk. She had asked one villager if she could have some cheese at a cheaper price than he was asking. Take it, as much as you want, he had told her.

Isa immediately brightened up at this news. His wife cooked macaroni and cheese and it was a good family meal.

Isa's feelings were oscillating. He could be disapproving—about the clock—and then playful with his wife and kids. And he would grow hopeful and excited, watching the Albanian and German news on Riza's TV.

Riza and Isa gazed at the TV and watched their fates play out. There were the two old hands at diplomacy, Martti Ahtisaari and Viktor Chernomyrdin, a Finn and a Russian, moving around Europe, trying to bring all this to an end. They were a good combination, as Tim Judah notes in *Kosovo: War and Revenge*. Finland was on the invisible line between the West and the Slavic world: Militarily neutral, close to Russia, and part of the EU. Chernomyrdin had close relations with the Americans and, compared with many Russians, had limited sympathy for Serbia while remaining its standard-bearer in the talks.

Isa watched with the world throughout late May as the mediators inched closer to a deal that would be acceptable to NATO and Milosevic. NATO couldn't let this go on much longer. Its three-day war had turned into a two-month war and it had not prepared a serious ground force for a possible invasion in the event that NATO leaders decided that Milosevic would simply never give in. Even though it was only early summer, there were also hundreds of thousands of refugees living in tents in places that would eat them alive in the brutal Balkan winter. They had to go home soon.

Milosevic, realizing the Russians were not going to come to his aid militarily, and facing a resurgent KLA, a future as president of a devastated country, and NATO threats of intensified bombing of infrastructural targets, decided he had to deal. On June 3, the Yugoslav parliament approved the peace agreement that Ahtisaari and Chernomyrdin had fashioned.

Two days later, military leaders from NATO and the Yugoslav Army began talks in Macedonia about how the changeover of military forces in Kosovo should proceed. Isa and Riza watched pictures of the big tent in Kumanovo where the generals spent days hammering out the details. On Wednesday, June 9, the two sides signed an agreement on the withdrawal of Yugoslav military, police, and paramilitary forces. The next day, NATO planes stopped dropping bombs on Yugoslavia and the moving began. The NATO force, named KFOR, crossed over into Kosovo. The KLA rushed in. The Serb forces began to pull back. Albanian refugees began to make their way to the borders and Serb civilians began to turn themselves into refugees. The hard-line paramilitaries rushed to find last-minute loot and revenge. Isa and his family stayed put.

Chapter 10

The Illyrian Wolves

At the side of the road we stood and waited, but we weren't quite sure what for. And then, out of the darkness, came our ride—a furiously loud tractor with its headlights on. And I had thought we were supposed to be silent, covert. After all, these hills were apparently riddled with Yugoslav soldiers. The most curious thing about this tractor, though, was the way its driver and already numerous passengers expected to carry us and our bags up the hill to wherever we were going. There was no room on the small wooden platform to the rear of the driver's seat. Still, the four or five young men already on the platform hauled our bags up and then Phil and Julian and I clambered up and held on to each other and to the tractor like a troop of blind acrobats. I got a particularly bad deal, my butt resting on the edge of the rickety wood, my left hand grabbing Phil's jacket, and my right holding some metal piece of the tractor. After a few minutes, the wood plank that had been supporting the bulk of me snapped off and I had to dangle off the tractor for the rest of the journey. After our recent slapstick attempts to get over these mountains one last time, this was not a good sign.

It was Friday, June 11, and it had been a rough few days. With the war appearing to be nearing its end in early June, Phil, Julian, and I agreed to head in a counterintuitive direction by avoiding the NATO rush into Kosovo from Macedonia. We wanted to cross the mountains once more and see what was happening in the uncontrolled part of Kosovo, around Pec, where the KFOR troops were due later than they were in the eastern part of the region. It seemed like a good plan but we had had problems. To begin with, I had failed to get into Montenegro because of the presence of the Yugoslav Army at Montenegro's border with Albania, where I was on June 3 when Milosevic accepted the peace deal worked out by mediators Martti Ahtisaari and Viktor Chernomyrdin. Then, after crossing into Montenegro a few days later from Croatia, the three of us took a boat trip down the coast to avoid a Yugoslav Army checkpoint. At one point a Yugoslav Navy gunship had followed our tourist dingy.

Rozaje had not been much better. Haki and his family were hiding there. The soldiers were everywhere. To talk in safety we had to walk through back streets and along the Ibar River before we could find a safe restaurant in a basement.

There, Haki told us the fate of the two Albanian guides we had hired on our last trip and who had not returned home. They had been caught on the way back by the army, held for a week, beaten until one of them had a blackened torso, and interrogated. The men, understandably, told the soldiers everything they knew. So now Haki was a wanted man and we had to keep a low profile in Rozaje. Haki would not go back over the mountains with us. There was more bad news: There was no sign of his mother and Xhafer and Shahe. The Serbs had attacked the area and Haki could not go back to check up on her.

So, through Haki, we found another Albanian guide. In spite of our concerns, he insisted on leaving at night from Balotici. We walked into the darkness and after a couple of hours became completely lost. We spent the night curled up on the forest floor, trees preventing us from rolling down the mountainside.

The next day we found another English-speaking guide. When his mother found out what he was planning to do, she fainted and he had to take her to the hospital. Our plans kept falling apart. At the last minute, we had latched ourselves onto a KLA supply train that was run by paid Montenegrin Muslims and a handful of young KLA soldiers. Hamed, the leader of the Muslim Slavs, spoke German and demanded a lot of money for his services. It was at his bidding that we were now hanging off the tractor, chugging through Balotici.

After about ten minutes, the tractor pulled up at a house that was buzzing with people and I fell off it with relief. It was about one o'clock in the morning and the stars were clear overhead. Several ponies stood outside the house. We went inside and sat around the living room with some of the young men and the family whose house it was. They brought us coffee and we smiled and thanked them and sat awaiting orders from our German-speaking friend, Hamed, who ignored us. We were already tired.

More young men came in and out, each new one who appeared carrying some sort of weapon, mostly Kalashnikovs and pistols. Hamed saw us looking at them.

"Don't worry, it is for your safety," he said, grinning. Only a few hours earlier he had assured us that there would be no guns. Now that I thought about it I didn't mind. We were going with a KLA supply train and if the Serbs intercepted us then I would rather the people we were with did have guns. Before they shot, the Serbs would be unlikely to call through the dark woods first to ask if there were any unarmed, purely objective foreign journalists who wanted to step out of the line of fire.

After an hour we set off. There were about ten or a dozen men, some Albanian, some Muslim Slavs, four horses, and the three of us. The horses were loaded up with tightly packed bags of something firm but soft. We persuaded our companions to let us each add a bag to a horse. For this trip, we had to take a lot of equipment with us because we knew we were not coming back anytime soon. So we took a pack each on our backs and the overladen horses carried the rest.

From the house we made straight for the trees and the hillside. Just like the night before, the light in the forest was almost nonexistent. It is a strange experience to walk for hours with your eyes wide open and to be able to see barely more than the vague outline of the person or horse in front of you and perhaps some trees to the left and right of you. You could easily get separated from the fast-moving group.

For the first two or three hours, the ground was rarely visible but it always sloped upward and was often soft with mud and water. At one tough point, a young Albanian beside me grabbed my hand to give me support. Another told Julian to hold onto the tail of a horse for help. The horses snorted now and then. Sweat dripped into my eyes. My boots had been saturated long before and my pants were becoming coated in mud. We rarely talked, and then only in a whisper. The walk was hard.

After maybe three hours we came close to the crest of the mountains, the trees parting to allow the moon to light up an alpine clearing. I filled a water bottle at a stream and had to stride to catch up with the supply train. The men never stopped to rest.

Cars were close by, to the right, to the south. There was the strained engine of a truck going uphill in low gear. And another one. We were into Kosovo, cutting through Serb lines, right next to Savine Vode. And that was the sound of Serbs leaving Kosovo. There was something dangerous ahead of us. I knew, because we had all stopped for the first time. A face appeared out of the moonlight beside me and a finger came up to its lips. Three men with Kalashnikovs moved toward the road and stood in the clearing, protecting us from whatever might be on the road, their guns leveled toward the sound of the cars. In small groups of three or four, we half-ran across the clearing, the horses going with us. None of them whinnied or snorted.

The hike continued through forests and valleys and uphill and downhill and the sun began to come up and we could see where our feet were falling. The morning came fast and the sun grew hot and by the time we had reached a stony red pathway that ran along the side of a ridge inside Kosovo it was high in the sky and strong. We recognized where we were. This ridge was one or two closer to the road than the ridge we had perched on during the last trip. In fact, we were walking in full view—if anyone had cared to look—of Savine Vode. You would have had to have been a fine marksman to hit one of us from there but it could be done. Nevertheless, the men made the barest effort to conceal the supply train, cutting off green branches from bushes and threading them into the ropes that held the sacks on the backs of the horses. The KLA and their helpers were suddenly confident. Across the valley we could see and hear Serb vehicles leaving Kosovo. It was Saturday, June 12. NATO forces were already in Pristina and would soon be in Western Kosovo, accompanied, whether NATO liked it or not, by the KLA.

Around the mountainside, down into a valley, and there in front of us was the tent city. It was empty. Many of the tents were burned. And then a brief drama. A man in fatigues in the tent city ran from a tree to the cover of a bush and disappeared. Our KLA men and suppliers dived behind trees and bushes and pulled their guns from their shoulders. It took ten minutes of welcome rest to discover that the man in the valley, and his teenage son, were KLA.

It was perhaps around ten o'clock in the morning when we arrived. We didn't even know where we were being taken and we were so tired we had almost stopped wondering. It was a small compound, hidden in a valley that lay north of the tent city. A stream ran down its center and on one side was a single tent, made of sticks and plastic sheeting, and a cooking and living area sheltered by a tree and loose branches woven into a camouflage canopy. A sheep wandered around the place, nosing for spring grass.

"Welcome," said a gentle voice. It was the senior officer, a handsome man in his mid-twenties with kind brown eyes, a beard, and long black hair. "You must be tired."

He looked like a hippie, not a soldier. We sat down at a white plastic table with limitless gratitude for his impeccable English and his manners. One of his teenage soldiers brought us sweet coffee. It was his duty, he said, to host us. He seemed to be expecting us.

His name was Xhavit Gashi and he was twenty-five and, like Luan Shala, was a former English student. His group of fighters called themselves the Illyrian Wolves. Albanians believe, with some historical justification, that they are the descendants of the ancient Illyrians. "The Illyrian wolf lived in these mountains," Xhavit explained. "He would fight off everyone before he would leave and he survived alone."

Narrow shafts of sunlight flowed through the leaves overhead as he told us about his earlier battles in the war, how the KLA had been overwhelmed by the Serbs in this part of Kosovo, and how the Illyrian Wolves had escaped up the valley and had been hiding ever since. The Serbs in Studenica, Radvac, Jablanica, and all the other villages north of Pec had been too strong. The KLA had a few enclaves inside Kosovo, but they were tiny and further south.

In the last days of the war, the guerillas on Kosovo's border with Albania had begun to mount a serious attack on Serb lines, threatening to break through and perhaps alter the course of the ground war. But up here, the Serb paramilitaries were still strolling around the villages, burning, burning as they went. So Xhavit and his dozen men—most of them teenagers or in their early twenties—were lying low.

They had slept in the tent together for weeks and it smelled. Dank mattresses lay on the ground covered in dirty blankets and pillows. There was always someone in there, cleaning a gun or playing a game or getting some sleep. One of the teenagers had his girlfriend with him and they giggled at the back of the tent. He pointed at her and said to us, "Beautiful?"

It was Saturday afternoon and Phil and Julian had to file soon for their paper but I had more time, because of the time difference between Europe and the United States. So I asked Xhavit if I could go into the nearest village—Little Jablanica. Xhavit said we would go in an hour or two. I lay down in the tent and slept.

Just beyond the trees, in the village of Radvac, the area's paramilitaries were burning their last Albanian homes. Filling the blue sky, the smoke rose and flattened into dirty clouds. Xhavit wasn't sure that the paramilitaries who had controlled Little Jablanica were completely gone, so he and three of his men came heavily armed. Xhavit carried a weapon that can do damage to an armored personnel carrier. The others had Kalashnikovs. His brother Avni carried a rocket-propelled grenade launcher. One of them scouted ahead, peering across the trees and across the fields as we walked down the country pathway toward the village, past abandoned tractors and burned-out shells of Yugo cars and the rotting carcasses of cows fermenting in the sunshine, decomposing and blackening just a little bit more each day.

A dog ran out to meet us as we reached the first house in the village. It was a big house, two stories, with a large front yard area surrounded by nine-foot walls, making it almost like a ranch or a compound. The two swinging steel gates that let cars and people into the grounds were off their hinges. The constant gurgle and splash of water was the only sound. This house belonged to a man called Sadiki Mavraj, Xhavit said. It was a ruin. Blackened, a large hole in the red-tiled roof, stripped of all its furniture and valuables. Inside, red terracotta tiles mixed with splinters of charcoal from the roof beams, clusters of brick and mortar, curls of wiring, and shards of glass. The water came from a burst mains pipe and was pouring from the top floor down the stairs and through the ceiling to the lower floor. This is what Mavraj and his family would come back to, assuming they were still alive.

"It was a very beautiful place," Xhavit said. "We were here before this happened."

A horse ambled into the yard and stared at us. A cockerel was crowing somewhere. Ravens sat in the trees.

We moved on to the next house. It too was behind a high wall and someone had spray-painted the Serbian sign of four Cyrillic S's. Only Unity Saves Serbs. In the garden, the fruit on a pear tree had turned black. Bees buzzed in and out of untended beehives. There was the frame of a burned Yugo in the front yard. There were no burned BMWs or Mercedeses in Little Jablanica.

"Any car that was in good condition they stole," Xhavit said. "Any that were not, they burned."

Slowly, through the destruction and the midsummer heat, we pushed on through the village. There were about two hundred homes there. We found one that wasn't burned. Like everyone, I suppose, I had wondered if sometimes the refugees who fled Kosovo might have exaggerated the extent of the destruction and violence they were fleeing. It would have been hard to do more damage to a village than was done to Little Jablanica. Only bulldozers and tanks could have done a more thorough job.

The horse reappeared and ran through the deserted streets, kicking up stones from the dirt-track roads, then rushing in through the busted gates of another house compound. Most of the homes here lay behind what Xhavit told me were the traditional high walls of Albanian homes. Now the walls were just broad canvases for Serbian graffiti: "Albanian bitches sit on Serb cocks." "King Slobo." There were a couple of quite skilled drawings—one a complimentary caricature of Milosevic in red paint, another a neatly brushed and elaborate Serb Orthodox cross.

In one house, Xhavit told me that below the rubble were the bodies of four women. I don't know if that was true.

Sifting through the debris in the front yard of another, one of Xhavit's soldiers, at forty the oldest of the group, picked up a smashed musical instrument, the two-stringed *ciftelia*. He used to play this, he said. This was his house.

"I was up in the hills looking at my house as it burned," Hajdar Elezaj said. "What could I do? And of course, it wasn't just my house."

He had watched as the Serbs razed his village in three installments. Two months earlier a group of paramilitaries had spent a day burning about ten houses. A week later they took care of another fifteen. Only two weeks ago had they returned to finish the job, taking care of the rest.

He stared at the mess of his house and smiled and said, in English, "Home sweet home."

Outside we passed the smashed up hut of a post office. Opposite was a shop, looted and partly charred. I hadn't seen one television, VCR, microwave. Not even broken or burned ones. Everything was gone. And this seemed like a well-off village. These were not peasant houses. They were the homes of hardworking farmers on fertile land who probably had family members in Germany or Switzerland sending them envelopes of hard currency in the pockets of friends who came back to visit or wired to the many travel agencies of Kosovo.

Down the road was the village school. From over the trees the smoke from Radvac seemed very close. One KLA soldier stood beyond us, further down the road, and another crouched behind a corner. We were very close to the Serbs and Xhavit was uneasy. Earlier in the war there had been a gun battle at this spot between the Serbs and the KLA, Xhavit said. The KLA had lost. There were used shell casings on the ground. We didn't stay long and hiked back to the camp.

I wanted to cry with exhaustion when Phil poked his head into the tent that evening to say that Xhavit had decided that tonight was the night that we would take the supplies that came on the back of the horses with us over the mountains to another KLA base further inside Kosovo. Nothing could have made me happier than the Illyrian Wolves' short-sightedness in not getting around to strapping down the packs—which were full of uniforms—until it was dark. The knots weren't good and so the packs fell off the horses' backs and no one could tie them back on properly. Xhavit aborted the mission until the next night. We slept.

The not very menacing Illyrian Wolves pushed into another wrecked village the next day. Kaliqan was as bad as Little Jablanica.

"There's an old man in the village," Xhavit said. But when we got there, the old man was nowhere to be found. His name was Ali Arifaj and Xhavit, who had been there earlier in the day, said he was scared and unsure of where he was. He was in his nineties, the old man had told Xhavit, and he was hungry. The Serbs had let him live and his house was smashed up but untouched by fire, unlike every other house in the village. The only electrical appliances left inside were an old electric sewing machine and a battered refrigerator. All the windows were shattered and what little furniture was left was either turned over or broken in pieces. Family photographs littered the garden, images of a bride in her wedding gown, a middle-aged couple relaxing on a beach, and teenage friends with their arms around each other. Along one outside wall were spray-painted the words "Freedom for Serbia." In a bedroom the sprayed words "King Voja" seemed to drip down a mirror. Voja, the soldiers said, was a Serb commander.

In what was left of the village mosque, burned pages of the Quran lay on Arabesque rugs. Most of the floor was covered by the red tiles and rubble of the roof.

We picked cherries in an orchard and a black-coated kid goat followed us back up the valley and bleated and ran around inside the tent.

"Dinner," said the soldier who was in charge of cooking, grinning at the kid.

That night we set off for another all-night hike, this time into the heart of Western Kosovo. We walked through trees, heard vehicles trundle past somewhere in the night, ran along a stretch of road that the Serbs were still using, and, at three o'clock in the morning, watched in awe as Savine Vode was lit up by back-to-back traffic. The headlights formed a slow sparkling snake all the way from the plain to the top of the mountains and then they disappeared. It was the early hours of Monday, June 14, the day that NATO was due in Pec. By the time the sun started to rise and we were arriving in a KLA base in a village called Ruhot and the Italian troops were beginning the journey to Pec, the traffic over the mountains was at a trickle.

Chapter 11

A Silent Town

I t took a while but after breakfasting with a new group of soldiers in the kitchen of the house, washing our faces with the water that we pulled up in a bucket from the well in the garden, and handing our mud-caked pants over to a young female soldier to wash, we were led in to see the commander in his headquarters in the living room. Julian now wore baggy pants like a genie's, and they were the color of a shamrock. I had also borrowed pants—bright yellow jeans. In spite of the outfits, the commander took our requests seriously. Two English-speaking soldiers translated.

"Yes, we can show you bodies," said Agim Elshani, the gray-haired commander of the 133rd brigade of the KLA. He was a tired-looking man with a tolerant smile. "You will go with my men later. It is not far. But it is not safe to go to Pec yet. The Serbs are still there."

It was Monday, June 14, two days after NATO troops had arrived in Pristina, but KFOR had yet to secure control of much of Kosovo. The first handful of Italian troops had arrived in Pec on Sunday afternoon but some Serb forces lingered there. Most of the region was in a volatile limbo, with armed men of three different forces—KFOR, the KLA, and the Serbs—sharing the roads and heading in unpredictable directions.

Ruhot, where the KLA had found an unburned house and had turned it into a base, was predictably devastated but not quite on the level of Little Jablanica and Kaliqan. The village sits just off the northern road that leads from Pec alongside the main road in Kosovo from Pec to Pristina. Pec was a few kilometers away down that bumpy track of a road. Albanians lived along the road and so the Serb authorities that controlled Kosovo in the 1990s were never much inclined to pave it.

Surrounded by fifteen young Rambo-types, weapons dangling from their shoulders, bandanas knotted around their heads, we made our way along the road to nearby Nabergjan. There we stopped at a building that had been an Albanian medical clinic, then a Serb paramilitary base, and was now a wreck. On one outside wall was a graffiti picture of a palm tree and, in Serbian, a message: "Welcome to Serbia. The Palm Inn. Rooms ten rubles. Death for free."

Rubles. "Russians were in this group," Elshani said. "My men killed one."

Pulling up stakes two days ago, the paramilitaries had left behind four glasses and two white ceramic bowls sitting on a garden table under a tree. There was a knife sticking in the wood table. A pair of black socks hung from the tree, drying in the sunshine. Beer bottles, cigarette butts, shell casings, an ax, and cracked red tiles from the building's collapsed roof littered the ground.

There was other Serbian graffiti in the village. "We are going to fuck Hillary." "Monica will suck us." Messages like that to the incoming NATO troops. There was even a caricature of Monica Lewinsky sprayed on one wall.

Back toward Ruhot and on the other side of the road was the local mosque. It still stood but inside the far wall was charred.

Ambling through the long grass of the field around the mosque, the KLA men almost looked like a group of friends out for a summer walk. The rumbling of engines turned them into soldiers in an instant. It could only be Serbs. No one else had cars or trucks. Elshani waved his men into position behind the bushes and trees that lined the road. Some stayed back. With every second the vehicles were coming closer. Some of the soldiers would be within almost point-blank range. Phil, Julian, and I stayed back about thirty yards behind bushes and waited for an eruption of gunfire and rocket-propelled grenades or for the vehicles to pass by. There was a cease-fire in place. And there was a lifetime of vengeful fury in every KLA volunteer's being.

The vehicles passed. No one fired a shot. There were tire tracks in the mud on the road.

One fighter threw his red bandana onto the road as the KLA emerged from the greenery. Others sat down and one pounded the ground in frustration. Elshani had ordered them to hold their fire. At last, they had had a chance to pick off Serbs. "Why didn't we shoot?" one asked, knowing the answer. Another said that the Serbs had seen him and another soldier and had hurried on. There was a small truck and an armored personnel carrier. Target practice in an ambush like this. A few sitting Serbian ducks after eleven weeks and ten years of hundreds of thousands of sitting Albanian ducks. Elshani said he too was frustrated but that it was his duty to respect the cease-fire. I wondered if he would have been as respectful if we had not been there.

Elshani was right about the bodies not being far from where we had slept that night. It was out of the side door in the garden, along a lane, through a deserted farmyard, down a slight slope on a path that passed between thick trees and into a small, flat, grassy patch of land surrounded on three sides by trees and a small river on the fourth. There, in the clearing, I trod on someone's vertebrae. It wasn't the only one hiding in the grass. There were some ribs, too. A dog milled around the shallow graves. I noticed that the ribs had been gnawed and stripped bare.

One young volunteer, wearing the conical *plis* hat with a KLA badge sewn on the front, had brought a shovel. His name was Nexhat Berisha and he went about his task silently, scraping away the loose earth on the surface of one of the two graves, which sat side by side, each about two yards by three. He wore thick rubber gloves. Once he had moved aside the topsoil, he dropped his shovel and grabbed two red, rubber-coated wire cables that sprouted up from the ground. He gave them a tug but they barely gave. So he dug a bit more, gently. The clearing began to smell as he uncovered more earth. He put down his shovel once more and gave the red cables another tug and a decomposing head appeared from the ground. The cables were wrapped around the man's neck. It was hard to breathe because the smell filled the open air as it might have filled a tiny sealed room. The man's face was falling off his skull like an ill-fitting mask and his eyes were putrid. The young soldier let go of the cables and covered up the body again.

In the other patch, a skull and more bones poked up from the ground. Some of those bones were blackened by fire. The skull seemed to be the size of a child's.

Milazim Berisha, Nexhat's twenty-six-year-old cousin, had buried the ten people in these graves on May 18. Also a KLA fighter in this group and a local, he had been on patrol in Ruhot that day when he had found the bodies. He had had to work fast because he could hear Serb soldiers nearby. Using a wooden wheelbarrow that still stood by the graves, he had collected the bodies and had then buried them in these shallow graves. He stood and watched quietly as his cousin dug.

Burned articles of clothing and shoes were scattered around the field, along with the bones. The black jeans and navy blue running pants of two of the dead men hung from a nearby tree where Milazim had placed them when he had buried the bodies in May. The white inside pockets of the black pants were stained with dark blood. The victims' shoes sat below. Milazim Berisha said the men were cousins Beqir and Deme Osmanaj, forty and forty-five years old, respectively. One of them was the man with the red cable around his neck. Milazim had found the Osmanaj cousins down the hill, one lying by the stream next to the clearing with the cable wrapped around his neck, the other next to a nearby hedge.

Then he had discovered the charred bodies of two adults in a farmyard, their remains lying among the ashes of a haystack. In a nearby cowshed he had discovered three more bodies, one of a child under the age of ten. Again, patches of hay lay around the site of the fire. In another adjoining farmyard were also the burned bodies of two adults and a child. The Serbs had not realized how difficult it is to fully burn a human body, which is made mostly of water. They had left evidence not only of a killing but also that of a cover-up.

Milazim showed us the places where he had found the bodies.

"They were so burned that when I pulled out their bodies their bones cracked," he said, gazing at the scorched earth of the farmyard. We walked back to the clearing.

When the gunfire started a moment later I knew it was serious because of the lost look on the faces of the four KLA youths we were with now. They stood still for a split second and looked abandoned, young, bemused. Then they dove for cover behind the nearest bush or tree. It was clear that no one was in charge. Julian, Phil, and I scrambled for shelter.

I think we all had only one thought: The Serbs had come back in force, the ones who had passed earlier and who had seen the two cocky KLA soldiers standing in the side track for all the world to see.

At first the automatic fire came from perhaps two or three guns. It was desperately loud and that meant it was coming from just behind the trees, where the road was. Within seconds, more weapons had begun firing. There was a lot of lead flying about in the very near vicinity. The four KLA lads with us didn't fire back. They had nothing to shoot at, just leaves and bark.

One of them sprang up from behind his tree and sprinted across a log that spanned the two banks, his body bent over, making it safely to the next field and hiding behind a slightly thicker and slightly more distant tree trunk. It looked like a good idea. Every moment the gunfire was coming closer. Julian went first. Then Phil and me. I felt like a running bull's eye in my buttercup jeans and I found the time to wonder if I was about to make a fool of myself by actually falling off the log and into the river. Like Phil and Julian, as I learned later, I really didn't feel like getting my clean new pants wet and muddy already. So I kept my eye on the log and scuttled like a cockroach along an electrical cable. Once behind a tree I rammed my hand into a patch of nettles. By this time Julian and Phil were further down the field and judging by the increasingly close gunfire, that seemed like the place to be. But it was a wide-open patch of ground. I went for it.

"Stop, stop, it's OK, it's OK," called out one of the two English-speaking KLA soldiers we were with. The shooting petered out. The confused fighters stood up and came out from behind their selected foliage. "It's OK, it was just our guys shooting in the air. NATO is in Pec. And so is the KLA."

We regrouped at the graves. Like so many of the celebrating gun-carrying people of the world, the soldiers chose to ignore the dangerous laws of gravity—what goes up must come down—and began expressing their own delight at the taking of Pec and their relief at not being mowed down by Serb soldiers at the last minute. Standing among the charred and gnawed bones of their countrymen and neighbors, they shot at the sky. One offered me his Kalashnikov but I can't think how he got the impression that I might want to use it, seeing as I was crouched on the ground with my hands over my ears.

The next morning, Tuesday, June 15, some Italian journalists who had driven into Pec behind the Italian troops showed up in Ruhot. We hitched a ride with one of them to Pec.

At first I thought I had made a terrible mistake throughout my reporting on the war: Stories from Montenegro about the razing of Pec and the eviction of its people. The first section of Pec we passed through, its industrial zone on the eastern side of the city, seemed untouched. Tito-era factories lay silent, many of them closed years earlier. Towering over the district, to the left of the road, were the vast white cylinders of the Pec Brewery. To the left was the disused factory that once made spare parts for Zastava cars. There was no one around. None of it was burned or shelled.

But we were not yet in the town. The town proper was across the railroad tracks and it smelled.

At first, there was the faint scent of an autumn bonfire. On the other side of the tracks, it sharpened into a bitter bouquet of molten plastic, cracked bricks, charcoal window frames, and burned-to-a-crisp car frames. There was a mixture of smells, some old and weathered, some fresh on the air currents of the town. They were all the smells of fire.

Nearer the center of town, most shops were without windows, looted and torched. High-rise apartment blocks still stood but nearly every café, store, and street-level building was damaged. On the sidewalk and street were glass, bricks, soda cans, socks, shop signs, chairs, curtains. Further into the town there was more. Some parts seemed relatively unscathed—the odd burned house, the shops looted. A predominantly Serb-owned street was untouched. One woman pushed a wheelbarrow down the deserted street. The blinds were down in the houses. Pinned and stapled onto the trees that lined the streets were the death notices of young Serb men in army or police uniforms who were killed in action and old Serbs who appeared to have died of natural causes.

Other quarters of Pec, especially the Long Quarter, were almost flattened. You could see what had happened here. A tank had rolled down the main street, nudging into a row of jewelry stores, causing them to collapse in peaks and crests of rubble. Small groups of people gathered in the town square, opposite the Hotel Metohija, where the Italians had parked a few of their tanks. The people were Serbs and they were terrified of what might be coming from the KLA and their returning neighbors and so they stayed within sight of the Italian soldiers, now their protectors.

The management had fled the Hotel Metohija, for a decade the temporary home of paramilitaries, army officers, and Serb businessmen. Albanians had not been allowed there for years. We took keys from behind the desk and helped ourselves to rooms. A very nervous young Albanian introduced himself and offered his services as a translator. We hired him and found him hard to trust. How had he gotten to Pec so quickly? It was hard to trust anyone.

Across the Bistrica River lay Kapesnica, Karagac, and Zatre in ruins. Many buildings still stood but they were charred, looted, spilling their contents out into the streets like guts. Wires fell across the roads. Everywhere, Serb graffiti. Only Unity Saves Serbs.

Slowly and quietly, a gray-haired woman walked in sandals along a street in Kapesnica, stepping through the rubble and holding a sprig of green from a tree in her right hand. She was a Serb called Smila Jovanovic and she was fifty-six.

"The NATO bombs didn't do all this," she said, looking at the rubble next to her feet. "All this came from the President. The big man, Milosevic."

She raised her head and in front of her, over the horizon of the devastated Albanian neighborhoods, were the alpine mountains, cutting dark lines in the blue sky. A couple of people on their balconies in the sunshine looked down toward us from the concrete apartment buildings on the other side of the Bistrica. There seemed to be no Albanians around and more dogs and cats than people. Occasionally an Italian armored personnel carrier rumbled along a street. But the town was deserted, uncontrolled, quiet.

Two other Serb women came up, one holding a freshly baked loaf of white bread. They stopped to talk. They were sisters-in-law.

"Now there are about a hundred people in the town," said Radica Milovanovic, who was forty. "Serbs and Albanians. In total."

"In three months, the whole city was destroyed," said Jefimija Milovanovic, Radica's sister-in-law, who was carrying the bread from her home to the house in the center of Pec where she had been sheltering from NATO bombs throughout the war. "We spent three months in the center. We don't know who to escape from. NATO, the KLA, or the paramilitaries."

None of them were keen to talk about the paramilitaries.

"I don't know anything," Jovanovic said. She would say only: "Some of the people tried to kill Albanians."

We talked on. Minutes later: "They killed lots of Albanians and whoever was lucky is now in Albania."

And most of the Serbs of Pec were also elsewhere now—Montenegro, Serbia. They had left in fear of the KLA, the women said. And they were scared too. They had drunk coffee in celebration when the Italians had arrived but they didn't feel safe.

"Only God can help us now," Jovanovic said. "We have nothing now."

Still holding her unexplained greenery, she said good-bye and walked off. The Milovanovic women moved on. There was only one open store in the town. It was Serb-owned and sold almost nothing. Food was hard to come by and we were getting extremely hungry. That night the three of us shared a single ration meal that the Italian soldiers gave us. We needed food, a car, and a translator. So we called Ibrahim and Anna in Rozaje on a satellite phone and persuaded them to come over the mountains in any car they could find and with as much food as they could bring. In the event, a *Wall Street Journal* reporter also procured their services and together they drove over from Montenegro through Savine Vode the next day, Wednesday, June 16. Pec was chaotic, full of fear.

The new "mayor" of Pec, a shaven-headed KLA commander named Ethem Ceku, greeted visitors with a few cans of beer and his Kalashnikov leaning against the wall of the conference room in the publisher's office he had taken over as his base. He had no mandate and no authority other than the guns his men carried. He promised that all innocent Serbs would be treated fairly.

Apparently unconvinced of this, dozens of terrified Serbs milled around the bucolic gardens of the Pec Patriarchate, home of the Serbian Orthodox Church. Uncertain about what to do or where to go, they were safe here only because of the Italian troops and tanks just outside the gray stone walls.

Acts of revenge, and reasons for it, were easy to find.

In one house near Ceku's base, blood was sprayed on cream-painted walls. It lay in hardened pools on the floor and had been used as paint on another wall to write the word "Serbia."

Serb houses started to erupt in flames as Albanian houses had for the eleven weeks of the bombing. I saw KLA men near the newly burning houses. The Italians and the KLA made little effort to stop the looting of Serb-owned businesses.

The KLA erected checkpoints and the soldiers now looked powerful, impatient, and unpredictable. Serbs coming in from Montenegro had shot one of our English-speaking Ruhot soldiers as he manned a road-block on Savine Vode.

Anger, violence, and revenge had become commonplace. And then, on Wednesday, the 16th, someone in the small crowd that lingered outside Ceku's base mentioned that the man over there with the moustache had suffered a great tragedy *after* the final military deal was struck in Kumanovo. The man with the moustache took us to his house nearby and showed us blood on the sofa and bloody clothes that he had tied up in a ball and left at the end of the road next to an overflowing dumpster and he waved his hands around as he told his story so loud and so fast that Anna had trouble keeping up. And we visited his wife in the hospital. She sat cross-legged on her bed and talked and was heavily bandaged. Her cuticles were caked in dried blood, her light brown hair was un-washed and tangled, and she had one old brown blanket for cover. Unasked, she lifted her stained white T-shirt to show her large, naked breasts. They slowly seeped blood and they were violet, bruise-yellow, black, and tender-red because a bullet had passed through them. Her name was Halise Bala.

Chapter 12

The Killing

MacDuff: I cannot but remember such things were
That were most precious to me. Did heaven look on
And would not take their part?
—William Shakespeare, *MacBeth*, IV.iii

It sounds like a gun battle has erupted all over Pec but that can't be. There is no enemy for the Serbs to fight against in the town. Halise is scared. The Serbs are going really crazy at last.

"There must be an agreement," says Isa, who has been following the news on his neighbor's television ever since his satellite link went down. "Don't worry. These are crazy fools and they even celebrate their defeats."

It is Wednesday, June 9, and the Serbs have lost another battle of Kosovo. This time, unlike in 1389, the outcome is clear. It really is a defeat. Six hundred and ten years earlier, a draw on the plain of Kosovo Polje had marked the start of the decline of Serbia as an independent country and so, in due course, the famous battle came to be seen as a defeat. But this time, it is a defeat. There is no mistaking that this agreement Milosevic has come to with NATO constitutes a loss, and unlike in 1389, most of Kosovo's Serbs are not staying around to see how things will turn out after the conflict.

Even though his side has won—NATO and the KLA guerrillas—Isa is scared. Beaten soldiers can turn on civilians as they retreat. And ordinary people, neighbors, who have to flee their homes through little fault of their own, might not be as gentle as they had been during the last eleven weeks. During the night, Isa sits at the window, worrying that someone will come to their house. The Balas are among the only Albanians left in town and lots of people know by now that the family is there. They make an easy target for someone wanting to vent his rage. Isa looks down into the dark street and watches the headlights of overladen cars, weighted down with clothes, valuables, and children. First his Albanian neighbors left like this and now his Serb neighbors are beginning to abandon their homes and their city. They are even on tractors, just like the Albanians before them, passing through Pec from the Serb farming villages outside the town on their way over the mountains to Montenegro.

Perched at the window the next evening, the day NATO stops its bombing campaign, Isa sees a four-wheel-drive Lada Niva, camouflaged in the blues and purples of the police force. He knows it belongs to Nebojsa Minic. He has seen it drive by many times during the war and he has always prayed that Minic would not notice that the Balas are still there. He has heard about Minic over the past weeks and he knows that it is best if Minic doesn't know they are there.

The Niva is at the head of a parade of about fifteen slow-driving, single-file vehicles that makes its way up Dushan Mugosha Street past Isa's house. Behind the Niva are the other cars with other paramilitaries driving and gazing out of the window. Some of the cars are black and have a slash of lightning on the side. Minic's gang is called *Munje,* or Lightning. Isa looks and thinks, "They have enough guns to fight half of Europe."

Minic's Bosnian Serb refugee girlfriend Rada sits in the passenger seat next to Minic, who holds a megaphone in one hand as he drives slowly along through the streets of Pec.

"Brother Serbs," Minic's tinny voice calls out around the streets. "Don't leave Kosovo. Kosovo is ours. Do not leave Kosovo."

And then he starts to sing Serbian songs, folk songs of nationalist pride and victory.

Behind, the other cars carry banners: "Serbia—Kosovo Is Ours."

The parade passes Isa's house and moves on to other parts of Pec, the megaphone becoming ever more distant before the convoy returns twice more on a circuit of the town.

"He was desperate and he wanted to reorganize his men and join the guys from the army and police and other paramilitaries who were willing to stay and wait for the Italians," recalled one Serb soldier, "Djorde," who knew Minic during the war and worked closely with *Munje*. "They were supposed to protect the remaining Serbs who had decided to stay. I mean, to defend the city itself from the KLA as long as the Italians hadn't come. I don't know how many of them there were. I fled two days before the end."

On Friday, Isa watches the civilian Serbs in the neighborhood continue to ignore Minic's pleas, this time in large numbers. They drive past Isa's house and on to Montenegro. Only a few people remain: The few Albanians who have stayed and survived, the Serb civilians who are willing to risk the KLA and NATO for the sake of their homes, and the occasional paramilitary. By Saturday evening, Pec is quieter than it has been for days.

This evening the electricity is off—the power cut came at lunchtime —so the Balas get ready for bed even earlier than usual. Musa spent the morning at Riza's. He took round a two-liter bottle of *raki* and by the time he left a couple of hours later there was less than a liter left. Now he's drunk and sits in silence on the couch, smoking one cigarette after another.

Halise begins to warm up some beans on a gas ring in the living room. There's no point staying up in the dark much longer and besides, the kids are getting grouchy. They sense that their time of release from the house, after nearly three months inside, is close. Yesterday, Halise made the air-light doughnuts of Kosovo, *petlla*, and after the children had dipped them in the tray of icing sugar and quaffed down all the *petlla*, they had rushed to Halise and kissed her hands. There was a feeling of celebration. Tonight, that feeling lingers among the children, even though Isa is anxious. Halise and Vjollca make sure the children put on their pajamas before they get ready for the beans and then bed. Isa helps with the kids, laying out the mattresses in the living room for his family and in the side room for Musa's family, as usual. Tomorrow, the television has told them, NATO will arrive in Western Kosovo.

~

Isa's old friend Rama Gashi holds a cigarette in his thin, brown fingers and blows its smoke into the night. It is just after eight o'clock and it is dark. Rama sits on a chair outside his house on Kosmonaut Street in the little courtyard behind the high metal gate that leads onto the street. He is finishing his cigarette and thinking about his family's survival in Pec. They are among the handful that have stayed and remained alive. Among the ten thousand who were driven from their homes to the basketball arena and then told to go home the next morning, they made two other attempts to leave but were sent back to Pec both times. The Serb military police and paramilitaries know the family is there. Rama even went with Isa to the court on the day of Musa's trial. He remembers Backovic's words.

From outside there comes the sound of car engines and brakes. Suddenly there is a banging on the gate. Rama stays silent and doesn't move. "Open up," a man shouts from outside in Serbian. "Open up." Rama still doesn't move. Perhaps whoever it is will just go away. Inside he has a wife and eight children, including three teenage daughters—Shpresa, Shqipe, and Valbona. He thinks back to the day when the NATO bombing started and remembers the threats of a man he knew by reputation. He was a big Serb called Nebojsa Minic and the Serb had come to Rama's house demanding money, threatening to rape his teenage daughters if the old man didn't come up with cash immediately. Rama is sixty-five and his health isn't so good and he retired from his work as an engineer some years ago. Money is tight, but he handed over much of what he had to Minic that day. So now Rama hopes that whoever this is, it isn't Minic, the devil he knows. Rama's children have by this time gathered at the windows of the house that look out on the courtyard and they are staring at the gate. Then Rama hears the scrambling sound of men climbing and he sees black, fingerless gloves and then khaki forearms appear over the brickwork that runs along the top of the gate. He knows he can do nothing now.

A face appears, streaked with black paint. "Open the door, motherfucker," the face says.

"Oh, hello, hang on a minute, I'll just let you in," Rama calls out cheerily.

He opens the gate and Minic and his men are standing there. About thirty of them, all in camouflage combat gear, all without identifying insignia, all with their faces covered in lines of black makeup. They have come in six four-wheel-drive vehicles.

One of Minic's men puts a gun to Rama's throat and leads him into the living room. The children start to scream. There are now about nine men in the house.

"Shut up," one of the men says, waving his gun at the children.

Minic sits down on the purple, blue, and black patterned couch in the living room, which is to the right of the front door, and runs his hand through his short black hair. Two of his men join him inside. From where he sits, he can call out instructions to those of his men still in the courtyard. He has a radio and it crackles and Minic seems to be getting orders from another man. In the meantime, he busies himself with talking to the family. He seems to be in an unpredictable mood, threatening murder one minute, apparently seeking sympathy the next.

"These are hard times," he says, sweating heavily in his police uniform. It is warm in the living room because that's where the family's white stove heater sits. "They're really hard times. I know I'm going to be killed but just tonight, I'm going to try to save your lives."

Minic's black-smeared face looks tired and his breath smells of alcohol. Rama and his children have seen the tattoos on his body before and can see some of them again—the ax, the JNA initials of the army veteran, the cobra writhing over his shoulder from his back, the four Cyrillic S's of the Serbian slogan, and the knives. There's a real knife hanging from his belt and a pistol tucked into a pocket in his olive-brown T-shirt. They know his nickname is *Mrtvi*. Tonight, the Dead wears two crosses around his neck, one gold, one wooden.

Minic and his men don't laugh and they don't joke around. For long periods they sit in silence, apparently awaiting orders from the voice on the radio. Now and then, Minic speaks up, as if to explain himself.

"We are warriors," he says to the family, who nod, "and we won't leave this place until the last of us is dead. NATO will never come here while we're alive."

Later he explains what they're doing tonight: "We're cleansing the center of town, finally."

An hour, perhaps an hour and a half, passes, and then Minic gives an order.

"Joska, take him and get him to show you the house," he tells a man Rama recognizes as Dalibor Banjac, otherwise known as Joska. Banjac has short blond hair and is about thirty years old. "You know what to do."

Rama gets up and, terrified, is led outside by Joska and a tall man with a dark beard and another man. They put him in the back seat of a black car that is waiting outside. Rama feels the seat of his pants getting suddenly wet and he puts his hand on the seat and he brings it close to his face and it is covered in blood. He directs them to the house of his friend, Isa Bala, the butcher.

At Isa's house, Joska and the bearded paramilitary go up to Isa's front door while the third man stands with Rama outside. Agon needs to be tired out a little bit more before he's ready for bed. He's at that hyperactive stage before the toddler exhaustion of evening hits him like a cartoon mallet bringing about instant sleep. So Isa takes him on his shoulders and carries him around the house.

"Daddy, I want to go to school," the preschooler squeals as he rides the thick shoulders of his dad around the house.

"Sure you can," Isa says.

"Can I have a school bag?"

"Yes, I'm going to buy you a gold school bag."

"I'm going to have a *gold* school bag," Agon shouts, between laughs.

"Why aren't you going to buy us gold school bags?" ask one of Isa's other kids, who are watching.

"I'm going to buy you all gold school bags," Isa promises his kids and they jump up and down.

"And I'm going to buy you all diamond bags," Halise says, and the family is happy.

The shouting comes from down at the front door. It's about half-past nine in the evening. People don't come around at this time, especially when the electricity is off. It is a man's voice and it is in Serbian. Isa takes Agon from his shoulders and puts him down on the floor.

"Open the door. Open the fucking door. I'm going to fuck up your God. Open the fucking door."

There's no use in keeping them out. Isa rushes downstairs with his key in his hand but he's trembling and just as he is about to slip it into the lock he drops it on the ground. The electricity is off and it is dark. He bends down and fumbles around for it. Dardane appears at the top of the stairs.

"What are they going to do with us? What are they going to do with us, Daddy?"

"Go upstairs, sweetie. Don't worry."

Isa's big fingers feel metal and he has the key. He unlocks the door.

"Don't you want to open your door?" asks a sneering voice.

In front of Isa are seven or eight men in fatigues, carrying Kalashnikovs, pistols, knives, and grenades. One waits next to a car at the gate. The others burst into the house and Isa turns and hurries up the stairs with the men shouting behind him. Even in the darkness Isa can tell that he has never seen them before.

Musa is at the top of the stairs and he says, "Here, take my watch," as if that will make the men go away.

"Keep your watch," one man says, derisively. "Everyone get onto the sofa and stay there. Now."

The Bala family obey and they line up on the curving velour couch that arcs around the front wall and the western gable end of the living room. The room clears of all but two of the men.

"You are Musa and Isa Bala?" one of the men asks.

"Yes. Don't kill us, we have young children," Isa says to the men.

"They won't kill us," Hajri reassures his dad. "They won't kill us because we're just children."

The men wear black knit hats and are heavily armed. One of the men in the living room is Joska, but for now the family don't know who he is. The other man is tall and has a dark beard. They light a pillow with a cigarette lighter and one of them waves it in front of the family to see their faces, to take a look at their captives, and perhaps to make sure they have the right family.

"Where's your money?" they ask Isa and Musa. Isa gets up and walks to a back room in the house where he uncovers a wad of three thousand marks.

"Come with me," Joska says to Musa and Isa. "The rest of you stay put."

Outside there is another paramilitary with Rama Gashi. One man stays to guard the house but all the others get into the black car that is waiting outside on the street and drive the short distance up Dushan Mugosha Street, across Yugoslav People's Army Street and round the corner to where Rama's house is the first on the right. Nebojsa Minic is waiting for them when they arrive. Isa recognizes him immediately. Minic. *Mrtvi.* Dead. The man who bought sausages in the shop, who lives nearby, who drove in his Lada Niva along the road the other day urging his fellow Serbs to stay. He is clearly in charge of the men gathered at Rama's. And he seems to know a lot about Isa and his family.

Joska hands Minic the money.

"Three thousand?" Minic says.

"Yeah."

"No. There's much more. Take them out and break one of their legs and they'll come up with more. We'll kill your children if you don't give us the money."

He says it casually and then he takes out his pistol and smashes it into Isa's skull.

"I have another forty-nine hundred," Isa says.

"Joska, take him and get the money," Minic says.

Joska and Isa drive back to Isa's house.

Rama and Musa stay with Minic in the second living room in Rama's house, to the left of the front door.

"Would you like some coffee?" Rama asks Minic, as if to a respected guest.

"Yes, I want coffee, old man," Minic says.

"Me too," Musa says.

And the three of them sit there in silence while one of Rama's daughters makes Turkish coffee and brings them the drink in tiny cups that she places down on the white lace covering on the wooden coffee table. Rama, skinny and weak, but smart, hopes he has established a small bond with Minic over the coffee. He wants Minic to feel like a guest, with all the Balkan politenesses that that role imposes. If you enter an Albanian's home, of course, he has to protect you with his life.

"Listen, will you save my life because of all the children I have?" Rama asks.

"It's going to be very hard to save your life but tonight I will try," he says. "But after tonight it will be very difficult because I have my orders."

Rama doesn't really understand what that means but he doesn't push it, thinking he has some measure of good will from Minic. Rama believes that Minic is the second most powerful paramilitary in Pec now, and if Minic says someone should die, then that person will die. It looks like the Gashi family have at least one more day of Minic's grace.

At the house on Dushan Mugosha street, Isa fetches his other hidden stash—the third of the original bundles of marks has been spent by this time—and he gives it to Joska.

"How much more money do you have?" Joska asks.

"This is it, forty-nine hundred," Isa says.

"Are you sure?"

Isa thinks that Joska wants to keep any extra money for himself, not share it with his boss, Minic.

"I'm sure."

Joska believes Isa. "OK, let's go," he says.

Back at Rama's house, Minic takes the 4,900 marks and seems convinced that there is no more money at Isa's house.

"Take him back," Minic says, moving his hand toward Isa.

"What about me?" Musa asks.

Minic smiles. "We're keeping you."

Joska and Isa drive back to Isa's house. Musa stays and looks panicked now. "Take him away," Minic says to two of his men. And Musa obeys as the men take him outside and Rama hears a car start and drive off.

On Dushan Mugosha Street, Isa and Joska climb the stairs and join the family and the other bearded paramilitary in the living room. Isa sits beside his favorite, Agon, and affectionately squeezes his thick neck.

"If I had a gun I would kill them," Agon whispers to his dad. Isa hugs his little boy.

Joska looks at Vjollca and gestures to her with his gun. "Stand up," he says, and Vjollca gets to her feet.

The bearded man stands in the living room guarding the family with his Kalashnikov while Joska leads Vjollca to the back room adjacent to the room where Mahie lies. The old woman hears the muffled cries of her daughter-in-law as the rest of the house remains silent. After several minutes, the door to the room opens and the Serb leads Vjollca out. She is disheveled and quiet.

"What did he do?" Isa asks her.

"Nothing," she says, as her rapist leads her back to the couch. "Nothing."

The bearded man swivels his gun around and smacks it into Isa's skull as punishment for asking the question.

"Daddy, Daddy," one of Isa's children shouts.

"Shut up or we'll kill you," the man says.

As they walk back towards the couch, Joska and Vjollca stop and he tells her to give him her jewelry. Her rings, her necklace, her earrings, her bracelets. She takes off every piece of gold she has and hands them to the man.

Vjollca is ashamed. A man has just forced himself on her while her family sat in the living room at gunpoint and her mother-in-law listened. Every member of the family old enough to know knows that she has just been raped and those who are too young know that the man probably did something bad to mommy, to auntie Vjollca. It is a blessing that her husband, who may be dead by now, isn't there. He may never know.

Vjollca only suffers her shame for a few more moments. As she is taking her place on the couch again, the two men level their Kalashnikovs at the family and one says, "Is everyone here?"

"Yes," Isa says. "Everyone's here."

Without another word they slide back the actions on their AK-47s and squeeze the triggers.

They shoot at the children first.

Halise does what any mother hopes she would do. She throws herself in front of her children, trying to take the bullets. She doesn't have a chance to beat the bullets. As she dives along the sofa, the lead slugs slam into her children, ripping through their bodies, pulling pieces of skin, bone, and internal organs with them as they pass through toward their exit. And when the bullets exit they are dragging enough bodily matter with them to cause much larger holes in the back than when they first enter the bodies. Then the bullets pass through the velour of the couch and into the white-painted plaster walls. Some drill into the floor. Others pass through the purple blinds and the double-glazing.

When the shooting starts Veton runs and in a second he is at the French window that leads onto the balcony. He pulls the chrome handle down and opens the door and leaps over the balcony and down into the front yard. It is a long way for a little boy but his bones are supple and the jump seems like nothing to him at the time. He doesn't notice that he's grazed his leg jumping over the steel railing on the balcony. Right behind him comes Isa, who has seen his son get up from the couch. He must protect him. He has already made the instant decision that those left behind don't have a chance. Only Veton has a hope of surviving. So Isa dodges the bullets and throws his big frame over the balcony railing and down onto the ground. It's a heavy fall but he picks himself up and takes his son by the hand and he runs down the street into the night. Already, there is a man at the window who strafes the street with Kalashnikov fire in the hope of finishing off the two escapees. Isa and Veton run and they are not hit. They make it to a Serbian neighbor's house, but the neighbors are too afraid to help and so Isa moves on to Riza's house where he leaves Veton. The sound of sustained machine-gun fire still fills the street but nevertheless, Isa goes back to his own home after a few minutes.

In the chaos of Isa and Veton's escape, another child runs. Unnoticed by the men in the darkness, tiny Roni darts off the couch and runs back into the house along the corridor. He runs to what he knows as safety— his grandmother. Mahie is lying there listening to her family die. And suddenly here is a grandson in her arms. She is probably next, she thinks. But perhaps my body can protect Roni. So she takes the little boy, the smallest of the seven, and she hides him down by her lifeless legs. It is the first time they have had any use for years and this time they save a life. When the men come to her door, they decide she is not worth killing and they do not see the child under her blankets pressed silently close to her body. Perhaps they have lost count of the children. Perhaps they think he ran down the stairs and out into the dark street. Perhaps they have plans to burn the house and with it, anyone left inside.

When they are done, when they think they have killed the whole family except the old woman in the back room who doesn't seem worth killing and the father and son who escaped out of the window, they light the pillows again and leave them to burn.

"They fucking asked for it," Halise hears one of them say to the other as the two men leave, their boots sounding heavy on the pine floor where the pool of blood is spreading rapidly over the boards and into the cracks between them. Shell casings sit like islands in the blood. "Those dogs called for NATO."

"I shit on their Albanian souls," the other replies.

"Look, let's throw in a couple of grenades so that the house will burn down. Better not to leave anything here for people to find."

The men pull the pins out of two hand grenades and leave them on the staircase, which is completely wooden and should catch fire easily. Quickly, they run down the path and through the gate. Lying on the couch across the bodies of her children, Halise hears two explosions. One grenade blasts a hole through the wood of the first small landing on the staircase and into the concrete below. Shrapnel bursts into the walls. A little further up, the second grenade rips out the step it is sitting on and shatters a couple of the banisters. Shards of pine and metal fly through the smoke from the grenades into the walls. The little fireballs caused by the grenades don't catch on the wood and there is no fire. Perhaps the men don't really care about the house burning down because they don't come back to check or to torch it again. Perhaps they are too busy. NATO troops are in Pristina and in less than twenty-four hours they will be in Pec. Perhaps the men need to pack up their belongings before they drive over the mountains to Rozaje.

About thirty minutes have passed since the paramilitaries arrived at Isa's house. It is now ten o'clock.

Joska and the bearded man return to Rama Gashi's house and say nothing. They nod at Minic.

The big Serb has been eyeing Rama's daughters, who are slim and pretty, their eyes wide open in fear and usually cast down modestly at the carpet. Minic's men are interested too. One by one, the daughters are led into the living room on the left by the men and the door is closed. But in spite of Rama's fears, inside the men are trying to chat up the girls. It's everything the girls can do to hold back their tears.

"Shake out your hair and turn around," Minic tells Shpresa, Rama's oldest daughter.

Minic sits on the couch, looking up and down Shpresa's body, and at the long brown hair that now falls down her back.

"Now, come and sit on my lap," he says.

Shpresa does what he says. He strokes her hair.

"I'm resting my eyes, looking at you," he says. "What's your name?"

"Shpresa."

"How old are you?"

"Eighteen. I'm younger than you think, you see?"

"Look, nothing's going to happen to you. But do you want to sleep with me?"

"No, please, let me go."

"But why don't you want to sleep with me? You don't find me attractive?"

"I'm saving myself for my future husband," Shpresa says, the tears beginning to slide down her cheeks. "Please let me go."

Shqipe and Valbona suffer the same interviews with Minic. They are seventeen and fifteen years old, respectively.

Some time later Minic tells Rama that he and one of the other men are taking the two older girls, Shpresa and Shqipe, for a ride.

"Please, please don't," Rama says, but it's useless.

Minic makes an odd promise. "I swear on this cross that nothing will happen to them," he says, touching one of the crucifixes around his neck.

And he's true to his word. For a killer of Albanians, he shows remarkable restraint. He and his friend drive the girls around town and do their best to persuade Rama's daughters to have sex with them. The girls refuse. Minic drives to a house, which he says is the house of his commander. The four of them sit outside and Minic says, "If you don't sleep with us you'll have to sleep with him. He won't be so understanding."

Shpresa and Shqipe won't give in. Minic gives up. They drive back to Rama's house and the girls whisper to their mother that they are okay, that the men didn't touch them.

For the Gashi family, it's nearly over. Minic tells his men to go outside and get ready to move on. It's nearly midnight by now. Minic is looking tired again, sad.

Just before he leaves, Minic looks at Rama. "We're going now but I must tell you something—Isa and his family are dead. I'm sorry it had to be that way but it did. We had to kill them."

Also on Dushan Mugosha Street that night is Djorde, the Serb soldier who knew Minic. He and his colleagues are loading their truck with some final loot from one of the houses on the street. "The people were beset with madness," he remembered after the war. "You could hear shootings everywhere in the city. You didn't know where it was coming from or where it was going. Suddenly one man came to us pale in his face. 'They killed them. The man is not dead, I think, but the children are dead. That is insane. What's the purpose of that? I can't believe it.' The guy next to him replied, 'Is that what we were fighting for?' And another guy with me said, 'We should go. It is over with us. Kosovo is gone. Minic has gone to dick. They are not normal. This will put an end to the Serbian existence in Kosovo. It is over, folks. Let's go.'

"Then we finished with the truck and sped away. Afterwards *Munje* were rampaging around the city. That night I also met some civilians on the streets, real nut cases. They were commending *Mrtvi*. 'He is our hero. He will defend us from the KLA.' These people were fit for the lunatic asylum. I didn't believe that *Mrtvi* would stay to defend the city. What happened to their newly reorganized brigade, I don't know. Everything is real bullshit.

"I have to tell you that I don't approve of such things but as you know Albanians had been doing much worse things to us. I am sorry because of the children but one day they would have become terrorists and would have done similar things to Serbs."

Five of the seven children remain on the couch, their bodies punctured by the bullets. Four of them are dead. Nita is unconscious and bleeding but still alive. Her mother Vjollca is also dead. Her aunt Halise has been shot eight times. Through both her arms, her torso, her breasts. The men think she is dead. Halise thinks she will be soon.

Halise pulls herself up and stares at the dead children on the sofa and at Vjollca. They are slumped over each other, bleeding through their clothes. She drags herself through the house, looking for survivors, and she finds none. Mahie and Roni are silent in their terror. She looks in the bathroom and the basement and she smears blood on the floor and leaves red streaks on the white walls. Back in the living room she sees that Nita is still alive but terribly wounded.

"Oh honey, we have to go now," Halise says. "We have to go to the hospital."

"I'm not leaving my mummy," Nita says. "I'm not. She's going to wake up soon."

Halise tries to persuade her niece to come with her and Nita refuses again and again. She won't leave.

Ten minutes after the shooting, Isa comes back to the house alone. He is terrified of what he will find there. The killers, bodies.

Inside the house are Halise and Nita and the bodies and the grenade damage and the smeared blood and the dark pool on the living room floor. Isa closes the windows to keep flies out. Halise and Isa talk in rushed, nonsensical bursts, neither really listening to the other, neither thinking rationally. Isa tries to take Halise away from the house with him. He is terrified the men will come back. But now it is Halise's turn to refuse to leave the bodies. It is sinking in. Her children are dead and she has been shot so many times and is bleeding so much that surely she will die soon too. She wants to stay with them.

Isa leaves the house again to check on Veton and when he gets back to his house, Halise is gone. She has panicked and has jumped off the balcony at the back of the house into the garden, through the holes in the back garden fences and into Riza's house.

Later, Riza writes in his diary: "I opened the door for her. She could barely stand. I helped her inside, and discovered that she was covered in blood. We put her in the cellar as the safest place. She said she was wounded in the chest. She kept groaning—crying for her children, saying that life was worthless since she had lost her children; she had no more will to live. It was very dark; we couldn't even see where the wounds were. Her child was crying. Isa didn't show up. I realized that she had a serious hemorrhage and might die from it, but how was she to be helped? We didn't dare light even a single match. The shooting continued without interruption and from various directions. We were full of apprehension. Now we were barred from even going outside. How could we leave the wounded woman alone? Taking her with us was impossible, for she was in no condition to walk, but carrying her would be too hard, because she was fat, weighing more than a hundred kilos. So we resigned ourselves to fate."

Still in his house, Isa finds Roni in the back room and decides that the two of them must not go to Riza's. The family should split up to increase the chances that they will survive more paramilitary attacks.

Isa leaves his mother in her room and takes Roni with him down the stairs and into the street. Nita refuses to leave her mother and she lies there among the dead, her own wounds seeping blood onto the already soaked couch.

In a corner of a burned-out house two doors down from his own, Isa steps through the rubble and charcoal on the floor of the house. Its roof is still intact. There is a two-month-old smell of burning. This house was one of the first in Brzenik to be torched. Somehow the flames missed one of the beds and Isa takes Roni and the little boy curls up and sleeps. Isa cannot sleep. Roni wakes up during the night and grabs at Isa's clothes and body through the dust storm of his bad dreams. "Don't be afraid," Isa murmurs in his ear. "Go back to sleep."

Sitting on the mattress, leaning against the wall, Isa rubs his neck. It is painful, tight, stiff with grief. This is the first time he's had to think. He has seen his children killed. His brother is missing and he is remembering Backovic's promise to kill him with knives, to cut him up.

Riza writes about the nighttime: "During the whole time Halise remained composed, no wailing, no noise. She kept begging pardon for the trouble that she had brought us, did not complain about herself, asked to go home, so as not to cause any harm to us. I could really see in her a big and generous heart and spirit. The shooting was still going on. After a while Halise said, in answer to my question, that she was feeling cold. We covered her with a blanket and put her on a couch, and I advised her to keep still, not to move, so as to lessen the loss of blood. Isa had still not shown up; we feared that they had killed him."

At about five o'clock, Isa wakes Roni up and they rush along the road toward the military police headquarters. Riza spots them and is delighted to see that they are still alive.

"After about half an hour Isa arrived with Musa's son," Riza writes. "He said that he had been at headquarters, and they had promised that emergency aid would come to get Halise and Nita."

Isa has found a Serb police officer he knows as Kaplan who agrees to take them in their police car. Isa is afraid of Kaplan. The Serb asks him who did this.

"Nebojsa Minic and his men," Isa says.

"I'm sorry," Kaplan says. "That's not right."

He drives Halise and Nita to the hospital that lies on the western side of town on the road to the Patriarchate and the Rugova valley. Halise holds Nita close in the backseat of the police car, their blood seeping together nearly twelve hours after they have been shot. They are very weak.

"Thank God you're safe," Nita whispers to her aunt. "You're going to take care of me like my mother, aren't you?"

"Yes, sweetie, I am."

Halise feels Nita's soft hug.

Resolutely there in spite of the what surrounded them throughout the war, the handful of Albanian nurses rush Halise and Nita into surgery. It's a Serb surgeon who's on duty. His name is Jovica Marinkovic. There are no Albanian doctors left in Pec. Marinkovic is a military doctor, an officer in the army, in uniform. He looks at the woman and the girl and says to Isa: "We need to give them blood, fast."

The doctor asks what blood type Halise and Nita have.

"How many members of your family were killed?" the doctor asks Isa.

"Five, and my brother is missing."

Marinkovic crosses himself. "How could they do that? How? Look, I'm going to try to save them. Don't be afraid because I'm a Serb. I'm going to do my best."

Isa leaves the hospital as soon as he has dropped off his wife and niece. Suddenly there's an energy in him. He can't bear the idea that cats might be licking at the bodies of his family or that they might be rotting in the June heat and so he goes home and finds some plastic sheeting and lays it out on the cool concrete floor in the basement, where the children used to sit when sheltering from NATO bombing raids. Riza is there and he helps Isa. One by one, they carry the bodies out of the living room, down the stairs, and down into the basement, laying them on the plastic.

Riza can't help but see that the top of Dardane's head has been blown off. As Isa is carrying her, a piece of her skull and her brains tip out and onto the floor. Isa has to pick up his daughter's brains with his hands. A bullet has also torn away part of little Agon's head.

When they are all in the basement, Isa wraps the sheeting carefully around the bodies so that no animals can feed on his children. He works quickly, worried that the paramilitaries will come back. NATO is still a few hours away, the Italians giving the Serbs time to pull out of Western Kosovo. Minic may send his men back to finish Isa and Veton off.

Once he has finished he goes to Riza's house and fetches Roni and Veton and he borrows a car from a neighbor and does what he has never before done during or before the war—he carries his mother out of the house and puts her in the car. They drive through the back streets to the devastated Kapesnica neighborhood and Isa finds a house that belongs to a Serb who has fled. This is to be their home for a few days.

At the hospital, Marinkovic operates first on Nita. She is the weaker of the two patients. She dies during surgery at three o'clock. Five of the seven children are now dead.

After he saves Halise in the operating room, the doctor tells her that she was shot eight times, six times in the body, twice in the arms, and he tells her she was lucky to make it after losing so much blood and being shot so many times. He says that she will be in hospital for two months and must rest and he says he is sorry about her children. And he tells her that Nita is dead.

Operating on the Balas is just about the last thing Marinkovic does before he leaves Pec. The first Italian troops from the NATO forces arrive in Pec at about two o'clock that afternoon and the KLA will be close behind them. Marinkovic must know that as a military man, his life will be in danger if he stays. So he makes the drive to Rozaje along Savine Vode, which is quite quiet now.

The Italian tanks rumble into Pec and the KLA filters in behind them, setting up roadblocks and standing by while some of the few remaining Albanians loot Serb-owned stores. Some Serb forces are still in town and they continue to pull out.

Halise is in the hospital. Veton and Roni are hiding in the Serb house in Kapesnica, which Isa has taken over for a few days now that the owners have fled. The Gashi family stay inside their home. Musa is still missing.

Serb and Albanian civilians emerge from their homes and walk alone through the devastated streets of the town as two military forces replace the one that has controlled Pec for so long. The Serbs who are left congregate in the Korzo, right next to the Italian headquarters in the Hotel Metohija. The Serbs are scared. No one is really in control of Pec at the moment. It is dangerous for everyone.

On Monday morning Isa and a dozen local men, including five Serbs, go to Pec's cemetery and start to dig six graves. The Serbs, a police detective and an army reservist among them, curse Minic aloud as they dig. They begin at eleven in the morning and sweat through the day, finishing at half past five, just as the sun's power is beginning to wane. Isa borrows a car and goes to his house to fetch the bodies, still wrapped in plastic in the basement. In a visit to the hospital he has collected some body bags and now he places each of the dead into their own plastic sack. Once he has taken them to the gravesides, he goes to the hospital and collects Nita's body.

During the day, some women in Pec who have heard about the killing come to clean the house. They scrub the pine and the couch and the green carpet and they roll the bloody clothes into a big ball. Isa takes the stained ball to the end of the road and leaves it there, where is sits near an overflowing dumpster for days. The women do not manage to get all the blood off. Some remains on the wall of the back room where Vjollca was raped. There is some on the pine banisters. The upturned couch is still encrusted with brown stains, as is the green carpet on the floor. And in the bathtub they have left some dampened rags and a sponge that bleed a small trickle of red water to the plug hole. Bullets are lodged in the floor and the walls and the purple blinds shake now and then as a breeze whistles through the bullet holes in the windows, the only sound in the silent house.

At the cemetery, Isa and his friends bury Vjollca, Nita, Rina, Dardane, Agon, and Hajri and they say some prayers for the souls of the dead. Before Isa places Dardane in her coffin, he rolls up her skipping rope and slides it into her pocket.

At Isa's request, Riza has found a piece of sheet metal from the burned-out house that stands between the two men's homes. Riza has cut out six rectangular pieces and, with green paint, he has brushed on the names and dates of birth and death of each person. Isa nails the nameplates onto wooden grave markers that Riza has cut from seasoned wood. The butcher goes alone to the cemetery and leans on the tops of the planks until they are secure in the red-brown soil at the head of each grave.

Chapter 13

A White Plastic Bag in the Long Grass

The war was over. KFOR had control of Kosovo. Few Serbs remained and the Albanians who had poured over the borders began to re-build their homes and enjoy a new freedom and dominance. NATO's leaders visited Kosovo on victory trips and the first street demonstrations began in the mangled Serbia against the regime of Slobodan Milosevic. It seemed like one of the cleanest military victories in the twentieth century, a model of how and why the West would wage foreign wars in the future: From the skies and with a clear moral mandate.

In many respects, the NATO leaders were justified in enjoying their adulation in the streets of Pristina. Wars tend to involve considerably more mess, both physical and moral, than did the war over Kosovo. But in many of the homes and hearts of the region, the war continued to torment. The ground war, a battle between the peoples of Yugoslavia that barely involved NATO forces but which nevertheless lured NATO into the war, had left terrible scars.

After a postwar break in Israel, I returned to look at those scars. There were fates to discover in Pec: Zejnepe and the other old people in the hut; Luan. Who lived? Who died? I knew which military force had won the war and which had lost, but not which individuals had won and lost.

~

Tony had won and lost. He left Kosovo a rich man, unable to sleep in peace.

We met him at an outdoor café on the outskirts of Podgorica, just next to a gas station. There was a gentle breeze and we drank strong milky coffee. Twenty-six years old, he wore a lime polo shirt and black jeans. He spoke softly, thoughtfully. He wanted to confess and to strike back at, to expose the organization and the country to which he had sold himself for a few weeks in the first half of 1999. He was not a killer, but I think he felt like one.

"Our group was not so patriotic, nationalistic. We were a small group and it was strictly business. It was not like a holy war, a sacred war. There are many evils I want to forget as soon as possible. I don't want to call those things to mind."

An oil smuggler before the war, Tony was now wealthy. "I have a good car. I bought an apartment here. But it's not so much. If I had only 1 percent of all the goods that passed through my hands I'd be the richest man here . . . I came away with 200,000 marks. It's the foundation for a decent life here, an apartment. I haven't decided what to do with the rest of the money."

Tony sat uncomfortably with that money in his pocket, I felt.

"I've withdrawn to a certain degree. I don't want to think about it. I wanted to get out of there, that hell, to finish the job and go. It wasn't my war."

Some memories pushed their way into Tony's sleep. Two or three things he could not forget.

"We were in a village before the units came and cleansed it. All the houses were ruined. There were only a few houses left. The Serb houses were spared. In one house lived an old woman and her granddaughter, who was sixteen or seventeen. They were both Serbs. We stayed in that village for two or three days, a bit longer than usual because we were waiting for a shipment from another place. We were supposed to meet there. That girl was cooking for our unit for two or three days. On the third day four guys got drunk and stoned and they raped her. I remember as we were leaving that village, the grandmother took her black scarf off her head and she addressed us with the worst curses."

There was a worse memory. It had been raining overnight and Tony's unit woke up to a fresh morning and sat outside the house they were staying in, sipping coffee, smoking cigarettes, and getting ready for the day's work. One of Tony's friends needed to correct the telescopic sight on his rifle.

"An old man was alone with his cows in the fields. It wasn't his war. He didn't know what was happening. He wasn't guilty."

Tony's colleague raised his rifle. It was fitted with a silencer. He aimed it at the old Albanian man, obliviously tending to his cows. Phud. The muffled shot sped toward the man but he continued to tap his stick against the flanks of his cows. The paramilitary lowered the rifle and corrected the sight. Another shot. Another miss. Another correction. And on it went for several more shots, with Tony and the others passively watching, until the old man fell silently to the ground around the feet of his cows.

"There," Tony's colleague said, putting down the rifle. "It's fixed."

Some of his colleagues were putting their money together in postwar business ventures.

"I'm trying to get out of this business and break off all connections with these people and live a normal, decent life. If I hadn't been there someone else would have done it. I was just an operational officer. I didn't burn houses or expel people. I have no one on my conscience— I know the money I earned was not decently earned and I have a bit of a troubled conscience about that but people here committed worse sins than me."

Why was Tony telling us all this?

"I want to tell someone," he said. "I don't have anyone here to tell the story to. People are too stupid here to understand. I know it's not good that I did that job. But I entered into it and it's impossible to go back. I'm not very happy with it. I definitely wouldn't go and do it now even for double the amount of money. When you see such things . . . I can't erase them from my memory."

I saw Tony again more than a year later, and still he talked with a determination to tell as much as he could safely give away. But he seemed less pale and had put on some weight. There was a relaxation and warmth in his manner, even though he searched me to see if I was wearing a hidden recording device. I wondered afterward if he was now free from his nighttime memories. Or was the confessing only a temporary relief, like occasional raindrops cleaning a dirty leaf that will only be covered in a film of desert dust again in the morning?

In the early afternoon of August 3, my translator Enver Doda and I drove to Big Jablanica to find the Zekaj family—Haki, Naim, Jeton, Emrush, Merita, and, hopefully, Zejnepe. With any luck, with any fairness, Zejnepe would be there too.

The road is the same one that leads north out of Pec to Rozaje. We passed unfinished and burned houses and a few houses still intact. Off to the left there were two dark cotton-candy clouds of smoke rising from two other buildings, out of sight from the road. Serb homes, I was sure, or perhaps gypsy homes. But I had long since stopped driving to these fires to see who started them, who suffered from them, because I knew the answers. The KLA and some Albanian civilians were reducing themselves to the level of the Serbs they so scorned. I pushed on past the midsummer-green trees by the roadside and Enver and I quickly rolled up the windows as we passed the rotting carcass of a horse.

To get to Big Jablanica you take the last road to the right before Savine Vode starts to meander up the steep mountainside to Kula.

Standing around in the red dust and pebbles of what passes for the center of Big Jablanica—there's nothing big about Big Jablanica, it's just that Little Jablanica is less big—was a group of men and boys. A little boy led us to Haki's house, which we had already passed by mistake. It stood opposite the mosque, which was large and unfinished and charred on the inside. The little boy banged on the gate as he ran into the Zekaj home and shouted that men had come to see Jeton. The little boy urged us along the side passageway next to the house and into the back garden. And like Veronica Lake in a war zone, Merita appeared on the balcony, blonde hair streaming down her healthy body that two months earlier had been slow and thin. She was wearing a pretty, long blue dress. And she was glowing. When last I saw her—in the shack on the mountainside—her skin was watery pale and she was sharp-featured, shy, and wearing a tatty running suit. Her belly partly explained the transformation into radiance. She was about four or five months' pregnant. A mountain baby, perhaps.

She came down to the garden and shook hands, still a little shy.

Pulling back the clear plastic cover from the white garden furniture, she asked us to sit down.

"Jeton's away in Rozaje but he'll be back soon," she said. Merita's face was always calm and didn't tell stories. I could not see in it whether there was any more mourning being done in the Zekaj family.

"How's Haki?" I asked.

"Very well," she said.

She paused, her eyes flicking aside to gaze at the grass. Otherwise, her face stayed the same.

"His mother was killed," she said. "And his aunt and uncle."

"I'm very sorry," I said.

It is not really a young Albanian wife' place to convey family news to two visiting men and so we made small talk for a few minutes. Merita said that her father-in-law, Emrush, would be along soon. So we waited until Emrush came to join us for sweet Turkish coffee.

Wiry and confident as always, he took our hands and we sat down and the now-silent Merita waited on us.

"I'm sorry to hear the news," I said.

"It's very hard for Haki and Naim," he said, sipping coffee under his moustache. "With their father killed too, they lost four members of their family."

We waited for his son, Jeton, but time slipped past quietly and slowly and we said we would come back another time. Emrush gave us directions to the Zekaj house in the western part of Pec and he told us where we could find Naim. The younger Zekaj brother had already opened a café just across the road from the police station and the Soliter apartment buildings.

Chanting slogans and carrying banners, hundreds of people were marching slowly up the street and Naim and Haki stood outside Naim's café, watching.

"Hundreds are missing in Serbian prisons," one banner read. "Bring back our brothers."

The war was over but the Serbs had taken prisoners back with them. It was good to see Haki and Naim. They stood in the sunshine and looked relaxed. I told them I was sorry to hear about their mother and they thanked me. Naim looked me straight in the eye, as he looked at life, and Haki cast his gaze around the busy street, perhaps wishing to be alone with his parentless sorrow.

"Come to the house tomorrow," Haki said. "My sister is here from Switzerland and we're going to visit the graves."

Just before twelve noon the next morning, we arrived at the Zekaj house. Inside, the living room was Spartan but we sat on couches that were among the only items of furniture remaining. Luckily, the Serbs had not burned down the house but had only used it as a place to sleep and as a source of household goods to take back to Serbia. So there wasn't much left.

Jeton was there. I was pleased to see him.

In a convoy of three cars, we drove the familiar route toward the mountains, taking the Radvac turn-off along the bumpy road to Big Jablanica. This time, we didn't make it all the way to the village, pulling off to the right to park with the right side wheels of the cars mounted on a grassy bank next to a fence.

Haki and Naim had their *salihus* with them. Round and concave, about the size and shape of the shields of ancient Greece, *salihus* are Albanian memorial wreaths of woven flowers, twigs, and leaves. Some ingredients are natural, some plastic. Pec's florists were having an unusually busy time making *salihus* at the moment. They advertised on the streets of the town by leaving an especially large and elaborate wreath on the sidewalk outside the shops. For Haki, Naim, and the family, a florist had prepared four *salihus* of dark leaves and bright red, yellow, and white plastic flowers. Wrapped in transparent plastic to keep the rain off, they were each bound by a cummerbund of scarlet on which were written the names of the deceased.

> *Musa Zekaj.*
> *Zejnepe Zekaj.*
> *Xhafer Zekaj.*
> *Shahe Zekaj.*

Elderly people, all of them, but none of them dead of natural causes.

Luljeta Dresh, Haki and Naim's thirty-three-year-old sister, had brought her children from Lucerne to see their grandparents' graves. Part of the Kosovo diaspora, it was she Zejnepe had tried to call on the satellite phone in the mountains. But Luljeta had not been at home for a final talk with her mother. She wore a navy pantsuit. Haki's wife Drita wore a long burgundy slip of a dress and struggled with it as we climbed, one by one, over the fence by the side of the road. The men wore jeans and short-sleeved polo shirts tucked in at the waist. Four young children squirmed in their mothers' arms and picked wild flowers, but they were quiet.

Along the fence ran a line of trees in full summer strength, casting a midday shadow on the graveyard. Small, unshowy gravestones cast smaller shadows among the tall grass and daisies and bluebells that had not been mown this year and perhaps never were. Two larger and newer and carefully carved headstones stood out in the tiny meadow. Hidden from the road, left alone to grow unkempt and with a view of the mountains to the north where Zejnepe, Xhafer, and Shahe had died, Big Jablanica's graveyard was a decent place to be buried.

Musa Zekaj's grave was identifiable by a roughly hewn wooden marker that the family had pressed into the ground before fleeing into the mountains and some weeds and heads of grass had appeared through the lumps of earth. Lined up next to Musa's were the three more freshly dug graves: Long, raised piles of dun earth that had been displaced by the coffins lying several feet below.

Haki and Naim and Jeton placed the *salihus* at the feet of the graves and the two women bound bouquets of orange and yellow and white flowers with thick masking tape to the tiny wooden markers at the heads of the three newer graves. And then they stood back and looked at the graves and the ground, and sometimes Haki cocked his head toward the mountains and no one said anything. Naim didn't like the weeds on his father's grave and he moved forward and started pulling them out and throwing them into the long grass, scaring away a small lizard that had been basking on the top of a nearby headstone.

White clouds passed gently overhead, north toward the mountains. The breeze made soft castanets out of the leaves on the higher branches around the cemetery and unseen crickets trilled in the grass. A horse in a field behind the trees snorted. At twenty minutes past noon, the wordless rite was over.

"You must come for lunch," Haki said, once we were all over the fence again and about to get into the cars. I was sure he was being polite.

"Not on a day like this," I said. "This is a family day."

"No, no," he said. "It's tradition. We always eat a good meal after paying our respects to a loved one's grave. You must come. It is our duty to feed you."

In the Zekaj house, we climbed upstairs and sat down in a circle on the large foam cushions that can double up as mattresses in Albanian homes. Merita came in holding a plastic jug and a bowl and she poured water over our hands, which we rubbed and dried off on the towel hanging from her forearm. Not a man stirred or offered to help.

The platters of food started to come in; cheese pie, sausage, bread, cheese, cucumbers. The pie is called *flia* and serving it to a guest is a traditional sign of respect. I asked the Zekaj men what had happened up there on the mountains.

"My mother didn't want to leave," Haki said, pulling off a piece of the round cheesy dough from the *flia* with his fingers. "Remember—she told you she would go back home again. She wanted to come back here to the house so much. And Shahe said she wanted to die in Kosovo, and nowhere else. My uncle wasn't so sure but he had to stay with her, of course. And then, you know, my mother was very upset about the death of my father. Very."

Along with Phil, Julian, Marko, and myself, Haki and Naim had reached Montenegro safely after our trip over the peaks. Haki never returned home because by the time he wanted to, he had heard from other mountain crossers that only a man bent on suicide would try to get into Kosovo now.

First came the shelling. It was eight days after we had left Kosovo. The valley full of tents and the old and sick were not the target—the Serbs were looking to shake out the KLA and the men like Jeton and Emrush who were on the hillsides. They blasted into the trees and the gorges.

Then the ground troops came in.

"The first day they burned some of the tents," Jeton said.

Emrush left his cow and took a couple of guns he had stored in his tent in the valley and climbed up the mountainside. He had said that he would hide in a cave if necessary. In fact, he hid in the trees, under the partial cover offered by a large boulder. Down below he could see the soldiers sweep into the tranquil hideout of the displaced Albanians. The Serbs torched most of the tents and carried the old people away on the backs of tractors, out of the war zone. The KLA was still in the region, Emrush knew, but they were few in number, tired, and nowhere to be seen. I wondered about Xhavit and the young kids in the Illyrian Wolves and whether they heard the shelling and the shooting from over the next ridge in their guerrilla bowers and their smelly tent.

All but two of the tent dwellers survived, according to the Zekajs. One young man and an old man, a *hoxha,* were shot and killed.

Jeton also stayed in Kosovo for a while during the shelling and the burning. A few days later he saw that the Serbs were also advancing from Montenegro. The family would be caught if they stayed put.

"You have to leave—now," he said forcefully, knowing that Zejnepe would likely refuse.

And she did. And Shahe and Xhafer said they were staying too. Zejnepe said something about not wanting to go over the mountains without a guide but she knew that Jeton knew the way and could lead her to Montenegro.

This was getting tight. Jeton couldn't wait any longer. His young wife was pregnant and his mother was old and he knew that he wasn't going to be able to lead them to safety the usual way, the way Haki came, the way we had come. For a superfit man like Jeton, that hike was a quick stroll. But now, with all these troops around, it would be too dangerous. And he was right. Later he would learn that a teenage boy who was sheltering with his two brothers in a slightly larger shack nearer the Montenegro border—the boy we had spoken with briefly just after crossing into Kosovo—had been shot and killed by Serb soldiers coming from Montenegro. So Jeton took his wife and mother the long way around the mountains. The walks I had taken had exhausted me. I can't imagine this: It took them ten hours, over the very tops of the mountains, where the wind and snow were at their harshest, and they went at night. They left at ten in the evening and walked until eight the next morning. After they crossed into Montenegro the sun came up and they were spotted by soldiers who shot at them through the trees.

Emrush tarried behind for a few more days, trying to persuade the three old people to come with him, but they wouldn't leave.

Zejnepe repeated her mantra. "My husband is dead and I've left my home in Pec and my home in Jablanica. They're going to have to burn this down before I leave it."

"God be with you," he said, as he left the hut one night and crossed over the moonlit mountains to Rozaje. As soon as the war ended, as soon as the Serb traffic out of Kosovo ebbed, the Zekajs joined the massive rush of Albanians back to Kosovo. The family arrived in Pec and found their house in one piece. In Jablanica there was some damage but they had been lucky again. But at neither house did they find Zejnepe, her brother-in-law Xhafer, or his wife Shahe.

From the house in Jablanica they gazed up at the mountains and quietly decided to form a search party. Quickly, Haki, Naim, Jeton, Emrush, other members of the family, and some of the villagers found the huts. Up the valley, where the Zekajs had hidden for so many weeks, Zejnepe's hut was just charcoal. The sooty metal stove stood in the center of the plot, its flue crashed to the ground.

By now the mountainside was snowy only in patches. Where the sun had burned away the snow, long spring grass coated the slopes and dandelions and daisies and other wild flowers pushed up toward the sunshine. Through the patches of white and green Jeton and the others spread out and began to search the mountains in the direction of Rozaje and Balotici. Perhaps they had made it quite far after all, and were sheltering in the forest on the Montenegrin side. Jeton had hidden supplies of oil, flour, sugar, and coffee and these things had gone. Perhaps that meant they were still alive. The villagers searched and looked and came up with nothing.

On the fifth day, a strong breeze blew on the mountains. The search team was about to set off from the huts again. Then one of the cousins, Mohammed, noticed a white plastic bag fluttering in the tall grass as the wind broke in waves over the hillside. It was about one hundred and fifty meters up in the woods, in the direction of Kosovo, not Montenegro.

188

Mohammed walked up to the bag and saw Zejnepe lying face down in the grass, her hand holding the quivering white plastic. She had been shot twice in the shoulders. Nearby was Xhafer, a bullet wound in his head. And there was Shahe, shot two or three times in the back. It looked like they had been running for cover in the woods, heading back into Kosovo. And they had died in Kosovo, as they had insisted on doing. Jeton would not let Haki and Naim see the bodies.

The search party returned and gathered together a group of about thirty men from Jablanica and they carried the bodies down from the mountains. The next day the Zekajs buried Zejnepe, Xhafer, and Shahe in the village graveyard.

Jeton, Haki, and Naim were sure that the Serb attack on the mountains that had resulted in the death of their mother was part of the ongoing campaign to clear the KLA and civilian Albanians out of Western Kosovo. The shelling of the mountains had started long before my trip to visit Zejnepe and had continued thereafter. But perhaps Jeton, Haki, and Naim are wrong. Perhaps my trip and the story that appeared in *Newsday* a few days later had been the provocation. Had I contributed to the deaths of three people and the beating of two others, the guides?

In many respects, the two guides were free agents. They had laughed at our inability to find our way over the mountains the first time we had attempted it with Haki. To them, it was a quick stroll through the trees to the border. They would not go further and we did not need them. They had turned back without any trace of anxiety about them. Without pressure, they made their decision to help us and to accept our money. On the other hand, they would never have been in that situation if we had not asked them to help us. They would not have been beaten if we had not showed up in their lives and offered them a hundred dollars each.

For Zejnepe, Xhafer, and Shahe, there are similar questions. They knew the risks of helping us, of telling their stories, of staying in the mountains, and of refusing to leave even when they knew that soldiers were on their way, even when Jeton and Emrush urged them to flee. In my story, I had tried to be as vague as possible about their location. The Mountains of the Damned are full of huts, full of valleys, and it would be hard to locate Zejnepe's that quickly. Furthermore, the Serbs knew that those mountainsides were the haunts of small KLA units like the Illyrian Wolves (we had met other armed men on our trip to see Zejnepe). And without provocation, the Yugoslav Army had ethnically cleansed Albanian villages inside Montenegro and had killed refugees inside Montenegro. The attack on the mountains where we had been was inside Kosovo and therefore fit the standard pattern for the army's actions during the war. Perhaps the mountains, like so many villages and neighborhoods, were just next on the army's list.

But perhaps it was not a coincidence. The possibility remains that the authorities in Belgrade saw my story and immediately ordered an attack in reprisal. Also, I had used a satellite telephone there and it is possible that the Serbs had been loaned technology by the Russians that enabled them to locate satellite phone signals. (However, given the relative impunity with which the KLA used satellite phones throughout the war inside Kosovo, this seems less likely.)

If my reporting did provoke the attack, it raises a key question of journalistic ethics: Was I right to endanger individuals in the search for a story that I hoped would bring home to hundreds of thousands of American readers who were losing interest in the war a wrong that was being done to hundreds of thousands of Albanians? I believe strongly that news consumers tire very quickly of major news stories that are not neatly wrapped up in a few weeks. And I believe it is a journalist's duty to try to reignite people's interest, especially in stories of such great moral and political importance as the war in Kosovo. Very knowingly, I had decided to risk my life for that belief.

But that could be self-serving rationalization. No one gave me or any other journalist the right to bring about someone's death, no matter how good our intentions.

I shall probably never know whether I contributed to the deaths of these people. It is a question that I live with very uneasily.

Over a year later, in November 2000, I returned and had dinner with Jeton and Haki at Haki's home in Pec. We ate a good meal of warm beef and bread and pickled peppers. The men were quiet as ever but deeply committed to hating the Serbs. Jeton told me that a teacher at school had told him many years ago that the Serbs were evil people because the Americans had discovered a group of Serbs with evil genes and had transplanted them to Belgrade. Jeton still believed the story. Both men longed for revenge.

Their lives continued and their businesses flourished and they were having more children. I wondered if they thought that the world had learned anything from the war, if Musa, Zejnepe, Xhafer, and Shahe had died for something.

Haki and Jeton became quiet. After a while Haki spoke.

"The world learned," he said, "that if you support a people who have been oppressed you will have the support of honorable men."

In early August 1999, I met Luan by chance. He was working as a translator for a Czech aid agency in the Hotel Karagac, which had been used as a paramilitary base during the war.

We agreed that I should stop by after his work one day and go to his family's apartment near the Korzo. We talked there and also later in a café. This was his story.

On Sunday, April 18, the morning after we left Rugova, the Serbs began their offensive from Montenegro. If the Serbs had attacked from there, the KLA reasoned, they would for sure attack from both ends of the valley, as well. Luan and his frontline reconnaissance unit headed down the main valley in Rugova, situating themselves near the tiny collection of houses known as Little Shtupeq, which sits next to the river gorge on the north bank of the Bistrica. The soldiers hid in the woods all day and all night, expecting the Serbs at any minute. The sun rose on Monday morning and still the Serbs had not come.

"We were waiting for their attack. We knew they would attack because they had started from Montenegro."

Luan's group was fifteen strong. With their potluck selection of weaponry and minimal training, the young men in patchwork uniforms and fake designer jeans waited for two nights among the pines for the well-equipped Yugoslav Army, which numbered about forty thousand in Kosovo during the war.

"On Tuesday, they attacked. We withdrew. They were shelling us. The Serbs came from so many directions."

Cut off in the confusion from their main KLA unit, Luan and two comrades slowly began to move as quietly as they could through the woods. Looking down the mountain Luan saw Serb troops kicking in the doors of a house in Little Shtupeq. Soon smoke rose from the farm buildings there.

"We decided to go along the middle of the mountainside. We started out at one-thirty in the afternoon. We went just twenty meters and then we would stop and listen. All three of us had binoculars. We would listen, hear nothing, and go another thirty meters. When we reached Big Shtupeq we went down to the buildings and went inside one of the houses and took some sugar and bread because we were hungry. I was left to guard. The Serbs had painted their four S's on the door in red paint. One of my friends put his finger on the paint. It was still wet."

For four and a half hours the three young men crept along the side of the mountain. As they approached Drelaj at around four-thirty, they spotted some civilians moving around. "We were afraid they were Serbs. My friend decided to call to them. They were Albanians and they were getting ready to leave. They were the last to move from the village but were leaving to avoid being massacred."

Between Drelaj and the village of Kuqishte, Luan and his two friends met up with the other KLA units that had been beaten back from the corners and mountainsides of Rugova. Eighteen men were injured. The commanders decided that a small group of fighters—about ten— should stay behind to observe and harass the Serbs in Rugova. It was risky but the trees, peaks, and caves of Rugova could shelter that number without much risk of their being discovered and killed. They were left supplies of wheat and oil. The rest were to evacuate over the mountains to Albania.

That evening, two hundred and fifty soldiers, including the eighteen wounded, began a terrible retreat.

"We walked for three days and three nights in the snow. Our feet were wet and frozen. My legs were numb. Even now the top of my big toe on my right foot, I can't feel it. It's much better than it was. The first day we had some food which we shared. We had some meat. I had two kilos of sugar that we'd taken from Shtupeq. We ate raw sugar with our hands. We had to give it to the others too, of course, so it didn't last long. Some soldiers ate the snow but I was too afraid of the cold, of having snow inside me. Some of the wounded were crying out, saying 'If I were dead it would be better than this.'

"We were carrying the injured men through the snow and we would often fall over with them. Some of our soldiers cried. 'I'm going to stay here and die,' they said. We had no doctors with us.

"We got near the triangle where Montenegro, Kosovo, and Albania meet. We passed the border and got to the first village. It was called Papaj. We stayed there for two or three days."

None of the injured died on the journey.

Luan went from Papaj to Tirana where he undertook two weeks of training. He stayed in Tirana for another week, awaiting orders, before making the journey to Bajram Curri, probably the most desolate, dangerous, and out-of-the-way town in the whole of Europe.

While Luan was at Bajram Curri, the war ended. Keen to get out of Bajram Curri as fast as every visitor was, he headed straight for Pec. He arrived there on June 13, a day before I made it to Pec. Oddly, we didn't bump into each other then, even though the town was almost deserted. Among the rubble, Luan was euphoric.

"It was really very good. I could see all the houses were burned but I didn't care. We will build better houses now."

It was the first week of August when I went back to Rugova. I drove up the valley from Pec, along and sometimes over the Bistrica, through the tunnels and gorges that the Serb tanks and troops had pushed through. Fourteen kilometers up the road sat the former headquarters of the 136th Brigade. The buildings had been torched, most of their roofs collapsed. Burned wooden beams lay among the bricks and mortar rubble on their floors. Bullet holes and the gaps left by shells had left the walls unstable. Lying around the rubble were playing cards, clothes, a washing machine, plates, a weighing scale, boots, an old tube of toothpaste. A group of half a dozen men were beginning to clear out one of the buildings.

Three kilometers further on lay Drelaj. Every single house was burned. The fields were unkempt and empty of animals. Some families had come back and were living in tents of plastic sheeting and branches.

They told of escaping the village once the shelling had started, carrying food into the mountains, and sleeping in caves before crossing the mountains into Montenegro. They felt forgotten by the aid agencies and were terrified of the coming winter. In Rugova, a tent in winter is useless.

Like all the others in the village, the house our group had stayed in was a shell. The floor we had slept on was no longer there; the walls were charred, the roof was gone. There was no sign of the tacky Mecca tapestry, no sheep under the stairs; no stairs even. And no family trying to rebuild.

Back down the valley I recognized the track leading up to Big Shtupeq. Sheltering under a tarpaulin next to their house were four members of the Nikqi family, including twenty-five-year-old Flora who had brought us the plates of *petlla* when we visited their house during the war and chatted with Joanna Carlsson and Selmon. This time she insisted on giving Enver and me mugs full of black currents and juice. The house we had drunk coffee in, from which Luan and his two KLA friends had desperately taken a bag of sugar, was burned.

On the front door of Luan's family's apartment was written in ballpoint pen, "Prof. Luan Shala, Brigade 136, UCK."

The two-room apartment in one of Pec's less attractive apartment blocks was now home to over a dozen people—including swarms of yelling children—because the Shala family home in Loxhe was still a bulldozed bed of rubble. I drank coffee and talked to Luan and his brothers about the war and the Serbs and the future.

Luan's older brother Ymer simply couldn't get used to cycling to Loxhe from Pec without being stopped by the police. Before, that journey had meant risking arrest, as Luan had learned so well.

His brother Mustafa, a surgeon, said he had finished with surgery forever. In a few weeks he had had to cut up and stitch together more people than he had anticipated performing on in his entire career. And without the proper instruments, medication, anesthetics, and convalescent care. His colleagues implored him not to leave surgery. He was insisting on a transfer to the pediatric wing of Pec's hospital.

The family's quiet warrior, Luan, was going back to university in Pristina to finish his studies. He would leave in a few days to share an apartment and schoolbooks with friends. He was as insistently polite and respectful as ever, vacating his chair and sitting on the floor when his older brother came into the room. He let his brothers do most of the talking. During the conversation, I asked the Shala brothers why they thought the Serbs had gone to war so often in the past decade? Luan's more boisterous brothers were silent for a minute, searching for an answer. Luan, still visited by Serb policemen in his dreams and by the friends he had lost in the war, sat on the floor in the center of the room and stared at me with lowered head as if he were about to charge. He said firmly, "It's genetic. Yes, it's genetic."

Chapter 14

New Roofs, New Coffins

I t's time to make the sausages. This happens once a week. It is Monday, August 9, 1999.

Ramiz Peshteri, one of Isa's two employees, drags out a five-gallon green plastic trash bin full of meat from the small room at the back of the shop. There are all sorts of cow parts in there. Solid sides of muscle, stringy legs of meat, fat in long white seams. Isa grabs the bin from Ramiz and pulls it around the steel table that sits behind the counter.

This is Isa's domain, his shop. It's a small place but as full of life as it is of death. People come in and out all the time, sometimes just to gossip but usually to buy dinner and gossip at the same time. They walk on a floor of square terracotta tiles and lean on the steel surface of the glass display case as they tell Isa what they want. If it's fresh steak for dinner, Isa will take his short, sharp knife with the black plastic handle and quickly come around the side of the counter to the large sections of cow that dangle on the fifteen butcher's hooks in the window. For a moment, the flies will buzz away from the unprotected meat while Isa slices off a section for his customer and then takes it back in his big hands to weigh on the scale that sits on an old, high wooden table next to the display case. It's a Zora—made in Yugoslavia—a Tito-era scale with a set of iron weights that are lined up Russian doll-style on the table. If the piece he has sliced off is too heavy and tips the Zora, he moves over to the massive cross-section of an oak tree, waist-high, that seems to grow up from the floor. On its round, scarred surface sits a rectangular cleaver. With unhesitating precision, Isa brings the blade down on the meat, a centimeter or two from the fingers of his other hand.

At the end of the day, the sides of beef hanging in the window find a home in two big refrigerators that line the wall on the right, in front of the scale.

Just past the huge upturned oak log is the door to the back room. This is where more meat is stored in another refrigerator and where the shop's sink is. There are often deep steel trays full of the useless parts of a cow sitting on the floor and the blue and white tiles of the wall are daily smeared with blood. A lot of chopping up happens back here, the kind of butchering that customers prefer not to see.

Still, the people of Pec aren't too squeamish about their meat. On the walls of the square white ceramic tiles in the front of the shop are a few framed posters that make no effort to conceal where the meat comes from. There's a bouncing spring lamb on the wall behind the counter and a merry goat on a mountainside on the left wall as you walk in, and a little further along is a dark brown goatskin stretched out on the tiles. Also on the walls are a cheap electric clock, the old photograph of Pec, the portrait of a local Albanian prophet Isa's father knew, and a price list. "Beef with bones—55 [dinars per kilo]. Beef without bones—70. Veal with bones—65. Veal without bones—80. Lamb—70. Smoked meat—170. Lungs—40. Kebabs—70. Sausages—80." The sausages. People come to Isa Bala, the proprietor of the Grand Butcher, for the dark sausages that dangle from the dozens of hooks along the walls and in the window of the shop. They are chewy and spicy and they make your mouth water.

Isa's back is arched over, almost humped between the shoulders, exposing the many moles sprinkled over his back and neck. He sticks his hands into the bin and hauls some of its contents onto the steel table. Thin white membranes and specks of blood and fat cover the red muscle tissue. Isa's sweat and the moisture from slabs and chunks of meat have matted down the dark hair on his forearms. His white apron becomes smeared with the rusty stains from the beef. His moustache curls into a smile. He loves making sausages.

He flicks a switch and the thirty-year-old grinder roars into a bellowing rotation. It's screwed to the table, on the right side as Isa stands. There's an open cup for him to feed in the chunks of meat. At the bottom of the cup is the huge turning screw that forces the beef through the small holes at the end of the grinder. The meat and fat wiggle out like well-disciplined teams of red and white worms and they form a huge pile on the table until Isa or Ramiz sweep the ground beef into another five-gallon bin. As the beef dreadlocks squirm out of the grinder, they make a squelching noise loud enough to be heard over the roar of the grinder's engine. Offal goes in there too. The smell isn't so good.

Naser, Isa's other employee, appears at the door of the shop pushing a wheelbarrow. There's a cow's head there, stripped of its skin and every edible sinew and possible morsel of sausage-stuffing. It's just a pile of bovine bones and hoofs and ears. Happily, it remains in the back room and doesn't make its way into the grinder.

"I can't make enough sausages for my customers," Isa shouts, smiling, as Ramiz brings him an armful of fat. Isa, the man with the shortened finger, pushes all the meat and fat and offal into the grinder with his bare hands. He has an instrument that could do the trick, a sort of sawn-off rolling pin, but it would take far too long to do it that way.

Isa smiles when he sees Enver and me grimacing as the worms of fat slither out of the grinder. This is worse than being in a Serb village, Enver mutters.

"You earn money by your mind, not by force," Isa yells at us, apparently delighted to be teaching young men a life lesson. By now, I have spent a lot of time with Isa. I have never seen him happier. "A donkey is strong but he can't earn too much. Same with elephants. But I have fifty kilos of fat and I put it in here, into these sausages. That way I earn an extra six hundred and fifty marks. By throwing it away you don't earn anything."

Isa is happy but he's hiding. He stays as late as possible at the shop and finds any excuse not to go home. And tonight is no exception. It's August 9, and the war has been over for two months. There are still bullets in his living room floor and holes in his windows, awaiting the forensic teams from The Hague. He can't stand those bullets and those holes. And he's finding it hard to be around Halise, too. But Albanian men don't talk about trouble with their wives. It's not for anyone else to know about.

By evening, after the sausage making, things are quiet at the shop and Isa sits outside. It's growing dusky. We chat and then Isa pauses.

"They're digging up my family today," he says as he sits on the wooden seat of his steel-legged chair, his unmoving face staring at the sidewalk.

I have been with him for many hours today and at no point previously did he mention that the investigators and pathologists from the International Criminal Tribunal for the former Yugoslavia in The Hague were planning to push their shovels into the terracotta earth of the nearby cemetery where six of Isa's family lie buried in makeshift coffins. He's known about it for a week. He's ordered up six new coffins—proper ones—for their reburial the following day.

"The investigators are doing a report on my family," he says in an excessively off-hand way, trying his hardest to show no interest, to let greater powers—his God, the Tribunal—have their way as they bring him the justice he quietly burns for. "They want to examine the bodies."

About half a mile south of Isa's shop on Yugoslav People's Army Street, past the basketball arena and the bombed army barracks, lies the town's Muslim cemetery. Italian soldiers with near-black feathers sticking out of their helmets guard the entrance to the graveyard.

Inside, there's a funeral going on. Women are wailing. Among the gravestones are several freshly dug holes, where the investigators have started the exhumation process. Littered around the red earth are the white surgical masks and gloves that the investigators wear. At the bottom of one freshly dug hole is a bloody, earthy blanket. From somewhere among the gravestones comes the sound of digging. Trucks roar past on the road to Djakovica. Crickets rub their legs and the pulsating whistling noise makes the place seem calm.

The investigators have erected a huge khaki tent inside the cemetery. It's large enough to sleep a dozen soldiers, or in this case, to lay out several bodies at a time on the steel tables that stand on the ground inside the tent. The overworked pathologists are finishing their work for the day and walk around like busy professionals doing their job.

"The thing is," an investigator who prefers to remain anonymous tells me, "we have to check everybody and finish forensic work on all of them. It's important to get the numbers right, for a start. You'd be surprised how many families claim their relatives were killed by the Serbs but who actually died recently of natural causes."

At this stage, the investigators are not even close to starting the interview process. Isa sits on his chair half a mile away willing to tell anyone who comes knocking who it was who killed his family. But they're not asking yet.

"I'm particularly interested in the family of a local man named Isa Bala," I tell the investigator.

He nods his head toward the front of the cemetery. About a dozen white plastic bags, some about six feet long, some much shorter, lie in the long grass in the corner of the graveyard nearest to the road. They were the first things I noticed when I walked through the gate of the cemetery and I've been trying to ignore them. Enver hasn't been able to ignore them, even though he has put his shirtsleeve over his mouth and nose; he has left the grounds and is back at the car, his dark eyes staring at the ground, rather like Isa was staring at the sidewalk. He can't bear the smell.

Lined up next to the body bags are six coffins. They are made of pine, held together by heavy staples. They are all the same dimension— thicker at the head—in spite of the differing sizes of the bodies they will hold. It's cheaper that way. They cost a hundred and thirty marks each and the small paddle-shaped plank that lies unattached on top of each one cost twenty marks each. Carved into the paddles are the following:

HAJRI ISA BALA 1986–1999.
AGON ISA BALA 1993–1999
DARDANE ISA BALA 1988–1999
VJOLLCA TRAKANIQI BALA 1971–1999
NITA MUSA BALA 1994–1999
RINA MUSA BALA 1992–1999

"That's them, the ones nearest to us," the investigator says, pointing to the bodies next to the coffins. "They're doing them tomorrow."

~

If you stand still in Pec for a moment or two you can hear the same sounds every morning and afternoon echoing across the rooftops and around the streets. Two months after the war, men are standing on ladders and perching on gable-end walls, hammering nails through planks and into the thick pine beams they have laid across the burned-out roofs. Others are down below in their gardens, putting their shoulders to the task of sawing the beams and cross-planks. A few times a day, another sound drowns out the tapping of hammers and the bite of the saws. It's an explosion, followed by a small gray cloud rising from a field outside the town. That's where the Italians are disposing of the mines that the Serbs and the KLA left scattered over the area.

In the town center, shops that only weeks earlier were looted, charcoaled shells now have new windows and are fully stocked. There are VCRs and televisions and stereo systems for sale, along with every kind of food you can think of. The goods are pouring over from Albania, Macedonia, and, to a much lesser extent, from Montenegro. Some people, as people always do when wars end and demand is great, are getting rich quickly.

At night, it is hard to find a table at the many cafés that line the main streets and diners have to share tables at many of the restaurants. Just around the corner from the ruined jewelry district, which is now home to street peddlers and a flourishing market, is the Prizren Restaurant—all violet neon, faux Doric columns, and waiters with bow ties.

As the young people promenade around the main square, friends bump into friends they have not seen for months. I meet a musician I first met at the Rozaje bus station in late March, a teacher who was passing through the same place, several KLA soldiers I knew in Albania, and others from the camps of Montenegro. There's a lot of flirting going on in the Korzo. The girls are in tight clothes and wear lots of makeup. The guys stop to talk to them, or pretend to ignore them. The KLA guys, the "heroes," can just sit there in their favorite cafés, some of them without hands and feet, and just wait for the girls to come and talk to them.

Some people in Pec are living off money they kept from the Serbs. It turns out that a lot of people hid their cash and gold in their backyards. One family I meet shows me the big jar of pickles they dumped their gold into just a few minutes before they fled their house. It sat under the stairwell throughout the war and had even been opened by someone, but the gold was still there when the family returned. The house was gutted.

There is a feeling of true elation in the transformed town. It's not just that the war is over and they are home. For the first time in their lives, the Albanians of Pec don't have to live with the Serbs. By August, there's not a single Serb living in Pec. Although there are still thousands of Serbs left in Kosovo, Pec is not a place for them any more. There was too much killing in this town during the war for forgiveness, people say. Too much burning and stealing by too many Serbs. A Serb here would only be an opportunity for revenge and there would be hundreds lining up to seize the opportunity. Even a kindly old couple I met in mid-June are gone. They risked their lives to provide their Albanian neighbor with shelter during the war. The last time I saw them—just a couple of days after I met them—they were hiding in a locked pharmacy opposite the Italian base. A KLA man had called through their door that they had better be gone soon or they would be dead. In August, they are long gone.

Only at the Patriarchate just outside town are there any Serbs. Amid the bees and the trickling streams of the gardens, a couple of old people shuffle around, keeping the flower beds in order and making sure the churches are clean. There's always a priest or two in residence. And there are always Italian tanks and soldiers around the property.

A few minutes east of Pec, in the village of Gorazdevac, more Italians guard the dwindling population. The villagers, all Serbs, say they cannot work their fields because the KLA will shoot at them. They are defiant and hostile. We saw nothing, they say. We did nothing. Enver leaves shaking with hatred. "If I had an atom bomb," he says.

Most Albanians in Pec say they don't care about the Serbs in Gorazdevac. As long as they're not in Pec. Because now, for the first time in a decade, Albanians are walking the streets at night without fear. They are in many places that were out of bounds before. The cultural center, the library, a nightclub, bars, the beer factory. Albanians who opened the doors to these places in the 1990s could expect nothing but a serious beating. At the beer factory, they have already redesigned the label and it is now Peja beer, not Pec beer. The bosses there have reclaimed their jobs and they grumble, with a certain smugness, about how the quality of the beer deteriorated under ten years of Serbian management.

Albanian officials are back in the stained offices of city hall, sitting behind desks they last wrote letters on and filled out work orders on ten years ago. Unfortunately, they are out of practice and, given that Yugoslavia was still genuinely communist when they last had jobs, their ways of thinking about government are a lifetime out of line with the rest of the world. Ethem Ceku, the former KLA commander, now wears slacks and well-ironed shirts and he has let his head sprout a less threatening dark fuzz than the shaven-headed warrior style he sported when I first met him in June. He's the KLA-appointed mayor now and he doesn't look like he's quite sure what to do now that there's no enemy. Nor does Ceku have a budget or a mandate from the people. Legally, all the power in the town resides with the UN and NATO. But perhaps he'll learn on the job about administration and democracy and how to prevent his men from ordering innocent old Serbs from their homes on pain of death.

Pec is Albanian now. Its people are euphoric. But part of that euphoria is born of hatred. Part of the reason they are so happy is that they never have to see another Serb again on their streets. The people of Pec like their sameness. They can spot an Albanian from Albania a mile off. Even people from Prizren or Pristina are treated with suspicion. Once the euphoria is gone, the people of Pec will have to learn to like other people a little bit more. It'll be hard. Some of the last people who lived in the town who were different from them flushed them out like dirty water in a few days in early 1999. It's hard to like other people when you've been through that. Perhaps that's the war's lasting damage to Pec. It doesn't know how to trust. And it hates more than ever.

Driving back from the Tuesday cattle market, the morning after the sausage making, Isa's impassive facade cracks. He says that his doctor has prescribed medication for him to help calm him down. But it isn't really working. It's true that an Albanian man doesn't describe what's going on between him and his wife, but Isa can't keep it in any more. When Isa goes home Halise starts in on him, he says, blaming him, asking him why he wouldn't let her take the children away. Why, Isa, why? If he had, the kids would still be alive. Her kids. As he tells us this he bends his head over toward his lap and becomes silent. From the backseat I can see his big body jump slightly, as if he has received a small electric shock. And again. His hand comes up to his face. In front of other men, Isa is crying.

Halise says things to him like: "It's all your fault. You tried to be the cleverest Albanian, didn't you?"

She starts crying and then he cries. And it's not a good place for Veton to be at those times.

"I keep taking the medication. I go out early in the morning to get away. I can't sit in there. I can't drink because I don't like alcohol. But what's the point in living? I'm going to find a new house. The hardest part is when Veton asks for his brothers and sister. He asks me to buy him things and I have to buy him anything he wants. One day he was so upset he said to Halise, 'You have to make me other brothers and sisters.' She told him, 'My son, one day you'll grow up and get married and you'll have your own children and the house will be full again.'"

Now Isa's hearing rumors around town that he refused to leave because he wanted to protect his money. This kind of thing is stripping him of his faith, his belief in goodness. "What can we do? People are like that. Sometimes human beings are worse than animals. People are bad. We don't try to help, we try to destroy."

And then his anger turns to the men who are really responsible for this, not the gossip mongers.

"I hope God will do to them what they have done to me. Even if The Hague captures them they will get ten years in jail. They deserve to be dead. Anyway, I don't believe The Hague will get them. Look at Bosnia— how many years have passed and how many have they caught? But it means nothing, nothing, if you don't go yourself for revenge. The problem is that I can't leave the two young kids. Otherwise I'd go and find out where they are and I'd kill them. I'd be happy if they were in the electric chair and they were burned to death."

We drop him off and go to the graveyard.

For now, the investigators have moved on, leaving behind the tables with their blood stains and stench of old death. Crisp brown blood has dried on a scalpel left behind on one of the tables. Just outside the tent is an old wooden wheelbarrow.

There are more body bags out in the sun today. They must have dug up a few more. Now, there are twenty white bags, their zips running down the center of the plastic. One is on a stretcher. Between the bags, lost in the grass, are soiled and bloody clothes and the odd bone here and there. A stained T-shirt, a rib, a femur, a sock. The bones are easy to step on by mistake. Some of the bags have a distinctly human form inside. You can tell that the bulb-shaped contour at the top is a head with a nose. There are the arms. And further down, uniformly thin, are legs that end with the bump of feet. In others, it's not so easy to make out human shapes. These must have decomposed more, shrinking and collapsing in the earth of the graveyard over the last few months, or perhaps they were found at the end of the war in houses and fields, already decomposed, and then quickly buried and now disinterred. It is hard to tell that there are people in there. They look like suit bags dumped on a bedroom floor after a business trip. The smell is powerful and undignified. It seems unfair to be forced to rot in public, just next to a main road, when you've been murdered. A final powerlessness, an imposed immodesty, to produce a smell that gets into the mouth and onto the tongue of anyone standing or walking nearby. It's a smell that makes you want to spit but opening your mouth would let more of the sugary, plague stench into your lungs. And a lot of it must be coming from one bag in particular. Its zip is torn or perhaps just left open. The flesh that spills out is yellow and black and dry and the flies buzz around it, feeding. It is rotting in the Kosovo summer sun, naked from the inside out.

Five of Isa's friends arrived early in the morning in Isa's old yellow Volkswagen van, which he has recently bought. After the autopsies were finished they carried the bodies over to the coffins and sealed them, then drove them in the van over to the graves. Once they were in the ground, the *hoxha* raised his hands a couple of inches from his face, palms inward, and prayed in Arabic. "May their souls be in heaven," he prayed out loud. "May they be starting their new lives."

Now the five friends are finishing off, shoveling on the last of the earth, patting it down with the sides of their spades. The paddles, now grave markers, stand at the end of each grave. No one speaks. Suddenly there's a huge bang and a wind rushes past, pressing clothes to skin.

Everyone laughs. It's just KFOR in a nearby field, blowing up Serb mines they have collected.

Neither Isa nor Halise came to the reburial.

How could those men kill those children? How could they do it?

Just think about the happiness of children, fleeting and beautiful. It's there with the tenth, the eleventh, the twelfth jump in a row into the shallow end of the swimming pool, a jump just to feel the novel impact of the water. It comes when grandpa is on his hands and knees on the lawn, making roaring noises, a grizzly bear looking for a human snack. It comes when the soccer ball bounces on the neighbor's dog, giving it a fright. And it goes just as quickly, replaced by tears and dejection. A mouthful of chlorinated water, an over scary grandfather, a neighbor's broken window. In their turn, the tears are forgotten in an instant as a new joy appears out of nowhere.

It's enrapturing, this undisciplined emotion. In an adult, it would be horribly tiresome. In a child, it makes you fall in love. It is passionate and limitless and unconditional love—Halise threw herself in front of her children and took eight bullets for them—and it has a sworn enemy. In his memoir, *Experience,* which dwells frequently on the death of the young, Martin Amis describes his father Kingsley's feelings toward death. "It wasn't only that he feared death; he hated it, because it was the opposite and the enemy of love." Death is also the opposite and the enemy of children and when they meet, the world seems to jerk backward slightly in its orbit before continuing on.

Amis's memoir lingers on a barely restrained anxiety about losing his sons, a fear fueled by his loss of his twenty-one-year-old cousin at the hands of one of Britain's most prolific serial killers. After the discovery many years after her disappearance that Lucy Partington had been murdered, Amis brings a close death even closer in his imagination.

"For a while my mind kept conducting involuntary thought-experiments, or feeling-experiments: I would imagine each of my sons finding themselves, as their distant cousin had, in such a violent force field, and I would imagine the moment when they sensed the magnitude of the undifferentiated hatred that was ranged against them. The first time I did this I teetered backwards on my feet, and there was a palpable rush or whoosh, as if I had approached the entrance of a wind tunnel. And this tunnel a mere vent or flap, leading to the room occupied by Lucy's parents and siblings."

Amis is a parent and so his imaginings, his empathy with children, are perhaps to be expected. But what about the childless? How is it that the death of a child can galvanize newspapers, governments, and even individuals who have never been parents into coordinated action? Kosovo was no exception. It took images of refugees—the children always tug hardest at the heart—to convince most people in the West that NATO's bombing campaign was justifiable. This is the stuff of empathy, not sympathy.

Does this love have an explanation? Why is that fleeting happiness so seductive, so heartbreakingly lovely?

Perhaps it is because children are, in a sense, what adults aspire to be. It is an impossible aspiration but to look on a child is to look at a cleaner future. Like its perfect skin, a young child's soul is unmarked by sin or true malice. Unlike adults, most children have done nothing wrong. They are already ahead of the game. They are better than us. It barely matters that we know they will grow into complicated and sometimes harmful adults because, for a few years, they are all about hope. So to feel the death of a child is to feel the awful end of unconditional love, the end of innocence, and the end of hope.

It is an empathetic feeling and it is also genetically selfish. These little happiness hogs are not just morale boosters, an impossible but inspiring ideal, but they are also the people we rely on to continue our kind. The death of a child is a negation of ourselves. It is an affront to our furious need to keep going on the planet as a team even though we know we are doomed as individuals.

And then there is murder. If the death of a child jars the globe for a moment, the murder of a child can make it feel suddenly frozen on its axis. A speeding truck, a fire, a crib death, these things are bad luck or bad mistakes. But the Bala children were killed by other people. Somehow, these men felt they had no connection to these children. And so they squeezed the triggers on their Kalashnikovs and shot them to death.

How does the cord that connects most adults to children become severed like that? Perhaps some people are simply not born to empathize with children. They are indifferent and don't see the future in a child. Other things map out their future—money, revenge, ideals, tribal togetherness. The cord between such people and children has been snapped.

There was certainly no cord running invisibly across Isa Bala's darkened living room between the men with the guns and the seven Bala children who sat in front of them on the couch. There were just a few feet of air between them. The connection was made only with lead, lumps of speeding hatred.

I asked Tony, the paramilitary looter who spends so much time thinking about what went on inside Kosovo for those eleven weeks, what is in the heart of a man who kills.

"They have some feeling that they are important now—when you are master of life and death. Some told me that they feel like God. He makes a decision about who will die and who will live. It's a very exciting feeling. You wouldn't believe how some completely normal guy, when he comes to war, in that normal man you can see a monster. Man is a very complex being. Inside normally you have some feelings that you think are not important, they're marginal feelings, but sometimes those feelings reach the surface and become the leader. In this war and in Bosnia, you have normal men and when they get the opportunity to have the power to decide, then it is very easy to pull the trigger. Sometimes you want to feel how it is to pull the trigger—yes, no, how does it feel? Can you imagine? I give you a Kalashnikov now and then I beg for mercy. You enjoy it, you wonder and in some moment you pull the trigger. You feel excited and it becomes an addiction, like coke."

But to kill children?

"They have that feeling that I told you about before. They have hate still. Mix all that and you can't speak about a normal person. You speak about a mutation, a genetic mutation, who only physically reminds you of a human being. But it isn't a man. A guy I knew in the war killed a kid. I asked him how he could do that. His answer was, 'You just aim your gun a little lower.' It's no use talking to someone like that. Maybe you appear strange to him, like he appears strange to you. It is a relative thing. It depends on the number of men who say that something is normal. If many men say this is normal then it becomes normal.

"By the way," Tony said, "the killing of these five kids can't be justified by drugs and alcohol. . . . They knew what they were doing."

What severed the cord between these men and these children? Was the cord ever there?

The Balas have their explanation. And in the weeks after the war, it seems unsatisfactory to me. Their main theory is that Backovic had influence with Minic and *Munje* and persuaded Minic to take revenge on his behalf for the humiliation Backovic had suffered as a result of Musa's testimony. Perhaps Isa and Halise are right but the revenge seems excessive, even in the awful atmosphere of Pec at the end of the war. And why would Minic care about a whining Serb called Backovic who had spent a week behind bars, courtesy of a Serbian court? As I spend day after day with Isa, I still do not feel at ease with this theory.

But Isa and Halise need to live with some kind of explanation, with some kind of story that makes sense to them.

Amis writes that the reason the relatives of murder victims need to know how their loved ones died is to reduce to one the endless number of horror stories they cannot help telling themselves about the death of their daughter, sister, son.

Isa and Halise live in the wind room with their single story, a story they didn't have to be told by police investigators because they were there when it happened.

There is a narrator's voice in their mind. The voice starts the story in different places so that it's all jumbled up and lurching around like a crudely rendered modernist tale. And when the ending comes—the killing—it is no ending, just the jumping off point for another part of the story, another dab of memory. And that wind room they live in can be calm, as Halise makes sure Veton takes a bath or Isa is weighing two kilos of sausages for a regular customer. But without notice a hurricane can burst into the room with the violence of the bullets that ended their children's lives and the story starts again in some random chapter.

Isa and Halise know the story. They know who did it and they think they know the motive. Still they live in constant pain.

Isa intends to rebury his brother too, once the Tribunal investigators get around to digging up the body. A few days after KFOR arrived in

Pec, Musa was found by a friend of Isa's in a burned-out house. Isa buried him hastily in Kakariq cemetery near where Musa was found. Musa had been shot nine times and his body and feet were a criss cross of knife marks.

I have an appointment to see Isa and his family at home on a Sunday in August, the only day he spends away from the business. When I get there, Isa is nowhere to be seen.

"Isa's just running away from the house," Halise says. "Even on a Sunday, his day off, he stays away. Since the tragedy he just runs. He goes out early in the morning and comes home late, sometimes even at midnight."

Halise is doing a bit of her own escaping. "Twice today I ran away to my brother's house. It just comes to me like that. God gave those kids to me and God took them, but when the moment comes and I see in my mind what the Serbs did, I want to go crazy, crazy."

We sit on the sofa and drink coffee and soda. Halise's mind is a whirlpool. And one of the bits of debris caught in the spiral is the Chinese whisper that I have been to see Minic in Montenegro. I tell Halise that no, I have not seen Minic, but I have seen men who worked for him and who knew him.

"I wanted to know if he has kids," she says, staring at me. "I would put two hand grenades in his house. I wouldn't care for my own life."

Almost more than Isa, she thirsts for revenge, Albanian-style. The *Kanun* may have been outlawed in the Balkans but its influence is still strong in Western Kosovo. "I blame Backovic and his brother. Backovic doesn't have any children but his brother does and if I could I'd go and kill his kids. I wouldn't care if they sent me to The Hague. My only wish is to avenge my kids."

Her speech jumps about, as she sits on the floor and leans against the sofa. There are other female members of the family there—her mother, Isa's mother, a cousin—and Veton and one of his young cousins. Everyone lets Halise speak.

"I'm going to go crazy from thinking about that evening. I don't even have the heart to cut up a chicken now because that night I saw the blood of my children and my sister-in-law. I blame myself for my kids' deaths.

I put jackets on the kids but Isa said no, no, no, we have to stay. I blame Isa as well but most of all I blame myself."

Isa says he wants to have more children as soon as possible. Will she have more kids?

"I'm not sure," Halise says quietly, sucking in her upper lip and then dragging it out between her teeth. Her gentleness lasts but a second.

"Go and tell Isa that we lost the kids we had," she spits out. "New ones would never be like the kids I lost. You go tell Isa we already had wonderful kids. But now you want others?"

Chapter 15

The Butcher's Business

at an uncertain hour,
That agony returns:
And till my ghastly tale is told,
This heart within me burns.
    —Samuel Taylor Coleridge, *The Rime of the Ancient Mariner*

The man with close-cropped hair pressed his black leather jacket to his chest, making sure that my connection and I could see the handgun he was holding underneath. I thanked him for taking the risk of talking to me about what really happened to the Bala family and he replied: "I'm not taking any risks. I have my friend with me here. The only friend who's never let me down."

It was six o'clock on a late November evening in 2000, and it was already dark in the streets of Podgorica. We had picked him up on an appointed street corner and he had climbed into the front seat. I had met paramilitaries before. None of them made me feel safe. But I had always met them in cafés, in public places. This young man, twenty-six years old and with eyes of cold aggression, made my hands shake and messed up my ability to ask questions properly. I knew he was a member of *Munje* and a trusted associate of Nebojsa Minic, who I knew would kill me if he had the chance. It was a risk, I knew, but this guy was offering to give me answers to questions that had troubled me for over a year. I had come back to Kosovo and Montenegro one more time before finishing this book to fill in some gaps and find answers to these questions: How did the Balas survive for so long inside Pec? Why were they killed? If they were killed because Backovic wanted them dead, why did Minic and his *Munje* boys do Backovic's bidding? Wasn't the killing of the whole family, all those kids, wildly out of proportion to Musa's offense of being too frank at the trial and landing Backovic in jail for a few days? For some reason, the man in the passenger seat wanted to give me answers.

At his instructions, we drove to an unlit parking lot in a patch of wasteland between groups of Tito-era concrete apartment blocks. Some lights were on in the far-off apartments. It was cold but my palms were sweating. My connection translated from Serbian.

"Get out of the car. I'm going to search you."

I went to the back of the car and he made me turn my back to him and spread my arms and legs. With his foot he pushed my legs a little wider apart. He had done this before. I felt ill.

Back inside the car we began. He sat on the backseat to my right and his hand spent much of the time inside his jacket, apparently holding the gun, apparently pointed at me. I could see his face now. It was thin, the nose and chin protruding slightly, the mouth retreating back inside his head a little. He was nervous, which I didn't like. If he hadn't kept swiveling around, looking for enemies, I would have been much happier.

I told him the basics of what I knew about the Bala case.

"That motherfucker Isa survived? I can't fucking believe it. I can't understand how he could survive."

He was furious and I thought that my connection and I were now truly in grave danger. We were alone in a parking lot with an armed man who had killed people in Kosovo. Those dead people had not even posed a threat to him but I had just admitted knowing a lot about a killing he had been involved in. My stomach shifted around inside and I wanted to end the conversation, to get away from him. But it was too late. That would have just alarmed him. And another part of me wanted to stay, to hear and understand. A car drove into the lot and the man grew more anxious and told my connection to drive to another lot. We spoke as we drove around Podgorica.

This is what we said:

"Being a real Serb patriot I joined an organization called *Munje*," he said. "There were three goals. One, to fight the KLA terrorists. Two, to prevent the incursion of terrorist groups from Albania. Three, the cleansing of areas that had been shelled previously. At different times there were several groups called *Munje,* which was founded in Bosnia. Nebojsa Minic was there."

Was *Munje* a police unit?

"It was sort of a police unit. We had good cooperation with the police forces. We were the ones who were cleansing the villages after the shelling. We added more casualties."

Who was above *Munje* in the chain of command?

"The Interior Ministry was above everyone there. There were orders when there was a need for it, but not for other things. They didn't issue an order to kill Isa Bala. That was a local issue. The MUP was just for bigger things—we were part-time workers for the MUP. They controlled the most important criminals. That's how the state functions. No one could get rich quick. They controlled it all. The Frenkis and Tigers were there too in Pec."

Who was most powerful in Pec?

"We were very influential in the Pec area. Whenever Minic was on good terms with Arkan we were also powerful in other parts of Kosovo. But when he wasn't, we were mainly in Pec. It was all about business. We were businessmen."

But you were patriots also, right? "Yes. You hook up business and pleasure at the same time."

Did *Munje* kill civilians?

"It was a classic war situation. If you know anything about war operations, well, the primary goal was the destruction of the KLA and all who might be useful to them. Those people were supplying items, lodging, operations help, and there were many people among those categories. You call them civilians but they were supporting terrorists and supplying them with guns and food."

What was your relation to Minic? "At one stage, I was in charge of Minic's security detail."

How many people were in *Munje*?

"There were several groups, each with about thirty members. Only Minic knew the exact number. I don't really know."

What is Minic like?

"He is a man of the terrain. After the war he covered many people's debts. He helped them take a lot of money away. He's a successful businessman. He was good to the Serbs, as good to them as he was bad to the Albanians—he's a good guy, very dangerous. He's determined, his will to succeed is amazing. He has a will of iron. When that gaunt face and those iron eyes look at you—it's inspiring. He's a good person. A man of honor."

How did the business work?

"We organized taking money in various ways. First there was the transportation of rich Albanians for two to five thousand marks per person. Or we would resell cigarettes to Albanians. And we would send squads with lists of Albanians to take their gold, diamonds, money. But the most lucrative job was taking them out of Kosovo for money. Whatever you think of us we took out a lot of people for money and those who were spying and working for both sides had to pay with their lives."

I was not sure where this last bit had come from or where he was going with it.

"That was the case with the Balas," he said.

No, I thought, as a feeling of dread came over me.

"We were supposed to take them out but we were caught and they told the KOS [the army's Counter Intelligence Service] that we were dealing coke and had accounts in Switzerland and so on. The Bala family was well known and, believe it or not, they were informers for the Milosevic regime. If we hadn't eliminated them the Albanians would have done it at the end of the war. Many people came to the butcher's shop."

But what kind of information could a couple of butchers have to pass on?

He let out a kind of evil cartoon laugh. "How naive you are. By killing [Musa] he became an Albanian hero. If he had waited till July or August he would have been killed as an Albanian traitor. It's a big surprise to me that Isa survived the shooting. Those guys told me they had killed him. I can't believe that bastard is still alive."

We had come to a stop in another parking lot and the three of us were giving off a lot of heat and steaming up the windows. My connection asked if he could open the window for a bit. We sat in silence as the fresh, cold air replaced the stale air we had been breathing. We were not allowed to talk until the window was closed again. I needed the break. For the first time since I became a journalist, I had been told something I did not want to hear. I desperately wanted it to be untrue but already the holes in the story seemed to be filling in. It made awful sense. Even if Isa had betrayed his people, could I betray him? Hadn't he suffered enough, a million times over? My connection pressed the button and the electric windows closed.

"Musa and Isa were working for the Serbian secret service," the *Munje* man continued. "They publicly said that we were taking rich Albanians out for money. . . . And then they wanted to slander people around *Munje* as men who were dealing with Albanians in narcotics projects in Switzerland. . . . That wasn't a complete lie. There was a small amount of cooperation. Business is business. But to mention that was a big mistake when they were caught by the military police."

So they and their families were killed in retribution?

"Maybe it shouldn't have been that way. I know that the kids were also killed. But Isa was a bit presumptuous. He thought we wouldn't do anything. He was cursing our Serb mothers. We had also been doing a bit of cocaine that night. . . . Many of my comrades won't be happy to hear about Isa being alive. A friend of mine messed up with Isa. I thought Isa had been hit with a few bullets."

Where were you at the time?

"I was nearby."

Was Vjollca raped? "I didn't rape her. My friend Josk—"

He held his tongue but most of the name was already out. I did not press him on it.

Why were the children killed?

"It's unfortunate. It's kind of unfortunate circumstances. Isa made rash moves. He jumped forward. No one is proud of that. . . . I don't think any of us like to think about that. You shoot and you don't see where you're shooting because the electricity is out. You can't see who you're shooting. It was an unfortunate event. I'm not sure if Minic knows the children were killed. The Serbian nation is a nation of warriors, knights. We do not kill children. We are not monsters. It wasn't anything personal. Just business. He ruined the business. Plus he was a spy."

Who gave the order to kill them?

"Who do you think? You already know that."

Minic?

"Yes."

We talked some more, just to clear a few things up. Minic had ordered the Bala brothers killed because of Musa's testimony at the trial. His statements in court had not only put the two Montenegrins and Backovic in prison and out of commission for ten very important money-making days near the end of the war, but the testimony had also revealed to the army's Counter Intelligence Service *Munje*'s secret and highly profitable racket of taking Albanians out of Kosovo. And that revelation had forced them to include the KOS in the deal. The KOS, remember, had control of the borders and no one was going to get past them without giving the KOS and their military police brethren a cut. Minic, *Munje,* and civilians like Backovic who were involved in the smuggling ring had been gypping the army's intelligence branches and the KOS and the military police were furious. Each group in the Pec area—*Munje,* the Frenkis, the Tigers, the army—were competing for Albanian loot and they knew they only had a short time to get it. As the end of the war became inevitable and the time for making money ran out, tempers became frayed. At this crucial time, to have business-damaging testimony coming from Musa, a man *Munje* considered an informer, well, the only thing you do with men like that is take them away and kill them. Painfully.

"And that's what we did," the *Munje* man said.

Toward the end I had a few more loose ends that I thought he could tie up.

What's Minic up to now?

"He's in Belgrade. He's a partner in a casino. He drives a fancy German car, an Audi A8, and he has an extremely good-looking girlfriend."

I had heard these details about Minic's new life from others.

Why are you telling me this? I asked the man.

"I feel relaxed after talking. It's much easier for me later, believe me. Although there's no logic to telling you these things it's easier on me later."

Like some of the other paramilitaries I had met, this man was like the Ancient Mariner. He felt compelled to tell his story, to confess.

Do you feel you have a burden to unload? I asked him.

He became defensive, angry. "I was defending my country, my people. I'm not ashamed of anything."

I ran out of questions. I knew I would have a thousand more later but I was exhausted. I could think of nothing else other than to start asking about names—who did the shooting? who were the Montenegrin men involved in the escape attempt?—but I sensed that the *Munje* man would get nervous and suspicious. It was enough. We pulled up at the side of the road. I leaned forward from the backseat and I shook his hand and thanked a man more evil than any I have ever met in my life.

But had he told me the truth? I spent a sleepless night. Two things kept me awake. Backovic and his brother, whom I had hoped to interview, knew I was in town and apparently wanted to kill me. So did two other men I suspected of involvement in Musa's escape attempt, Nikola being one. I had dined with a good friend of the Backovic brothers who warned me to stay away from them. The same went for Dalibor Banjac, who was in southern Serbia but would happily make the trip to Podgorica to silence me. They were all one or two degrees of separation away. I had miscalculated, expecting them to talk like the paramilitaries I had met before. The difference this time was that I was looking for very specific information, a task too similar to that of an investigator from The Hague. A book about their crime could only make their lives more difficult and dangerous. As for Minic: "The moment you see him will be your last," said the Backovic friend I dined with, a Pec resident who also knew Minic. So in the early hours of the morning, I lay alone in a rented apartment in a tower block—carefully avoiding the hotels—worrying that these men had found out where I was staying.

That worry alternated with an incessant set of questions about Isa. Was it true? What the man in the parking lot had just told me seemed horribly logical but how could I believe a killer over a kindly man with whom I had spent so much time, who had suffered so much pain?

Confirmation, one way or the other, was what I needed. Further information came quickly. Everyone even vaguely involved with the war in Kosovo seemed to know about the Bala case.

Three more paramilitaries independently confirmed that Isa and Musa had been close with the Serbs. But to these men, the Bala brothers were not spies, merely low-level collaborators.

"Zlatko," a senior figure in the Serbian criminal and paramilitary world, a man who had very close connections to Arkan until the latter's death and has now taken over a large part of Arkan's empire, had this to say. Yes, Isa was close with the military police. Yes, the military police were meant to be given a cut for every Albanian transported out of Pec—for the usual fee of five thousand marks. When the trial took place, Musa spilled the beans and most of the blame fell on Backovic. The judge had accused Backovic of "treasonous" acts. Backovic was humiliated and furious. Yes, Minic gave the order to kill, and yes, in the anger of the moment, the kids were killed on purpose.

"Minic is a mere executioner," said Zlatko, a man in his thirties with close-cropped hair, bloated, hard muscles, and a fast German car. "That shit is getting more influential now, more important. The only thing I appreciated about Minic during the war was his courage. But he's a petty cheat. It's a pity we let him get out of Kosovo."

Another man who is very close to Minic confirmed the story again, adding that Isa and Musa were very low-level collaborators.

I remembered something another man, Momo, who worked for Minic during the war had told me a year before: "There were a certain number of Albanians in Pec but many were hiding," Momo had said. "When you go some place you need informers."

And then I met with Tony, a man I trust. He only tells you what he knows and if he doesn't know something he will say so. We waited for forty minutes in a grim bar on the furthest outskirts of Podgorica. Every man there wore a black leather jacket and when Tony came in, a couple of them greeted him.

"I saw Minic and his companions in the north of Montenegro at the end of the war and I heard stories that they had killed some family," Tony began, after I told him what I was looking for. "I wasn't surprised by anything that came from Minic. I remember Isa. Once in the Hotel Karagac during the war my friends were there, with girls, and they were preparing a party. They had a lamb and they wanted it butchered, so someone said they should get Isa. I don't know if he came."

Tony was unmoved when I asked him if Isa had collaborated with the Serbs. "Of course," he said.

"In Pec many Albanian families were killed. It was quiet until June and the end of May. There were Albanian spies for the KLA. But if you agreed to be under the Serbian nation and respected Serbian laws you could stay. But at the end of the war a campaign started of cleansing every Albanian and the war became bloodier and bloodier. Everyone saw that the end of the war was approaching and everyone wanted to get more money, to kill someone, to enjoy himself, to remember something from the war. It's a strange feeling at the end—you want to take what you can. For some, killing is much more than money.

"To survive as an Albanian in Pec, even those who did favors for Serbs, the first thing you needed was to be lucky. If some crazy man notices you, your house, your pretty daughter, your jeweler's shop, you could have many problems. So you needed luck. I saw Isa only once after my friends talked about him at the Hotel Karagac. He was near the stadium talking with a military policeman. They were kind of friends, if that was possible at that time. Musa was a drunk. Isa was a wise man, a clever man in some ways, able to think in different ways. His success was to survive. He sold some meat during the war and tried to work to survive.

"At the end of the war everyone tried to make more money. In Pec there were different groups, different interests—the army, the police, the city clerks, the local gangs—it was a mixture of influence, a mixture of interests. Between them there were confrontations. Many of them didn't like each other and it could get violent. There were many killings between Serbs. . . . It was also an ideal time and place to do something if you had some bad experience, if you had to clear out the accounts and then you could just say it was the other side who did it. No one asked you anything.

"I had one short meeting with Backovic about some job. He wanted to sell a dentist's chair and other dental equipment for a low price. They took it from some Albanian dentist. He didn't call after that. When we met at the end of the war I asked about the deal. He told me that some Albanian garbage had spied on him, exposed some work of his. He worked with many Albanians, taking them out. But the secret police wanted to be involved in everything. So there was a conflict of interests. I think he was in jail some time. A week maybe."

Tony didn't know more than that. We talked about other things and after a couple of hours, went our separate ways. The evidence so far suggested that Isa had been close to the Serb authorities, but that the *Munje* man had exaggerated. After all, Isa had frequently volunteered stories to me about his attempts to stay friendly with the military police and his Serb neighbors. That was not the behavior of a man trying to hide an informer past. Perhaps the *Munje* man's conscience was helping him paint the Bala brothers in a worse light than they deserved to be in. Perhaps he was still working under orders from a branch of the Interior Ministry and had been told to meet with me to blacken the names of the Bala brothers.

I went back to Pec, sick at what I had to do: Ask Isa whether he had been a collaborator with the Serbs. Before I went I checked in with an Albanian friend in Rozaje, who knew the whole story very well. I led with a simple question—How did the Balas survive for so long in the hell of Pec?—and without prompting my friend told me, regretfully, that the Balas had collaborated.

On my first night back I bumped into another friend who was a senior commander in the KLA in the Pec region during the war and is now involved in politics. He would know. We had a beer in a quiet corner of a café and I asked him how the Bala family had managed to stay safely inside Pec for so long during the war when nearly every other Albanian had either been evicted or killed? By Isa and Halise's own account, the Serb authorities knew they were there all the time.

There was a long pause. My friend gazed at the table and then looked at me. "They had some kind of relationship with the Serbs, you know," he said.

I went to ask Ethem Ceku, now voted out of office but the local leader of one of the two parties that had emerged from the disbanded KLA. He was furious at my question. How could I even ask such a question about a man who had lost his family?

Over the next two days I spoke to my former KLA friend some more. And I spoke to another highly respected and prominent member of the Albanian community in Pec who knows about the case in great detail. As with the KLA veteran, this man brought up the issue of the Bala brothers' closeness with the Serb authorities without my directly asking him. Both men requested anonymity. Both painted the same picture of the Balas: Albanian businessmen doing what all Albanian business owners had to do during the 1990s to get by, with Musa perhaps having a looser tongue with the Serb police than Isa had. Isa was not a deliberate conduit for information, they said.

"They were of the lowest category and we knew about them," said my former KLA friend, who added that Ceku was just trying to protect the Balas out of sympathy for their tragedy. "They could not have damaged our cause."

There had been no retribution against the Balas after the war for two reasons. First, they had suffered terribly already. Second, the KLA leadership had immediately recognized that it would lose all credibility in the world community if it went around Kosovo after the war executing hundreds of Albanian collaborators. There would be no more Albanian blood spilled, the KLA leaders had decided.

The truth is impossible to pin down but it lies somewhere in the zone between the Serb authorities' view of the Balas as useful and the KLA's knowledge of them as unthreatening collaborators and nonpolitical businessmen doing their best to survive in an apartheid regime.

Isa and Musa Bala were not spies. They were not agents. They were not even true informers. They were Albanian business owners who had to remain on good terms with the Serb police in order to operate their shop. There was free meat. Perhaps some money too, going into Serb pockets. And maybe the brothers would pass on a tidbit of gossip about an Albanian and how much money he had or where his political sympathies lay. Perhaps a Serb police officer would simply ask, "Hey, that Rexhep is close with the KLA, isn't he?" And perhaps Musa would nod or shake his head without even thinking about it. Perhaps. I do not know the details.

On my last day in Pec, I went to see Isa and told him that I needed to ask him something in private. It had not been an easy time for the Balas. Since I last saw them in August 1999, Halise had become pregnant again and had given birth on May 7, 2000, to a baby girl. Isa insisted that they call her Dardane. The baby died an hour after she was born and is buried in the same cemetery as the brothers and sister she never met.

Isa was now considering selling the shop and the house and moving to Pristina, to get away from the memories. The brown goatskin that hung on the wall was gone. Musa had skinned that goat, Isa said. He didn't want to be reminded of his brother all the time.

"If I ever catch them here," he said of the killers one day, "I would turn them into bones like this." He seized a huge cow bone in his right hand. "I would put them into the grinder like that meat and then I would throw it to the fishes. If you meet them, tell them to come visit soon. I'd be very happy to meet them. In Germany, Turkey, wherever. I will fuck them up. They'll have to deal with me."

This morning, he came out of the shop and we stood on the street in the rain. He looked at me and waited.

How were your relations with the Serbs? I asked him.

"They knew me well because I was always polite to them and I never had a problem with them."

He looked a little offended, clearly knowing what I meant by the question.

"You have businessmen here who have saved factories, houses, everything because of their connections with Serbs," he continued. "Whenever the regular police, the traffic police, the financial police came they would always fine you or they wouldn't let you work. Sometimes I would give them twenty kilos of meat for free."

Did they ever ask you to pass on any information? "No, they just came to take money and meat."

It was time to ask Isa directly.

I was in Podgorica and a *Munje* man told me that you and Musa used to pass on information.

"He lied to you," Isa said. "We never passed on anything."

We talked some more and I gave him some more time and opportunities to alter his story but he was intent on it. I believed that Isa believed he had done nothing wrong. But I was equally sure that he and his brother had been of some, perhaps indirect, help to the Serbs. It is possible to be innocent and to have done wrong.

We said good-bye and pretended we had not had the conversation. Isa held out his arm and instead of shaking his hand, covered in blood and flecks of meat, I squeezed his forearm. It was the last time I saw him.

Later I found out a little more about Joska. For days after the killing of the Bala family, he lived in a drunken haze. It really got to him, what he had done. For a brief moment. By the end of 2000, he was planning to open a striptease club in a town in the southeast of Serbia. He had started to make good money again, this time from imported Ukrainian and Moldovan women. One of his business partners was the man I met in the parking lot.

The war over Kosovo may not have been a clean war but it was a just war. Isa Bala may not have lived a completely clean life but he is a man far more sinned against than sinning. It is hard to find pure good in a war and it can barely be found in the stories of the war that I have come across.

Motivated at least in part by morality, the Western powers waged a war for good but still killed Serb civilians, bombed China's embassy, bombed Albanian refugees, failed to unseat their enemy from his position of power, and did not have the courage or even basic military planning to threaten ground troops. NATO's political leaders, their eyes on opinion polls, would not risk losing a single soldier on the ground for the Albanians.

Motivated by a desire to protect his family, Isa Bala did what countless other Albanian business owners did during the years of Serb control in Kosovo. After all, his children did not die because he had collaborated with the Serbs. His children died because a group of killers whose stream of revenue had been interrupted wanted revenge.

Motivated by the dark, fluid anger inside him, Nebojsa Minic never wrestled with morality during the war as Isa and NATO's leaders did. Those eleven weeks were very good to him. He is now a wealthy businessman with a beautiful girlfriend in Belgrade. Sometimes he drives his Mercedes, sometimes his Audi. So far, he has not been publicly indicted by the International Criminal Tribunal for the former Yugoslavia. The Tribunal's investigators have interviewed Isa and Rama but officials at the Tribunal will not discuss the case and will not say whether there is a sealed indictment against Minic. Compared to the generals and ministers who orchestrated the whole war, Minic is small stuff.

But for Isa Bala, Nebojsa Minic has come into his life forever. Minic occupies an enormous space in Isa's life. It is the space that his children once filled. And where once there was love, now there is pure hatred.

Bibliography

Anzulovic, Branimir. *Heavenly Serbia: From Myth to Genocide*. New York: New York University Press, 1999

Carver, Robert. *The Accursed Mountains: Journeys in Albania*. London: Flamingo, 1999.

Di Giovanni, Janine. *The Quick and the Dead: Under Seige in Sarajevo*. London: Phoenix, 1995.

Glenny, Misha. *The Fall of Yugoslavia*. London: Penguin Books, 1993.

———. *The Balkans: Nationalism, War and the Great Powers*. London: Granta Books, 1999.

Ignatieff, Michael. *Virtual War: Kosovo and Beyond*. London: Chatto and Windus, 2000.

Judah, Tim. *The Serbs: History, Myth and the Destruction of Yugoslavia*. New Haven: Yale University Press, 1997.

———. *Kosovo: War and Revenge*. New Haven: Yale University Press, 2000.

Malcolm, Noel. *Kosovo: A Short History*. New York: New York University Press, 1998.

Merrill, Christopher. *Only the Nails Remain: Scenes from the Balkan Wars*. Lanham: Rowman and Littlefield, 1999.

Mertus, Julie A. *Kosovo: How Myths and Truths Started a War*. Berkeley: University of California Press, 1999.

Silber, Laura, and Allan Little. *The Death of Yugoslavia*. London: Penguin Books, BBC Books, 1996.

Sudetic, Chuck. *Blood and Vengeance: One Family's Story of the War in Bosnia*. New York: W. W. Norton, 1998.

West, Rebecca. *Black Lamb and Grey Falcon: A Journey through Yugoslavia*. London: Penguin Books, 1969.

About the Author

Matthew McAllester is the Middle East correspondent for *Newsday*. He shared a Pulitzer in 1997 with *Newsday*'s staff for coverage of the crash of TWA flight 800.